DATE DUE

OTHER VOICES

OTHER VOICES

The Struggle for Community Radio in India

Vinod Pavarala
and
Kanchan K. Malik

SAGE Publications
Los Angeles • London • New Delhi • Singapore

First published in 2007 by

Sage Publications India Pvt Ltd
B1/11, Mohan Cooperative Industrial Area
Mathura Road, New Delhi 110 044
www.sagepub.in

Sage Publications Inc
2455 Teller Road
Thousand Oaks, California 91320

Sage Publications Ltd
1 Oliver's Yard, 55 City Road
London EC1Y 1SP

Sage Publications Asia-Pacific Pte Ltd
33 Pekin Street
#02-01 Far East Square
Singapore 048763

Published by Vivek Mehra for Sage Publications India Pvt Ltd, typeset in 10/12 Calisto MT at InoSoft Systems, Noida, and printed at Chaman Enterprises, New Delhi.

Library of Congress Cataloging-in-Publication Data

Pavarala, Vinod, 1962–

Other voices: the struggle for community radio in India/Vinod Pavarala, Kanchan K. Malik.

p. cm.

Includes bibliographical references and index.

1. Community radio—India—Case studies. 2. Broadcasting policy—India. 3. Communication—Political aspects—India. 4. Communication—Social aspects—India. I. Malik, Kanchan K., 1968–
II. Title.

HE8697.95.I4P37 384.540954—dc22 2007 2007026991

ISBN: 978-0-7619-3602-2 (HB) 978-81-7829-765-1 (India-HB)

The Sage Team: Sudeep Kohli and Neha Kohli

To 'General' Narsamma
and
Shilwanti Biranchi
for keeping alive
our faith in community radio

CONTENTS

LIST OF TABLES

LIST OF TABLES

PREFACE AND ACKNOWLEDGEMENTS

'Be you, be new, and be true!' This was the advice offered by the irrepressible Louie Tabing, farmer and pioneering community broadcaster from the Philippines, to potential community radio operators in India assembled recently at a national convention in Delhi. This simple dictum underlined the need for community-owned and managed media in the age of homogeneous, formulaic, and misleading content in mainstream media outlets.

Tabing's sage counsel comes at a time when media activists and civil society organisations in India are celebrating the announcement of a community radio (CR) policy by the Government of India at the end of 2006 as the denouement of a decade-long struggle for the creation of a third tier of broadcasting in India, to co-exist with public and commercial radio. With increasing marginalisation of the concerns of the rural poor and the oppressed people in the market-driven media outlets, alternative media have a real potential to redefine notions of democracy, development, identity, and, forge a public sphere that is more egalitarian and equitable. Perhaps the celebration is somewhat premature, for the practitioners of community radio and the campaigners for democratisation of the airwaves are acutely aware that the task ahead is Sisyphean—creating awareness among community-based organisations of the possibilities of this medium as well as of the opportunities proffered by the new policy; building the capacities of non-literate rural people; exploring viable, cost-effective technology options; instituting more democratic governance structures; and establishing more ethical and responsible standards of media practice. All this if one were to realise the near-impossible dream of well-meaning bureaucrats envisioning thousands of community radio stations all over the country in the next couple of years, allowing a legitimate space on the radio dial for hitherto suppressed voices!

This book is about these 'other voices' that have been trying hard to be heard above the cacophony over the airwaves in India that had risen to a crescendo by 2005. The FM radio revolution has well and truly struck at the media consumption habits of people in the metros and beyond, with its non-stop film music and the inane chatter of a new generation. While this situation leads some observers to revel in a liberal-capitalist rhetoric of 'multiple outlets' and 'consumer choice,' one cannot help but invoke Brecht's lamentation in the late 1920s that radio had been reduced to only a distribution system, an 'acoustical department store.' He pleaded for turning radio into 'something really democratic' by making it a medium of two-way communication, enabling true participation by citizens in public affairs. This book not only offers a historical account of the struggle for community radio in India, but also provides a documentation of the efforts of non-governmental organisations (NGOs) and rural communities to realise the Brechtian mandate to use radio as a tool to build a robust civil society in the country, employing creative ways, in the absence of a licence to broadcast, to take their community audio programmes to the people.

Work on this project started in 2000 around the time when Vinod Pavarala participated in the drafting of the now oft-quoted Pastapur Initiative on Community Radio Broadcasting along with representatives of NGOs, media activists, communication educators, journalists, and policymakers. The document articulated the need for using communication technologies for the empowerment of local communities and argued that people must have access to media not solely as receivers and consumers but as producers and contributors of media content. Taking into consideration the experiences and policy precedents from other democratic countries, the document appealed for broadcasting in India to be based on principles of 'universal access, diversity, equitable resource allocation, democratisation of airwaves, and empowerment of historically disadvantaged sections of society.'

Since then, the inspiration we drew from this pronouncement took us to a number of villages in Andhra Pradesh, Karnataka, Gujarat and Jharkhand where exciting community radio projects, often referred to as the 'Big Four', have been attracting national and international attention. The palpable enthusiasm about the potential of community radio in India that we exude is an outcome of our interaction with the people who are part of these community radio initiatives. We are grateful to everyone at Deccan Development

Society, Pastapur, in the Medak district of Andhra Pradesh; Kutch Mahila Vikas Sanghatan in Bhuj, Gujarat; Alternative for India Development, in Palamau, Jharkhand; and VOICES in Kolar and Bangalore, Karnataka. We would never be able to forget the warmth and keenness with which they accommodated all the requirements of our study.

We would specially like to thank 'General' Narsamma, Preeti Soni, Mangala Gowri, P.V. Satheesh, Suresh Kumar, Ashish Sen, and all the community radio reporters who gave us their precious time, shared their experiences and offered every possible help to interact meaningfully with people in their villages. We are also indebted to Nandita Roy of the National Foundation for India for commissioning the Jharkhand component of this project and providing the necessary support. Kanchan K. Malik benefited from a modest travel grant from the Indian Council of Social Science Research (ICSSR), enabling her to visit some of the sites of our study.

We perused reference material at various libraries, including those at the ICSSR, the Press Information Bureau, the Indian Institute of Mass Communication, Publications Division, all in New Delhi, and the American and the British Libraries in Hyderabad. Uday Sahay, Prasar Bharati; P.S. Murthy, Director, Audience Research, AIR; and S.S. Thakur, Librarian, Research, Reference & Training Division of the Ministry of Information & Broadcasting, have been of immense help in giving us access to policy documents and other resources related to broadcasting in India. We feel obliged that the doyen of Indian journalism, B.G. Verghese, Anil Baijal, and Bandana Mukhopadhyaya spared their valuable time to talk to us about broadcasting issues in India. We thank Jo Tacchi, Queensland University of Technology in Australia for reading parts of our work and sending her critical comments. We are grateful to Ian Pringle of UNESCO, Leela Rao at the Manipal Institute of Communication, Anita Gurumurthy, IT for Change, Bangalore, Dorothy Kidd, University of San Francisco, J. Josephine of University of Madras, Anjali Monteiro and K.P. Jayasankar, TISS, Mumbai, and Shohini Ghosh of Jamia Millia Islamia for their inputs, comments and suggestions that have variously contributed to the final shape this book has taken. The cr-India e-group, especially Frederick Noronha, Sajan Venniyoor, and Stalin K., deserve special mention as they not only kept us posted on all CR matters in India and elsewhere, but also gave us a comforting cyber community with which we could share our own trials and tribulations. Padma Prakash, who was then at the

Economic and Political Weekly graciously offered a special issue on community broadcasting and published versions of some of the material we present in this book.

We are deeply indebted to the University of Hyderabad (UoH) for providing us with the apposite academic milieu for carrying out our work. We thank colleagues in the Department of Communication at the Sarojini Naidu School—B.P. Sanjay, P. Thirumal, Vasuki Belavadi, E. Sathya Prakash, and the late C.V.S. Sarma—for being a constant source of support. Kalyani, Janardhan, Srivani, Sunil, and Niranjana, students and research scholars, helped in conducting focus group discussions for different case studies and also transcribed and translated some of the recordings. We are also thankful to Natarajan, Rajani, Raghavan, Venkatalakshmi, Ramesh, and Madhu, non-teaching staff at the School for the cooperation they extended to us during the course of this work.

Omita Goyal, Mimi Choudhury, Sugata Ghosh and Sudeep Kohli saw this book through at various stages of its career with Sage. We also thank the reviewers and editors at Sage, especially Neha Kohli, for helping make this a better publication.

At a personal level, we both should acknowledge our respective family members and friends for bearing with years of CR babble from us and for reassuring us that we are on to something good.

For Kanchan: Aparna Rayaprol for her sincere and progressive counselling that gave me strength as a woman. I also draw a lot of inspiration from my sister, Kavita, whose 'power of focus' is exemplary. Rama and S.K. Mohindra made me feel at home during my extended stay at Delhi. My cousin, Sunil Arora, who helped me at a time when I needed it most. My parents have been my pillar of strength always and Parul is probably the most loving and understanding daughter in the world. Arun Malik has been a true partner in every sense of the word.

For Vinod: Surinder Jodhka and Sneha in Delhi and Tasqeen and Asad in Bangalore for their hospitality and warmth, Aparna Rayaprol for being such an inexhaustible source of strength, Ratna Naidu and Probal Dasgupta for their periodic reminders about my next book, my parents, my sister Vanitha for helping me keep track of media reportage on CR, and little Saranya, without whose help this book would have long seen the light of day.

Hyderabad
2007

Vinod Pavarala
Kanchan K. Malik

1 INTRODUCTION

Politics of Community Radio in India

> When radio fosters the participation of citizens and defends their interests; when it reflects the tastes of the majority; when it truly informs; when it helps resolve the thousand and one problems of daily life; when all ideas are debated in its programmes and all opinions are respected; when cultural diversity is stimulated over commercial homogeneity; when women are main players in communication and not simply a pretty voice; when no type of dictatorship is tolerated, when everyone's words fly without discrimination or censorship; that is *community radio* (José Ignacio López, 1997).

The satellite revolution and the unprecedented boom in Information and Communication Technologies (ICTs) have provoked a spirited public debate across the world about the role media play in the lives of the people. Certain discernible trends, including privatisation of media industries and services, deregulation of government controls on gigantic media corporations, relaxation of regulations on entry of foreign multinational companies and concentration of ownership of ICTs in the hands of a few media conglomerates based in the United States, Europe and Japan have led to an oligopolistic control over the terms of public debate and discourse and to cultural homogenisation. Popular resistance to media globalisation emerges out of a concern that the development of technology would ultimately cater only to state and transnational commercial and political interests. The paradox of multiplication of communication outlets and at the same time the diminishing plurality of information have eroded the diversity and quality of information in the public sphere, rendering civil society increasingly ineffective.

Throughout India, a number of civil society organisations are questioning the positions held and roles played by state-centred or market-run media and challenging the hegemonic intentions of the market to control the minds of the people. They are articulating the need for alternatives in the form of popular and community-based media—people's theatre, small local newspapers, community radio, participatory video and alternative documentaries. These alternatives, they suggest, would help revive the developmental prowess of media by promoting meaningful content that is change-oriented and socially responsible, as well as relevant to local contexts. The community radio initiatives by several groups across India for a share of the airwaves, which are 'public property', are one significant indication of this popular resistance. This book examines the burgeoning movement for community radio in India as a particularistic response to this universalistic phenomenon of media globalisation.

Organisations experimenting with participatory communication for social change across the world, citizen groups, community organisations and media activists have been pushing for an institutional space that can be effectively used for revitalising the civil society. A necessary condition for the creation of this alternative institutional environment is a progressive state policy that facilitates the development of new centres of symbolic power, which lie outside the spheres of influence of the state and the market, respectively. By taking stock of the political realities associated with broadcasting in India, we make a case for the functioning of radio in the country to be based on the principles of 'universal access, diversity, equitable resource allocation, democratisation of airwaves, and empowerment of marginalised sections of society' (DDS, 2000).

What is Community Radio?

> The historical philosophy of community radio is to use this medium as the voice of the voiceless, the mouthpiece of oppressed people (be it on racial, gender, or class grounds) and generally as a tool for development.
>
> Community radio is defined as having three aspects: non-profit making, community ownership and control, community participation.
>
> It should be made clear that community radio is not about doing something for the community but about the community doing something for itself, i.e., owning and controlling its own means of communication (AMARC[1] 1998).

Community radio gained momentum as an alternative to public and commercial radio in the late 70s. In the West, community radio fulfils the needs of self-expression for groups who have negligible access to the mass media. In countries with autocratic or totalitarian governments, community radio becomes a means for passive or active resistance. In the developing countries, as a Rockefeller Foundation report asserts, community radio is 'one of the best ways to reach excluded or marginalised communities in targeted, useful ways', and in giving them a 'voice' that matters most in development communication (Dagron, 2001).

Radio is an affordable medium in terms of production, management, as well as for reception and can reach communities at the very end of the development road—people who live in areas with no phones and no electricity. Radio reaches people who cannot read or write. Even in very poor communities, radio has a far-reaching penetration. It is more appropriate for cultures dominated by orality and helps enhance cultural identity and community pride. The widespread ownership of and familiarity with transistor radios make it potentially a people's medium. All over the Third World radio has a proven track record of being a catalyst for social change (see for example, Girard, 1992; Dagron, 2001).

Tabing (2002: 9) defines a community radio station as 'one that is operated in the community, for the community, about the community and by the community'. According to Tabing, 'the community can be territorial or geographical—a township, village, district or island and can also be a group of people with common interests, who are not necessarily living in one defined territory.' Thus community radio may be owned and managed by one group or by combined groups. It could also be controlled and run by people such as women, children, farmers, fisher folk, ethnic groups, or senior citizens. Tabing points out that a high degree of people's participation, both in management and programme production aspects distinguishes community radio from other media. Also, the principal sources of support for community radio operations are individual community members and local institutions.

Distinct from the other two forms of broadcasting, the public and the commercial, community broadcasting is a non-profit service. Community radio is a social process in which members of a community federate to design and produce programmes, and air them (Fraser and Restrepo-Estrada, 2001). Community radio is thus characterised by access, public participation in production and decision making, management by listeners, and its operations rely mainly on the community's own resources. This involvement of community members distinguishes it from the dominant state and/or commercial stations that are operated for profit, propaganda, power, politics and privilege but are neither accountable nor accessible to the public. Community radio works as a cultural broadcast mechanism that adapts perfectly to reflect the interests and needs of the community it serves and offers people of the marginalised sectors an opportunity to express themselves socially, politically and culturally. Community radio is recognised by AMARC (World Association of Community Broadcasters) as a unique contribution to media pluralism and an ideal means of fostering freedom of expression, development of culture and identity, and active participation in local life.

Federación Argentina de Radios Comunitarias (FARCO, Argentina) describes community radio stations as those that practice radio broadcasting as a community service and see communication as a universal right. Such radio stations develop pluralistic and participatory communication and exercise the right to communication and the right to information by challenging the traditional division between broadcasters on one side and listeners/consumers on the other. Community radio helps to put the community members in charge of their own affairs. A free marketplace of ideas and opinions is opened up. Important local issues are aired making community radio an essential partner in community development (Tabing, 2002). Community radio incorporates new languages, inventive formats, other sounds, novel music, unheard voices and innovative ways of pressurising the authorities. Community radio can thus be seen as part of a broader struggle for access to communication media and as a mechanism for social groups to reproduce their cultural identity, to voice their social and economic demands and to create new social relations.

Some of the characteristics of community radio compiled from AMARC (1994) and UNESCO (Tabing, 2002) documents are summarised below. Community radio stations:

- serve a recognisable community;
- promote access to media facilities and to training, production and distribution facilities as a primary step towards full democratisation of the communication system;
- offer the opportunity to any member of the community to initiate communication and participate in programme making

and evaluation. Encourage local creative talent and foster local traditions;

- use technology appropriate to the economic capability of the people, not that which leads to dependence on external sources;
- are motivated by community well-being, not commercial considerations;
- facilitate full interaction between the producers and receivers of messages;
- are managed and owned by the community members. Community or their representatives have a voice in the financing of radio programmes;
- promote the right to communicate, assist the free flow of information and opinions, encourage creative expression and contribute to the democratic process and a pluralist society;
- are editorially independent of government, commercial and religious institutions and political parties in determining their programme policy;
- provide a right of access to minority and marginalised groups and promote and protect cultural and linguistic diversity;and
- follow management, programming and employment practices which oppose discrimination and which are open and accountable to supporters, staff and volunteers.

Perhaps the best way to sum up the multiple features of community radio is in the words of AMARC's (1995) members:

> Community radio, rural radio, cooperative radio, participatory radio, free radio, alternative, popular, educational radio. If the radio stations, networks and production groups that make up the World Association of Community Radio Broadcasters refer to themselves by a variety of names, then their practices and profiles are even more varied. Some are musical, some militant and some mix music and militancy. They are located in isolated rural villages and in the heart of the largest cities in the world. Their signals may reach only a kilometre, cover a whole country or be carried via short wave to other parts of the world.
>
> Some stations are owned by not-for-profit groups or by cooperatives whose members are the listeners themselves. Others are owned by students, universities, municipalities, churches or trade unions. There are stations financed by donations from listeners, by international development agencies, by advertising and by governments.

Community Radio Worldwide

The right to communicate and to have affordable access to the means of communication is increasingly being acknowledged throughout the world as a fundamental human right. The Seventh World Congress of AMARC held in Milan, Italy, 23–29 August 1998 emphasised on the just and equitable access to and participation in communications media for strengthening the rights of indigenous peoples, minorities, migrants and refugees. There was also focus on education and training to enable people to develop their own media and communication skills. The Milan Declaration recalled and recognised several historic charters and pronouncements including Article 19 of the *Universal Declaration of Human Rights*, the *Beijing Platform of Action*, the *People's Communication Charter* and the *European Charter for Community Radios*.

All these endorse that communication resources (such as airwaves and outer space) should not be appropriated by private parties or monopolised by governments. Communication and information services should be guided by respect for pluralism, diversity of culture, language and gender, and the empowerment of historically disadvantaged sections of society. The AMARC called for international recognition of the community broadcasting sector as a vital contributor to democracy and freedom of expression and information, and for establishment of national, community level and international norms and measures to enable development of independent community broadcasting services.

According to Dagron (2001), radio is the most pervasive and economical electronic medium in the world with the potential to serve as an 'ideal medium for change'. For over 50 years now, radio has been the 'most appealing tool' for participatory communication and development and community radio stations have 'multiplied by the thousands' all over the world. Experiences from Latin America, dating as far back as mid-40s, have demonstrated the potential of community radio for social change. The first documented case of community radio being totally conceived, owned, run, as well as sustained by a section of society, and used to fight poverty along with social injustice goes back to the Miners' Radios of Bolivia, Latin America (Dagron, 2001; Fraser and Restrepo-Estrad, 2002; Girard, 1992). The Miners' Radios originated in 1949 with the birth of

Radio *Sucre* in the mining locality of Cancaniri while, at the same time, Radio *Nuevos Horizontes* started in the little city of Tupiza in the south of Bolivia. By the 70s, the miners' radio network comprised 26 radio stations enabling workers, families and communities to communicate, discuss and debate their situation (Buckley, 2000).

Latin America today has one of the most diverse and dynamic radio traditions in the world with hundreds of stations even in the smaller countries. Girard (1992: 1) has described the Latin American environment as 'a radiophonic salad of state, private, church, university, special interest and indigenous peoples radio stations', much of which emerged after periods of revolution or following the replacement of military regimes with civil government. Most of these are low power frequency modulation (FM) stations serving their communities with content that is appropriate to the local language, culture and needs, and thus enjoy immense amount of public support. At present, however, there is regulatory vacuum and legal uncertainty about the status of low power independent radio stations. The radio activists and independent stations are lobbying aggressively for the need to legislate for socially-owned media as an essential form of social communication especially for small communities.

In 1985, according to AMARC–Africa, there were fewer than 10 independent radio stations in the entire continent of Africa. The next decade saw remarkable political changes in Africa accompanied by an opening up of the airwaves to hundreds of independent private and community radio stations (Buckley, 2000). In a conference called 'Freedom for African Radios' held in Bamako, Mali in 1993, many countries formally recognised the important role that community radio can play as a tool to empower the disadvantaged majority and argued for legislation in its favour (Fraser and Restrepo-Estrad, 2002). Community radio is an emergent force in many African countries, notably in South Africa where it is supported among other wide-ranging radio services, by a distinct regulatory framework. The post-apartheid broadcasting policy in South Africa, spearheaded by the Independent Broadcasting Authority, articulates a three-tier system based on universal access, cultural diversity, democratisation of the airwaves and nation building. Being hailed as one of the most comprehensive and progressive communication policies in recent times, the South African policy seeks to address historical inequalities in: access for the disadvantaged, resource allocation (frequencies, human resources and finance), and language, cultural and educational programming.

Probably the first independent and non-commercial radio station in Europe was Radio Student set up by students of the University of Ljubljana, Slovenia in 1969 (Buckley, 2000). Starting with the UK in the 60s and Italy and France in the early 70s, the 'pirate' radio movement swept the conservative media environment of Europe, which was until then dominated by radio operated as centralised state-owned monopoly (Dagron, 2001). Through the 80s and 90s, most European states liberalised radio and allowed community broadcasting of one kind or the other. While public policy has most directly contributed to the development of community radio in many western European countries like France, the Netherlands and Ireland, in eastern Europe, Hungary provides the best example where radio stations run by civic sector organisations have been supported by public policy (Buckley, 2000; Dagron, 2001). In the UK, over 20 years of campaigning by the Community Media Association (CMA) followed by the pilot 'access radio' project by the Radio Authority in 2001 resulted in the passing of Community Radio Order in July 2004. The Community Radio Order legalised a new 'third tier' of very local, not-for-profit (or not profit distributing) community radio stations with the responsibility to deliver 'social gain' rather than a return to shareholders. So far, the media regulator OFCOM has awarded full five-year licences to 48 community radio stations across the UK (CMA, 2005).

Most of North America and Australia has a strong, entrenched third tier of broadcasting in addition to the state network and profit-oriented sectors. Locally owned and accountable community radio stations, licensed by an independent broadcast regulator, engage with and serve their communities. In Australia, community broadcasting has been allowed for nearly two decades on the condition that stations licensed under that category must be: (*a*) non-profit enterprises that reflect community purposes and interests; and (*b*) operated with the participation of community members. The objectives of the Australian policy include: promoting the diversity of broadcasting services, developing and reflecting Australian identity, character and cultural diversity; and providing programming material that is locally significant.

Similarly, the United States has a long history of community radio along side commercial and institutional broadcasting sectors. The Federal Communications Commission gave a further boost to the community radio movement in the country by announcing, in recent years, a new low-power FM radio licensing policy. This has enabled even smaller players to enter the fray. The policy objective for establishing community radio stations in Canada is the provision of public access to the airwaves with the aim of offering a unique type of grassroots local programming not generally available on the radio dial. Organised as a three-tier broadcasting system (public, private and community), Canada also provides for a simplified process for licensing low-power 'developmental' community stations that could serve as a training ground for the future establishment of higher power community stations.

The new Irish community radio broadcasting policy published in 1997 recognises the 'surge in community and voluntary activity over the past twenty years', especially in areas such as education and health, and identifies the third sector of broadcasting clearly with community and voluntary organisations (BCI, 1997). The Independent Radio and Television Commission of Ireland (now BCI: Broadcasting Commission of Ireland) has also started a Community Radio Support scheme to provide financial support for licensed community radio stations.

Broadcasting in Asia has been slower to shed its colonial past of state-controlled broadcasting. Philippines, Sri Lanka, Nepal, Indonesia and Thailand provide important examples where community radio stations have been permitted within the existing legal frameworks. But much of what is called community radio is conducted under the aegis of state-run broadcasters or other national institutions. At present, therefore, these countries do not offer much in terms of law that enables setting up of an autonomous community radio sector that can be a real alternative to state and commercial broadcasting. This, however, is the region to watch for dramatic transformations in the radio scenario, as there is a ferment that is prodding the state to share airwaves with community groups.

The first genuinely community-based radio to be set up in Asia was in the Philippines, as part of the Tambuli Community Radio Project of UNESCO in the 90s. The Danish International Development Agency (DANIDA) provided the initial capital and UNESCO set up a management and training team to cooperate with communities to organise independent community radio stations in less developed rural areas in the Philippines. These stations are run with community participation, on a not-for-profit basis with support from local or international NGOs or even some government departments.

In the South Asian Region, in May 1997, Radio Sagarmatha became the first independent station to get a license in Nepal. This FM station, run by the Nepal Forum of Environmental Journalists (NEFEJ) in the capital city of Kathmandu, represents South Asia's first major effort at autonomous community radio broadcasting by non-governmental groups (Noronha, 2000, 2003). The broadcast environment in Nepal opened up gradually after the introduction of parliamentary democracy in 1990. The bold National Communication Policy and the amended National Broadcasting Act of 1993 (Government of Nepal, 1993) ended the monopoly of Radio Nepal over the air waves as new broadcast policies, legislation and regulations allowed for the setting up of independent public-interest, community and commercial FM radio stations. Nepal's Broadcasting Regulations (Government of Nepal, 1993) specifies that primate groups can operate only on the FM band, but does not provide a clear distraction between commercial and community radio stations and between for-profit and non-profit broadcasters. The legal and financial obligations are similar, and all stations have to pay the license fees and a government levy of 4 per cent on net profits. According to Koirala (2002), the community radio stations are identified by their ownership and the power of the transmitters they use. Since licence fees are based on the transmitter's capacity, the communities prefer to use low-power (100 to 200 watts) transmitters because of their limited financial resources.

The FM broadcasting in Nepal may be seen as consisting of commercial and community radio stations. Out of the 22 independent radio stations that were issued licenses and were operational till 2002 in Nepal, five could be categorised as non-profit community stations: Radio Sagarmatha, Lumbini FM, Radio Madanpokhara, Swargadwari FM and Himchuli FM. Except for Sagarmatha, the other four are radio stations in smaller regions outside Kathmandu and started broadcasting regular programmes in/after the year 2000. The community broadcasters focus on locally relevant information and discussions and on national/local culture. The commercial stations are almost entirely entertainment-based and cater to the younger generation of music listeners, and claim to have public service content in their programming in one form or the other.

A report of the workshop on 'Community Radio in South Asia' organised in Kathmandu by the Institute of Development Studies, Sussex (IDS, 2002) in 2002 took examples from Nepal to discuss the different models of ownership and management of community radio that would be feasible in the South Asian context. In the case of Radio Lumbini, the ownership and management operations are carried out by a cooperative (Cooperative Model) formed by the local entrepreneurs and journalists. While the shareholders contributed to the initial setting up of the station, there are also 600 friends of Radio Lumbini each paying 100 rupees annually. Radio Madanpokhara is owned and managed by the locally elected Village Development Committee (Local Administration Model). With preliminary funding coming from UNESCO, Radio Madanpokhara was the first community radio station to be based in a rural area in Nepal. Radio Sagarmatha works on an NGO model and is run as a non-profit organisation. Initially funded by UNESCO and other NGOs, the licence holder is NEFEJ. According to Raghu Mainali, a community radio activist in Nepal, who runs the Community Radio Support Centre in Kathmandu, the most important thing is for community radio to prove itself as a social entity. 'This entails drawing on social, human and physical capital and is not just a matter of financial resources' (cited in IDS, 2002).

Radio came to Sri Lanka as early as December 1925 when the Ceylon Broadcasting Service (CBS) was established. The CBS was subsequently brought under the Broadcasting Act No. 37 of 1966 and is now known as the Sri Lanka Broadcasting Corporation (SLBC). The SLBC operates under the Ministry of Information and the Media with a mandate to promote public service broadcasting in the country. A Farm Broadcasting Unit was established within SLBC in 1967 and a daily rural service was aired from 1969. The programmes of SLBC's services for rural communities are broadcast in all three languages—Sinhala, Tamil and English—of the national and local services but focus more on teaching rather than on sharing experiences (http://communityradionetwork.org/leftlinks/comm_radio_ southasian/sri_lanka).

The Kothmale FM Community Radio Station began broadcasting in February 1989 and is one of the four community radio stations operating under the Mahaweli Community Radio (MCR) Project of the SLBC. The MCR Project was launched by the SLBC with the assistance of UNESCO and DANIDA and is regarded as a turning point in Sri Lankan rural broadcasting because of its participatory approach towards the socio-economic development of the settlers alongside the Mahaweli River (David, 1992). In 1998, UNESCO set up a pilot project in Sri Lanka to assess prospects of converging community radio and information from the Internet to determine its possible impact on development efforts in rural communities. The Kothmale Community Radio was identified as the site for this pilot project. The Kothmale Community Radio Internet Project uses community radio as an interface between the Internet and rural communities, and has become a global yardstick for participatory community broadcasting in the digital age.

Even after nearly 60 years of independence from colonial rule, India, Pakistan and Bangladesh, the three largest countries in South Asia with cultures more diverse than almost any other region of the world, have not permitted any real media decentralisation or diversity. In Pakistan, the government recently approved an ordinance to make community radio possible, but questions about the degree of control/level of autonomy for the new media still remain unanswered. In Bangladesh, there is an absence of a coordinated regulation for radio broadcast and the law needed to issue licences for community radio is yet to be prepared. In all the South Asian countries, civil society organisations are lobbying actively for independent media, but progress towards the establishment of community radio has been very slow.

Many of the liberal democracies in the world have enacted laws that promote independent and pluralist media, India being the conspicuous exception till recently. This book presents an analysis of broadcasting legislation and policies on community radio in the US, Canada, Australia, South Africa and Ireland, countries which have offered lessons for policy in India through their long-term, durable experiences with community radio. These countries, where community media are operating on a self-managed democratic basis, as an alternative to the media hierarchies of the official public realm, present us with a significant breadth of vision about the role of broadcasting in contemporary world.

Ferment for Community Radio in India

Facilitating Community Radio

The broadcast laws in India, until November 2006, did not permit community radio as conceptualised by media advocacy groups and

NGOs seeking democratisation of the airwaves. Radio broadcasting shifted from being a government monopoly to a highly commercialised broadcasting after Ministry of Information and Broadcasting (MIB) announced the Phase I of auctioning of licences to set up 140 private FM stations in 40 cities in November 1999. The Phase II of the private FM radio licensing policy announced in July 2005 has made access to the airwaves a whole lot simpler and feasible for the commercial players and 330 frequencies in 90 cities are up for bidding. It also cleared foreign direct investment (FDI) within the overall cap of 20 per cent. Radio entertainment in India is witnessing a revival of sorts, as the airwaves break free from government control.

The social sector, however, was left high and dry every time the government took a step forward in making radio more accessible. No one seemed to have an ear for the voices from the rural areas that were seeking a 'radio of our own' for using it as a tool to participate in and further their own development (DDS Website—Community Radio; Joseph, 2005; Malik, 2005). Several non-governmental and other civil society organisations had been campaigning to get rural communities the right to set up low-cost local radio broadcasting facilities, but to no avail. An articulation of these concerns is also discernible in the reports of a number of committees periodically appointed by the Government of India to evolve a comprehensive media policy for the country (Kumar, 2003b). Today, more than a decade after the historic Supreme Court of India ruling on 9 February 1995 (Appendix-I), which declared the airwaves as public property, the Government of India has been cautious in unshackling broadcasting, but to allow its use only for entertainment. The private commercial FM radio services have not been permitted to broadcast news and current affairs programmes even under the new policy.

The long-standing demands for a third tier of independent, not-for-profit broadcasting in the country yielded a confined 'campus' avatar of community radio in the form of 'Guidelines' issued in the first quarter of 2003 that allow 'well-established' educational institutions to set up FM transmitters and run radio stations on their campuses. This decision diluted somewhat the hegemony of the state and market over radio, but to open up the broadcasting sector for an urban, educated, elite coterie in areas that are already well-served by media violates the fundamental philosophy behind community radio. Labelled as 'community radio', the norms laid down for obtaining licenses include, as a mere tokenism, content guidelines that suggest that these campus radio stations air programmes on agriculture, environment, health and other development-related information. It is unrealistic to expect campus radio stations managed by young students to eschew fun and entertainment. There is no apparent fit between form and content in this new policy, even as marginalised rural communities continue to be denied the right to produce, own and operate real community radio (Pavarala, 2003a).

The stations of All India Radio (AIR), the public broadcaster, to a large extent, still remain centralised, government-controlled, and lacking in editorial independence. All India Radio has had some historic experiments in development. It also has a network of local radio stations in districts for serving the local communities but the stations have not proven to be locally relevant as they are not community-run (Mukhopadhyay, 2000). In the 70s, an experimental FM station was set up in Nagercoil district in Tamil Nadu. The project successfully elicited participation of the listeners and could have turned out to be a workable model for development-oriented FM stations. The station functioned with methods that did not conform to AIR's top-down approach. K. Anjaneyulu, the initiator of the project, asserted that 'Local radio should identify itself so completely with the interests of its local population that the heart of the people beats in every pulse of the programme it broadcasts' (Page and Crawley, 2001). This modus operandi could not be replicated in stations administered and staffed by an all-India cadre of broadcasters with only temporary local affiliations.

Radio, designated by several as a medium of the poor, seemed to have been hijacked by the elites. If it does not enable the marginalised, rural or poor populace to challenge the mainstream understanding of social issues, the whole purpose is lost. But the Government of India stubbornly refused to yield to the demands for opening up this sector, under misplaced apprehensions that secessionists, militants or subversive elements would misuse the medium. These so-called subversive elements do not need official sanction to communicate with each other. There are all kinds of simple as well as more sophisticated mechanisms by which such groups bypass the official communication routes. Pavarala (2003a) contends that this is just a bogey being raised by a government that is uneasy about the consequences of allowing autonomous broadcasting spaces to communities and the social sector. The question we should ask is: why does this government find Rupert Murdoch more trustworthy than a poor, unlettered, Dalit woman who wants to use a media channel to communicate?

Landmarks in Community Radio Campaign

For more than 10 years now, non-profit development organisations and media-activist groups have been campaigning for the right to set up low-cost local radio broadcasting facilities to support their community development work. They have also been attempting to network and further the cause of community radio in the country. The Bangalore-based communication campaign group, VOICES, convened a gathering of radio broadcasters, policy planners, media professionals and not-for-profit associations in September 1996 to study how community radio could be relevant to India, and to deliberate on policies appropriate for such an action. A Declaration (see Appendix-II) calling for the establishment of community broadcasting was signed. A suggestion to the effect that AIR's local stations should allocate regular airtime for community broadcasting was put forward. Requests were also made for grant of licences to NGOs and other non-profit making groups for running community radio stations (VOICES, 1996). Subsequently, UNESCO made available a portable production and transmission 'briefcase radio station' kit to VOICES to do experimental broadcasts of programmes for a hands-on learning experience towards the objective of setting up an independently run community radio station.

A UNESCO sponsored workshop from 17–20 July 2000 in Hyderabad issued the *Pastapur Initiative on Community Radio* (see Appendix-III) that urged the government to take its intentions of freeing broadcasting from state monopoly to its logical conclusion by making media space available not only to private players but also to communities. The document urged the government to create a three-tier structure of broadcasting in India by adding non-profit community radio to the already existing state-owned public radio and private commercial radio. Drishti Media Collective and Magic Lantern Foundation organised a 'Media and Human Rights Workshop' as part of the conference on 'Globalization, Social Movements, Human Rights and the Law' in December 2000 at Panchgani in Maharashtra. The last two days of the workshop were spent exclusively discussing the range of issues pertaining to community radio. In June 2001, a four-day UNESCO workshop on 'Community Broadcasting in the Digital Age' was held at Kothmale, Sri Lanka. Participants from India, Bangladesh, Nepal, Sri Lanka, Pakistan and Maldives resolved to make the struggle for community radio a South Asia-wide movement. A media-watch website, http://www.thehoot.org carried out an 'Internet Conference on Community Radio in India' from 30 November 2001 to 10 February 2002, the edited proceedings of which are available on their website. In March 2003, the UNDP–IIM, Bangalore workshop on 'ICTs and Cross Media Partnerships' focused some attention on community radio and brought the experiences in this field onto a common platform.

The spirited campaigning for communities' right to access the airwaves and innumerable representations by organisations, academicians and individuals resulted in the Ministry of Information and Broadcasting (MIB) organising a workshop supported by the UNDP and UNESCO in May 2004 in New Delhi to design an *Enabling Framework for Community Radio in India*. The workshop aimed at seriously exploring the possibility of creating a new frame-work for community radio in India. The basic purpose of the workshop was to study the experiences of different countries and organisations about successful community radio frameworks and practices as well as brainstorm on key issues of concern while formulating a national policy framework on community radio in India. The workshop brought together a large number of community radio enthusiasts, academics, NGOs and policy makers, who worked out a set of recommendations for a new community radio policy, one that would allow community groups to run their own radio stations. When Telecom Regulatory Authority of India (TRAI) issued a consultation paper later that year, they arrived at much the same formulations for community radio.

In July 2004, MIB prepared a draft policy based on the May 2004 consultations. Subsequently, community radio groups in India launched an online petition campaign, urging the inclusion of the right of communities within the community radio policy and thereby ending the discrimination against rural and poor communities. In October 2005, the draft policy was referred to a Group of Ministers, which took about a year to give its approval after deliberating upon several contentious issues such as advertising, news and information, license fee, spectrum availability and so on. In November 2006, the policy was finally cleared by the Union Cabinet, marking a much-delayed, but well-deserved victory to communities and civil society groups that have been waiting patiently for this right to broadcast to be extended to them.

Conceptual Framework

Broadcasting and Development

In the post-World War II period many nations emerged from colonialism and embarked upon an exercise of nation building, which involved a model of economic modernisation and liberal democracy. Scholars, policy makers and institutions often mobilised the media of mass communication in aid of this process. Print media and radio, initially, and television later, were seen as instruments for the dissemination of information related to the state's agenda for development. This process assumed a hierarchical, top-down and elitist character with one-size-fits-all prescriptions for planning and growth. There was little stakeholder involvement and local knowledge or participation of people at the grassroots was rarely considered essential in these efforts. Historically, radio has been used by the state within the context of this older paradigm of development as early as the 50s in India. The whole approach was prescriptive and pedagogical, and treated people as only passive consumers of information.

However, 'community radio', in the sense of a non-state, non-market venture, owned and managed by the community[2] is a relatively recent idea in India. This idea is today being articulated against the backdrop of participatory approaches to development that were popularised by the rise of new social movements and non-governmental organisations (NGOs). These movements and NGOs appeared on the Indian socio-economic canvas in the post-emergency years, as the state suffered from a severe crisis of legitimacy, giving rise to a civic ferment. These organisations have now, after two decades of grassroots work, reached a level of maturity, redefining politics and development in the country. After years of focusing on issues of livelihood, capacity building and mobilisation, some of these organisations have now turned their attention to deploying media technologies for empowerment of marginalised communities. They are envisaging democratised and decentralised media systems such as community radio as key agents for facilitating a self-propelled and self-sustained social change and a more democratic development process.

This book examines the potential of community radio as a medium for generating an autonomous, democratic, community-based communication environment with opportunities for articulating localised and people-centred development needs. Through case studies of ongoing experiments with community radio by civil society organisations, the study highlights the complex nature of participation in diverse social, economic and cultural circumstances and pinpoints important related concepts such as conscientisation and knowledge sharing. An attempt is made to gauge if an internal democratic process that puts grassroots expression at the heart of all programme production has been strengthened; and whether the democratic, dialogical and participatory process of community radio has helped in raising the consciousness and understanding of the community about their social reality, problems and solutions.

Media Globalisation

Freedom of expression and equitable access of communication media are seriously threatened in the twenty-first century, not by excessive use of state power as in an earlier period, but rather from the unhindered growth of media organisations into large-scale conglomerates. In India, the 90s were marked by a gradual easing of state monopoly over the electronic media. Globalisation and liberalisation of the economy inevitably meant greater power to market forces, which made their presence felt in the media sector. While the state and the market carved up the available media resources and made up iniquitous rules of access, people at the grassroots were left unrepresented. The consequences of this media globalisation for market, state and civil society and for the relationship between them are immense. If the realm of civil society must include, as Calhoun (1994) puts it, 'organized and substantial capacity for people to enter into public discourse about the nature and course of their lives together', a free flow of information to and from citizens becomes an essential prerequisite. But media globalisation diminishes freedom of information and restricts the diversity of information. This is evident in the fact that even as we have an expanded menu of media outlets, the uniformity of the content renders meaningless the increase in the number of information sources.

The global media juggernaut has been facing stiff resistance all over the world from citizen groups, community organisations and media activists. An expression of this widely shared anxiety could be seen in the countervailing public demand for greater decentralisation of political power and distribution of the benefits and control of media technologies. Alienated by an indifferent government and priced out of an inconsiderate market, many communities have been forced to think of genuine alternatives. A sustained critique of media globalisation has, almost as a parallel to the emergence of market power, yielded fresh perspectives, which emphasise horizontal communication, people's participation and indigenous knowledge. As realisation dawned about the ill effects of one-way, vertical communication processes, historically marginalised communities started mobilising themselves in order to make their views heard. The book examines the potential of community radio to stimulate a kind of publicness, which is neither part of the state nor wholly dependent on the autonomous processes of the market. This requires, in Thompson's (1995) words, 'establishment of an institutional framework which would both accommodate and secure the existence of a plurality of independent media organizations', free from the exercise of state power, but also unhindered by market forces.

Gender, Media and Development

Feminist activists and women's movements have argued that the conventional ideology of male superiority and the control of productive resources by men have affected women's options and opportunities for a better life. Gender is a significant dimension in community radio initiatives launched by community-based organisations that are seeking to deploy communication technologies for social change in general and empowerment of women in particular. By examining the intersections of development frameworks and feminist theorising, and how they have been influenced by debates and critiques of media globalisation, the book highlights the gender mainstreaming practices stirred by them, especially those that address issues of regional and cultural differences. Through the case studies of community radio initiatives, we explore the manner in which management, control and ownership of media technologies by marginalised women has provided them access to representation and decision making and helped in activating women's alternatives for fostering social change.

Forging Counterpublics

Our book investigates the possibility of how access to radio could not only transform the dominant public sphere, but also help establish counter public spheres controlled by the subaltern sections in India. It examines the potential of these *counterpublics*, established through the process of shifting control of media technologies to those excluded from the dominant public sphere, to expand the discursive space and facilitate collective action that could prove emancipatory for the marginalised.

Community Radio Initiatives in India

Even as the government was dithering over legislation to facilitate the functioning of community radio in India, a few community-based organisations had initiated radio projects to support their community development work. Some made use of available spaces within the state sector of broadcasting while others, fearing co-optation and appropriation, steadfastly resisted the offer to use state radio. They, in the absence of an independent licence, continued to creatively engage in narrowcasting, that is, playing back of programmes on a tape recorder or reaching the people through television cable. The Deccan Development Society (DDS), an NGO working with poor, rural, Dalit women in the Zaheerabad area of Medak district in Andhra Pradesh, for nearly two decades, set up a community radio station with assistance from UNESCO in 1998. A couple of young Dalit women from the area manage the station, produce programmes and take the audiotapes for narrowcasting in the village *sangams* (autonomous groups of women). One of the few NGOs in the country to apply for an independent license to broadcast, the DDS had to face rejection from the MIB (MIB, 2002b).

VOICES/MYRADA started an audio production centre, *Namma Dhwani* (Our Voice) in 2001 at Budhikote in the Kolar district of Karnataka and have been cable-casting (through television cable link) programmes made by rural men and women trained in the basics of radio production. The Kutch Mahila Vikas Sangathan (KMVS), Gujarat, an NGO working with rural women on their concerns in the villages of Kutch district, offers a different model for community broadcasting in India. KMVS built on its long presence in the area of doing development work and started airing a 30-minute sponsored Kutchi language programme on AIR's Radio Bhuj in December 1999 by purchasing a commercial slot. They have since acquired the AIR slot for two subsequent series. *Chala Ho Gaon Mein* is a community radio programme supported by the National Foundation for India (NFI) and produced by community representatives of Alternative for India Development (AID), a grassroots level NGO in Jharkhand. From August 2001, the programme has been broadcast from Daltongunj, a backward region in the Palamau district of the state, by using the AIR slot of the local station on terms similar to that of KMVS in Bhuj. The book includes detailed case studies of these grassroots-level projects, along with focus group discussions with the listeners of each of the radio programmes in order to gain an overall understanding of the role of community radio in rural India.

Methodology

Work on this research project started in September 2000, a couple of months after the release of *The Pastapur Initiative on Community Radio Broadcasting*. As stated earlier in the chapter, this document, among several others, is an important landmark in the narrative of the ferment for community radio in India. It was an outcome of the four-day stocktaking consultations organised by UNESCO from 17 to 20 July at Hyderabad and Pastapur (Andhra Pradesh) jointly with VOICES (Bangalore), the Sarojini Naidu School of Performing Arts, Fine Arts and Communication, University of Hyderabad, and the Deccan Development Society (Pastapur). It drew together the experiences of communication experts, media practitioners, researchers, educators, trainers, non-governmental development organisations, journalists, policy makers and students of mass communication and law. This group met to review the status of community radio in South Asia and to lobby for legislative action by Government of India to enable the functioning of non-profit, people-owned and managed community radio stations.

The Pastapur agenda explicates the community radio initiatives by several groups across India as a significant indication of the popular resistance to the positions held and roles played by state-centred or market-run media and their hegemonic intentions to control the minds of the people. It articulated the need for using communication technologies for the empowerment of local communities and argued that people must have access to media not solely as receivers and consumers but as producers and contributors of media content. This document not only provided groundwork for activists championing the cause of community radio in India, but also outlined the issues and discourses that nurture this fledgling movement. It included the voices from within the community that are seeking a 'radio of their own' and mentioned the efforts of some NGOs that are using audio technologies for empowerment at the grassroots level. However, despite the range of issues discussed on community radio and development, it pointed towards a remarkable absence of sustained, context-specific research undertaken on the potential of community radio and its sociological and political ramifications with respect to the media scenario in India.

For those seeking to examine comprehensively the demand for community radio in India and the politics behind freeing of airwaves, this document thus served as a legitimate starting point. Its contents and references formed a suitable basis for an exploratory study, which aimed at addressing a number of critical questions related to community radio through engagement with the stakeholders in this sphere. The aims and objectives as also the context of the research evolved from a perusal of pertinent literature on theory and practice in the fields of development communication and community organising in addition to interaction with resource persons in the area of communication for social change and media policy.

Aims of the Study

Set against this background, the study began with the intent of recording the methods and motives with which grassroots NGOs and media activists are pursuing the cause for community radio in India and their conceptualisation of public access to airwaves. Locating this movement within the context of globalisation of communication technologies, and how communication could play a more integral role in development, this study endeavoured to analyse how community radio is being hoisted as a medium for articulating more people-centred development needs in India and other regions of the world. In the face of the paradox of multiplication of communication outlets and the diminishing plurality of information, the research investigated the possibility of how access to radio could transform the dominant public sphere, by establishing decentralised public spaces for dialogue and collaborative action controlled by the marginalised sections in India.

A necessary condition for the creation of an alternative institutional environment that can effectively revitalise civil society is a progressive state policy that takes a fresh perspective on media and society. This study sought to explore conditions for the creation of an enabling environment for democratic media by taking into consideration the history of broadcasting and the issues that currently challenge the media policy formation in India. A comparative analysis of the legislative measures for democratisation of media by different countries of the world was carried out with focus on the status accorded to community radio.

The research proposed to address the critical issues related to the functional and efficacy aspects of community radio through case studies of ongoing experiments with community radio in the four states of India. An evaluation of the responses of the collaborators and participants in these projects was undertaken in order to make an assessment of the consequences of community radio as perceived by them. A deeper understanding of the social, economic, cultural and political dynamics and constraints that can variously enhance and negate the developmental and empowerment potential of community radio was attempted. Every objective was considered as a part of the whole, while determining the criteria to accomplish it.

Research Objectives

Against this backdrop, the study specifically proposed to:

(*a*) trace the growth and evolution of broadcasting in India from a media policy perspective, relating it with the role of the state in determining its form and structure;

(*b*) carry out a comparative analysis of the national broadcasting policies/legislations of different countries of the world along with the measures and provisions therein for facilitating a vibrant community media sector;

(*c*) analyse the ferment for community radio in India with a critical evaluation of the lobbying and capacity building endeavours by civil society organisations that are seeking alternative media spaces as a means for empowerment at the grassroots;

(*d*) undertake case studies of ongoing experiments with community radio by civil society organisations (KMVS—Bhuj, Gujarat; AID—Daltongunj, Jharkhand; DDS—Pastapur, Andhra Pradesh; VOICES—Bangalore, Karnataka) and investigate how the message development process of community radio by itself becomes a training ground for participation in the broader issues of development at the community level;

(*e*) to probe through case studies the extent to which community radio contributes to effectively enhancing access to information and the process of self-expression, public dialogue, collective action and empowerment.

Research Strategy

Based on the aims and conceptual framework of the study, a set of research foci were identified and corresponding research questions formulated (details in Table 1.1). This was done to assess the commonalities emerging from the findings across different objectives and case studies. Interview guides and checklists, as appropriate in particular situations, were used for the purpose.

Table 1.1: ***Research Themes and Questions***

Research Foci	*Research Questions*
Community Radio: Concept	What is 'community' radio: its features? What would people do with 'a radio of their own'?
Community Radio: Policy (India)	How has advancing democratic functioning of radio been a contentious item in the continuing debates for a comprehensive media policy in India?

Research Foci	*Research Questions*
	What enabling policy framework can government evolve in India to open up the broadcasting sector for 'community' radio?
Community Radio: International Perspectives	What kind of progressive policies/legislation is being adopted by various liberal democracies to facilitate radio for community empowerment?
Alternative Media: Lobbying	What is the ideology that drives lobbying efforts by organisations that are seeking community radio? What form does this lobbying take?
Civil Society	Does community radio contribute to the creation of a new relationship between media and civil society in accordance with the contemporary ideas of participatory democracy?
Communication for Social Change	How can community media play a constructive role in enabling rural people to manage their own development?
Gender, Caste and Class	How do the categories of gender, caste and class play out in both production and reception of the content?
Community Radio Initiatives	What are the different functioning models of community radio in India and their socio-economic, political and cultural contexts?
Capacity Building	How can technology be demystified for the marginalised and capacities of communities be enhanced to take control of radio?
Degree of Participation	What is the extent of community participation in different stages of the content development and distribution process of community radio? What is the sense of ownership among producers, volunteers and listeners of community radio programmes?
Power and Control	What role do power equations within the community play in control of media technologies?
Perceptions at the Grassroots	What are the perceptions of the members of the community about the role community radio can play in empowering them?

Research Methods

The research work used qualitative methodology for accomplishing the objectives of the study. The approach was to gain insight on community radio in India through application of multiple methods of inquiry. The case study method was used, involving in-depth and open-ended interviews and focus groups, along with analysis of documents. A comparative approach was used throughout the study. The study was located in the context of globalisation, participatory communication and social change and relied on meaningfully generated broad research foci and open research questions to discover important categories, dimensions, and inter-relationships for analysis. An attempt to problematise/operationalise the concepts that were the key to further investigations in the course of theresearch was made. Data collection and analysis continued throughout the study.

Following Patton (1990), the qualitative research done for this study was understood as a complex system that was more than the sum of its parts. We made direct contact with the people, situations and phenomena under study in order to gain insight on multiple interdependencies. Participation of rural audiences was sought in a more significant manner than as mere respondents in the interrogative context of a structured questionnaire. Thick description, inquiry in depth, direct quotations capturing people's personal perspectives and experiences formed the qualitative data to describe how people were experiencing the phenomenon. Our personal experiences, observations and insights form an important part of the inquiry and are critical to understanding the subject. We avoided getting locked into rigid designs that eliminate responsiveness and was open to adopting new paths of discovery as they emerged. Cross-case analysis to look for themes and patterns across diverse experiences was undertaken at a later stage, but the first level of inquiry treated each case as special and unique. Case studies were undertaken of all known ongoing experiments with community radio in India by civil society organisations, outside of the state and market sectors.

The four grassroots-level projects using community radio for development included: KMVS project in Bhuj (Gujarat); AID project in Daltongunj (Jharkhand); the DDS project in Pastapur (Andhra Pradesh); and the VOICES project in Budhikote (see Chapter 4 for profiles of organisations). In addition to this, the fieldwork involved collection of policy-related documents and interaction with resource persons in the allied areas of broadcasting, alternative media, development and policy formulation.

Throughout the study, the individual case studies were analytically connected through a common framework. By addressing the same issues in all cases, common *themes* that identify consequential features and patterns across the case studies were explored. The comparative method was also employed to study the international policy perspectives on community radio. We have also undertaken extensive analysis of documents. Document analysis of official publications, factual records, reports and declarations yielded excerpts, quotations, or entire passages, facilitating a historical study of media development, operations and legislative framework of broadcasting in India. Analysis of documents released by organisations involved in community radio initiatives helped in tracing the ideology behind them and the course of the lobbying efforts for community radio in India. In addition, audio material, websites of organisations and postings on the community radio e-mail list server were also examined.

In-depth interviews with members of lobbying groups, representatives of the various civil society organisations, programme coordinators, content producers and policy planners were conducted to generate productive information consisting of direct quotations from the people about their experiences, opinions, feelings and knowledge about community radio in India. Focus group discussions (FGDs) with listeners within the broadcast/narrowcast area were conducted with the aid of a moderator in the sample villages. The sample villages were selected for each case study, based on geographic and demographic variations. The focus groups convened consisted of 6–10 people as a smaller size limits the potential of gathering collective information and more than this makes it difficult for everyone to partake. They were organised in such a way that they represented gender, religion, caste and age depending on the socio cultural profile of the village. These discussions were audio-recorded and transcribed for detailed analysis. The focus groups were conducted in the local language and in comfortable settings where the members would normally gather to hold discussions in their villages.

Data analysis was not treated as a distinct end process and, as mentioned earlier, a substantial amount of parallel analysis was carried out as data collection progressed. We kept moving from data collection to data analysis and back. This reflexivity helped in looking out for more meaningful and in-depth information during the case studies that led to a deeper understanding of the existing circumstances. Informal visits to the villages as well as discussions at the many seminars and conferences, and consultations we attended over the last five years were some of the ways in which we gained familiarity with those associated with both the advocacy and the grassroots facets of the community radio movement in India. On the whole, the most fulfilling part of the project for us has been listening to community voices—women talking about their issues, men and women discussing the developmental concerns of their region, and community radio reporters and project coordinators sharing details of the programmes they produced.

Overview of the Book

The book contains eight chapters, including the introductory and concluding chapters. Chapter 2 compares community radio policies of five countries with a view to understand the contours and content of progressive state policy that promote democratic media. Chapter 3 traces the growth and development of broadcasting in India from a media policy perspective and attempts to probe within the historical and contemporary contexts, the issues, dilemmas and political realities associated with opening up of radio broadcasting for the non-profit social sector. Chapter 4 offers detailed profiles of the NGOs and their community radio initiatives that were examined in this study. Chapters 5, 6, and 7 are thematic chapters that knit together the empirical observations and analysis of case studies of community radio initiatives with the theoretical insights.

Notes

1. AMARC, the World Association of Community Radio Broadcasters, is an international non-governmental organisation for the promotion, support and development of community radio worldwide. The international headquarters is located in Montreal, Canada following the founding Assembly held in 1983.
2. For the purpose of community radio policy, the Pastapur initiative defines it as 'a territorially bound group with some commonality of interests'.

2 LEGISLATING FOR COMMUNITY RADIO

A Comparative Analysis of Policy Frameworks in Other Countries

The right to communicate and to have affordable access to the means of communication is increasingly being acknowledged throughout the world as a fundamental human right. The Seventh World Congress of the World Association of Community Radio Broadcasters (AMARC), an international non-governmental organisation for the promotion, support and development of community radio worldwide, held in Milan, Italy, 23–29 August 1998 declared that:

- the Right to Communicate is a universal human right which serves and underpins all other human rights and which must be preserved and extended in the context of rapidly changing information and communication technologies;
- all members of civil society should have just and equitable access to all communications media;
- the rights of indigenous peoples should be respected in their struggles for access and participation in communications media;
- the democratic participation of women in communications media should be guaranteed at all levels;
- communications media have a responsibility to help sustain the diversity of the world's cultures and languages, which should be supported through legislative, administrative and financial measures;
- community media can play an important role in strengthening cultural rights, and in particular, the rights of linguistic and cultural minorities, indigenous peoples, migrants and refugees by providing access to the means of communication;

- access to the means of communication must be supported by education and training to assist a critical understanding of the media and to enable people to develop their media and communication skills;
- the market economy is not the only model for shaping the communications infrastructure. People must be seen as producers and contributors of information and not be defined solely as 'consumers'.

The Milan Declaration recalled and recognised several historic charters and pronouncements including Article 19 of the *Universal Declaration of Human Rights*, the *Beijing Platform of Action*, the *People's Communication Charter* and the *European Charter for Community Radios*. All these endorse that communication resources (such as airwaves and outer space) belong to the 'commons'[1] and should not be appropriated by private parties or monopolised by governments. Communication and information services should be guided by respect for pluralism, diversity of culture, language and gender, and the empowerment of historically disadvantaged sections of society. AMARC called for international recognition of the community broadcasting sector as a vital contributor to democracy and freedom of expression and information, and for the establishment of national, community level and international norms and measures to enable development of independent community broadcasting services.

While these are laudable principles, AMARC has pointed out the existence of a number of barriers to access to communications infrastructure by citizens and communities. Some of these barriers include: insufficient or inappropriate spectrum allocation, poor levels of connectivity or insufficient access to bandwidth, market failure to deliver new systems based on appropriate technology at affordable costs of access, socio-cultural barriers to access, and, more importantly for this chapter, inappropriate/hostile public policy frameworks. A major hurdle for fostering community media all over the world seems to be the lack of a coherent, appropriate public policy framework to support non-profit access to broadcasting and public communications. However, as will be elaborated shortly, there are some countries that provide good workable models for community involvement in communication. These models underline the critical role played by progressive public policy in withholding or allowing access to the means of communication.

This chapter examines broadcasting policy frameworks in different nations of the world that are seeking to construct autonomous communication spaces and democratic media by sustaining the new tier of community radio. Such policy is shaped to a great extent by the forces and actors of the state and the market. Progressive policy efforts attempt to guide this influence in democratically productive directions, and aim to deploy broadcast media as a forum for participatory public dialogue that is essential for social change. Although the policies vary by country, political system, purpose and organisation, they are all based on the actual experiences of civil society organisations in organising such media on a self-managed, democratic basis, as an alternative to the media hierarchies of the official public realm.

Even though community radio stations are ensconced in their own geographic and collective universes, media scholars and community radio enthusiasts are aware of many successful and exciting people's media initiatives in different parts of the world (see Chapter 1 for details). Radio Pacifica in the US, the Tambuli project in the Philippines, Bush Radio in South Africa and Radio Sagarmatha in Nepal have all been, in varying degrees, sources of inspiration for the community radio movement in India and elsewhere. The way in which the fortunes of the public sphere are tied to the state and to contemporary political situation in a country can be seen clearly in the case of broadcasting policy. The primary objective here is to analyse broadcasting legislation and policies on community radio in Australia, Ireland, South Africa, Canada and the US which could offer lessons for policy in India either through their long-term, durable experiences with community radio or present us with a significant breadth of vision about the role of broadcasting in the contemporary world.

Hantrais (1996) points out that cross-national comparisons have not only served as a means of gaining a better understanding of different societies, their structures and institutions, but have also contributed in the area of social policy as a means of evaluating the solutions adopted for dealing with common problems. Price and Verhulst (1998) point out that the important snag to be addressed in the use of comparative media law methodology is that of context as what has proved satisfactory in its country of origin may not necessarily be applicable in the country that proposes to adopt it. Thus we have also analysed the political structures and the historical context within which community radio took off in different countries before examining the implications for a community radio policy framework for India.

Comparisons pertaining to these countries were made through perusal of legislative texts, policy guidelines and statements, articles and documents available on the Internet that dealt with:

- history of evolution of community radio sector;
- definition of community radio;
- licensing procedure;
- allocation of frequency and technical parameters;
- sustainability/funding;
- management and ownership;
- programme content; and
- regulation and monitoring.

AUSTRALIA

History of Evolution of Community Radio Sector

The advent of FM in Australia is seen as the starting point of public broadcasting. Before this, industry and government shared control of the airwaves through a parallel system of a national network and a commercial network. In 1946, FM services were permitted on an experimental basis in four capital cities, but they did not last long as the government and the industry did not perceive a need for FM in Australia. The closure of the experimental services in the early 60s gave birth to political and ideological struggles by many citizen groups, including radical campus communities, in the late 60s and early 70s that swayed policy formulation in favour of public access to airwaves and also promoted the idea of public participation in the operation of new radio services (Langdon, 1995).

Community non-profit radio operated under the amended provisions of the *Broadcasting Act 1942* until 1992, when the new *Broadcasting Services Act* repealed the 1942 Act and the control of services was placed firmly in the hands of a single regulator, the Australian Broadcasting Authority (ABA). The first non-profit service, the Adelaide Educational Radio station 5UV, went on air on the amplitude modulation (AM) bands on 28 June 1972. Community radio experienced phenomenal growth after the first fully licensed community (previously 'public') radio, 2MBS-FM went on air in Sydney in 1974 (Forde, Foxwell and Meadows, 2003).

Definition of Community Radio

It is the autonomous ABA, which is responsible for the regulation and allocation of Community Broadcasting licenses subject to the provisions made in the *Broadcasting Services Act 1992* and also to the availability of spectrum in a license area plan (LAP) prepared by the ABA. Community broadcasting services are defined in Section 15 of the Act as being services that:

- are provided for community purposes; and
- are not operated for profit or as part of a profit-making enterprise; and provide programmes that are able to be received by commonly available equipment and are made available free to the general public.

The ABA prefers a broad definition of 'community':

> Given the role that community broadcasters play in promoting the objects of the Act, the ABA believes the most useful definition of community is one that is broad and takes into account social, historical and cultural linkages. The objects of the Act include promoting the diversity of broadcasting services available to the public; developing and reflecting Australian identity, character and cultural diversity; and providing programming material that is locally significant.

Source: www.aba.gov.au/radio/services/licence_types/community/index.htm

Licensing Procedure

There is no cost involved in lodging an application for Community Broadcasting license. Access to spectrum is also free for community broadcasters. Only non-profit community broadcasting organisations, which represent a community interest, are eligible for the allocation of a community broadcasting license. The ABA decides whether, and to whom, to allocate a community broadcasting license, in keeping with the norms set out in section 84 of the 1992 Act. These include:

- the extent to which the proposed service would meet the existing and perceived future needs of the community within the license area of the proposed service; the nature and diversity of the interests of that community and that of other broadcasting services within the license area;
- the capacity of the applicant to provide the proposed service.

Source: www.aba.gov.au/radio/services/licence_types/community/alloc.htm

Allocation of Frequency and Technical Parameters

The Department of Communications, Information Technology and the Arts administers broadcasting within the Australian government. Its public broadcasting branch has a community broadcasting section. The ABA is the independent federal statutory authority responsible for the licensing and regulation of the broadcast industry in Australia (Price-Davis and Tacchi, 2001). The ABA ensures economic and efficient use of the radio frequency spectrum for broadcasting purposes by undertaking an extensive national planning programme to identify vacant radio frequencies and allocate new licenses. This is done through the preparation of a frequency allotment plan (FAP) and the LAP based on priorities such as identifying geographical areas least well served by existing services. Once each LAP is prepared, the ABA makes licenses available. The nature of those licenses are determined by the available frequency and perceived public need.

Sustainability/Funding

The Community Broadcasting Foundation Ltd. (CBF) is an independent funding body for community broadcasting. It was established in 1984 as a non-profit body for backing the development of community broadcasting in Australia. The CBF receives an annual grant from the department of communications, information technology and the arts plus a smaller grant from the Aboriginal and Torres Strait Islander Commission. All community broadcasting licensees are subject to a condition that prevents them from broadcasting advertisements, but they may broadcast up to five minutes of sponsorship announcements and a range of announcements and other promotional material that are not classified as advertising in any one hour (for more details see: http://www.aba.gov.au/radio/services/licence_types/community/sponorship/index.htm).

The ABA has developed guidelines for broadcasting sponsorship announcements and other promotional material on community radio and community television. Also, the *Community Broadcasting Code of Practice* (2002) of Community Broadcasting Association of Australia (CBAA) affirms that commensurate with the need to ensure active participation by the community in the station's management, development and operations, community broadcasters will adopt and implement—in consultation with their communities—a sponsorship policy which ensures that:

- sponsorship will not be a factor in determining access to broadcasting time;
- the content and style of individual programmes is not influenced by the sponsors of programmes; and
- overall programming of community broadcasting stations is not influenced by sponsors.

Management and Ownership

The community broadcasting code of practice put together by CBAA, a national representative and coordinating body for community broadcasters, defines the responsibilities of broadcasting to the community and to the principles of democracy, diversity and independence, and indicates that community broadcasting stations will:

- have policies and procedures in place, relating to the licensee's community of interest, which ensure access and equity and encourage participation by those not adequately served by other media;
- be controlled and operated by an autonomous body that is representative of the licensee's community of interest;
- have organisational mechanisms to provide for active participation by the licensee's community in its management, development and operations; and
- incorporate policies that apply to all station activities, which oppose and attempt to break down prejudice on the basis of ethnicity, race, language, gender, sexual preference, religion, age, physical or mental ability, occupation, cultural belief or political affiliation.

Programme Content

The CBAA *Code of Practice* also includes 'Guidelines for all programming' that reflects the principles of community broadcasting; breaking down prejudices and discriminations; and preventing the broadcast of material, which is contrary to community standards. For example,

- community broadcasting licensees will avoid censorship wherever possible; however, consideration shall be given to the audience, the context, the degree of explicitness, the propensity to alarm, distress or shock, and the social importance of the event;
- community broadcasting licensees will establish programming practices, which protect children from harmful programme material;
- news and current affairs programmes (including news flashes) should: provide access to views under-represented by the mainstream media;
- present factual material accurately ensuring that reasonable efforts are made to correct substantial errors of fact at the earliest possible opportunity;
- clearly distinguish factual material from commentary and analysis;
- not present news in a way that public panic or unnecessary distress to listeners get created.

Regulation and Monitoring

In recent years there has been a process of deregulation of the broadcasting sector in Australia and community broadcasting is largely self-regulated now. A term used by some is 'co-regulation'. The CBAA, mentioned earlier, is a membership organisation that provides advice and support to community broadcasters. It is dedicated to supporting the development of the sector in Australia and to the principles of local ownership and control. The CBAA has an established community broadcasting code of practice. The code includes responsibilities and guidelines for community broadcasters as well as rules on programming, sponsorship and volunteers.

The ABA allots licenses for a period of five years. The *Broadcasting Services Act 1992* was amended at the end of 2002 by the

Broadcasting Legislation Amendment Act (No. 2) 2002 giving the ABA more discretion to review community broadcasting licenses on renewal. When renewing community broadcasting licenses, the ABA can now take into account the same matters it had regard to under section 84(2) of the 1992 Act in deciding whether to allocate a license. The ABA will be able to refuse renewal of a community license where the applicant no longer meets these criteria. Renewals may be applied for no earlier than one year and no later than 20 weeks before a license expires.

IRELAND

History of Evolution of Community Radio Sector

Pirate radio stations have existed in Ireland since the early 60s, mushrooming in the capital in the 70s and throughout the country in the 80s. In later years these stations operated openly and often with the participation of elected representatives on the programmes. Radio Telefis Eireann (RTE), the state broadcaster, had in 1974 begun a community radio project in which a mobile unit visited towns in rural areas for two weeks at a time, producing programmes under local editorial control. The success of the project encouraged RTE to propose a national community radio scheme, but this foundered as the political climate changed in favour of commercial broadcasting.

In 1988, legislation was introduced which ended the state monopoly in broadcasting and established the Independent Radio and Television Commission (IRTC) to oversee the licensing of independent radio and television. The IRTC (now BCI: Broadcasting Commission of Ireland) was initially cautious about the community sector. During 1992, the IRTC decided to issue a single one-year experimental license to a Dublin conglomerate of community groups. Many of the community radio groups in Ireland were dissatisfied with this and continued to campaign for a full-fledged policy on community radio (Pavarala and Kumar, 2001a).

In 1994 the IRTC established an 18-month community radio pilot project to explore and evaluate the potential offered by community broadcasting in an Irish context. Under this initiative, 11 stations were licensed to operate until the end of 1996. Following the evaluation of this project, the Commission determined that community stations could develop into a viable distinct strand in Irish broadcasting, the other two strands being commercial and public broadcasters.

Definition of Community Radio

Recognising the 'surge in community and voluntary activity over the past 20 years,' especially in areas such as education and health, the new BCI policy on community radio identified this third sector clearly with community and voluntary organisations. The BCI policy provides a definition of community radio, which reads:

> A community radio station is characterised by its ownership and programming and the community it is authorised to serve. It is owned and controlled by a not-for-profit organisation whose structure provides for membership, management, operation and programming primarily by members of the community at large. Its programming should be based on community access and should reflect the special interests and needs of the listenership it is licensed to serve.

Source: http://www.bci.ie/licensing/radio/community_policy.html

Since the term 'community' is central to this definition, the Commission adopted the *AMARC Community Radio Charter for Europe*, as a statement of the objectives community stations should strive to achieve. This includes a commitment to working for 'social purposes' and remaining independent of government or large media corporations.

Licensing Procedure

The single regulator, BCI, first invites expressions of interest from parties interested in securing contracts for sound broadcasting services. Expressions of interest are expected to indicate in general terms the type of service that will be provided and are not regarded as an application for a sound-broadcasting contract. Expressions of interest for community licenses are expected to include:

- a clear definition of the community to be served;
- the level of current and expected participation by that community in the station;

- the type of programming service envisaged; and
- how they propose to fund their station.

As part of the decision-making process certain selected applicants may also be invited to make an oral presentation to the Commission before a decision is taken. After considering the expressions of interest received, the Commission decides whether or not to move to application stage. If a decision to proceed is taken, the BCI invites applications by public notice. The BCI continues to use its definition of community radio and *AMARC Community Radio Charter for Europe* as a reference point when assessing submissions from, and the activities of, relevant groups. In conjunction with the AMARC Charter, the Commission also uses the following three-dimensional framework to assess the community nature of relevant organisations and groups. Stations included in the community-broadcasting strand will be expected to:

- describe clearly the geographical community or community of interest served;
- promote and support active participation by this community at all levels in the operation; and
- operate in a manner which is in keeping with the ethos or value system which underpins community activity.

Allocation of Frequency and Technical Parameters

The number of licenses issued depends on the applicants meeting the required criteria, the availability of frequencies, the resources of the Commission and any other considerations which may be relevant from time to time, such as the totality of services in a specific area. The Commission reserves the right not to award licenses in an area where, in the opinion of the Commission, an application is not of a sufficient standard.

All stations broadcast on FM frequencies. Each contract is individually considered and the most appropriate frequency allocated. The maximum radius for transmission is normally five miles—though there are variations. For example, in certain remote rural areas, such as Connemara, the only form of local radio available is the community station, and the transmission area is larger than five miles to enable the geographically dispersed listeners to receive the station. In more densely populated areas such as Dublin City, the broadcast area is more localised.

Sustainability/Funding

The BCI suggests that the community should be funded from a diversity of sources, including membership fees, sale of services, collections, general fund-raising and on-air commercial activity. This is not only the most realistic option, but is essential if stations are to ensure that, primarily, the community served determines programming. The BCI regulates on-air commercial activity, and allows community stations to broadcast advertisements and sponsorship announcements, subject to the following conditions:

- no more than 50 per cent of income is secured from commercial activity; and
- a maximum of six minutes of advertising/sponsorship per hour.

The Commission limits community stations to broadcasting only those advertisements that relate to work opportunities that exist, events that are to occur, businesses that are carried on and services that are delivered in the specified area. The BCI provides support for a number of specific initiatives through the Community Radio Support Scheme developed in consultation with licensed community broadcasters through the Community Radio Forum. The Commission allows coordinated funding for community stations from appropriate statutory sources and endorses that community radio should be included in the support structures in place, and generally be developed for community and voluntary organisations.

Management and Ownership

In keeping with the definition of community radio, the BCI policy states that stations should be owned and controlled by not-for-profit organisations. Also, their structures are expected to provide for membership, management and operation of the station by the community served. It is important to have a clear definition of the relevant community and of developing structures to facilitate and promote participation of the community served at all levels. The station should be accountable to the community and the community must be in control of, and therefore responsible for, the station.

It is essential for community radio stations to employ paid staff, but the BCI reinforces the importance of participation in a voluntary capacity by the public at large. The extent to which members of the community served are willing to give of their own time, in a voluntary capacity, to support their station is seen by the Commission as a key indicator of the success of that station. As providing suitable training on a formal and informal level proved critical to progress in this area, it is the policy of the Commission to seek commitments in relation to training from interested groups.

Programme Content

It is the policy of the Commission to include in all contracts an approved Programme Schedule and Programme Policy Statement. Policy statements set out the station's programme philosophy and detail its plans to facilitate and promote community participation. Statements are expected to include clear commitments in relation to areas such as speech/music ratio, Irish language programming, music policy and externally produced programmes. The Commission endorses community broadcasting as a form of media with strong roots in the local community that it is licensed to serve.

The development of a viable community broadcasting service depends on a station providing a new and unique forum for communication between individuals and groups within the community served. The programming should be based on community access and reflect the special interests and needs of the listeners a station is licensed to serve. The AMARC Charter also states that community stations should promote and protect cultural diversity and inform their listeners on the basis of information drawn from a diversity of sources.

Regulation and Monitoring

The stipulated standard license term for stations in the community strand is five years but the BCI retains the right to vary the terms and conditions of each individual contract. It is the policy of the

Commission to seek information on how prospective licensees intend to approach the issue of community and audience evaluation, including the methodologies they propose to use and the frequency with which these will be applied. Authoritatively evaluating the relationship between a station and the audience is an important part of any assessment of the performance of a licensed broadcaster. The Community Radio Forum endorsed the qualitative approach to audience research. With regard to business, technical and programming aspects, a representative of the BCI visits the station at least once a year with the aim to inspect and to offer cooperation and consultation on these issues.

South Africa

History of Evolution of Community Radio Sector

The history of broadcasting in South Africa, had since inception, been characterised by politicisation of the broadcasting system and monopolised by the state-controlled South African Broadcasting Corporation (SABC). Broadcasting was used to entrench an oppressive political system that kept a large section of the population out of the public life of the country. In line with the apartheid ideology, broadcasting service provision was meant to favour the privileged according to the criteria of colour, class, geographic location and language. Apart from disseminating racial stereotypes and fragmenting the South African population on racial lines, content provided by the system was often political, particularly in the coverage of news and political events. The hallmarks of this broadcasting system were political censorship and the dissemination of propaganda on all services.

With the inauguration of a new democratic political system in the early 90s, a process was set in motion to re-regulate the broadcasting system. The airwaves in South Africa were opened for the first time in history with the creation of the Independent Broadcasting Authority (IBA) on 30 March 1994 by an Act of Parliament—the *IBA Act* of 1993. This ushered in a radical departure from state monopoly over radio broadcasting (Mtimde, 2000). When it took charge, the IBA had to contend with many inequalities in the broadcasting sector, including: inequality in (*a*) access, (*b*) resource allocation (frequencies, human resources and finance), (*c*) language, cultural and educational programming, (*d*) diversity and choice in services and programmes; and (*e*) empowerment for the historically disadvantaged.

The IBA began issuing community stations with temporary 12-month licenses from 1994. In 1999 a broadcasting Act was introduced. The preamble of the Act explicitly articulated the new broadcasting vision for South Africa as consisting of a three-tier system of broadcasting—public, commercial, and community—based on universal access, cultural diversity, democratisation of the airwaves and nation-building. In May 2000, the South African government created the Independent Communications Authority of South Africa (ICASA) through an Act, paving the way for the merger of the South African Telecommunications Regulatory Authority (SATRA) and the IBA.

Definition of Community Radio

The object of the *Broadcasting Act number 4 of 1999* is to establish and develop a broadcasting policy in the Republic of South Africa in the public interest and with a purpose:

(*a*) to contribute to democracy, development of society, gender equality, nation building, provision of education and strengthening of the spiritual and moral fibre of society;
(*b*) to encourage ownership and control of broadcasting services through participation by persons from historically disadvantaged groups;
(*c*) to ensure plurality of news, views and information, and provide a wide range of entertainment and education programmes; and
(*d*) to encourage the development of human resources and training, and capacity building within the broadcasting sector especially amongst historically disadvantaged groups.

The 1999 Act defines community broadcasting service as one which:

- is fully controlled by a non-profit entity and carried on for non-profitable purposes;
- serves a particular community;

- encourages members of the community served by it or persons associated with it or promoting the interests of such a community to participate in the selection and provision of programmes to be broadcast in the course of such broadcasting service; and
- may be funded by donations, grants, sponsorships or advertising or membership fees, or by any combination of the aforementioned.

Licensing Procedure

The current IBA Act includes two types of community licenses. These licenses are defined as those serving a geographical community and those serving a community of interest. The IBA grants 12-month temporary licenses as well as a permanent four-year community license. There is an application fee, which is non-refundable and community services also have to pay an Issue of License Fee and an Annual License Fee. The ICASA can reduce fees to promote community services in needy areas (Price-Davis and Tacchi, 2001). In considering any application for a community broadcasting license, the ICASA takes into account the following criteria:

- whether the applicant is fully controlled by a non-profit entity and carried on or to be carried on for non-profitable purposes;
- whether the applicant proposes to serve the interests of the relevant community;
- whether the applicant has the support of the community or of those associated with or promoting the interests of such a community; and
- whether the applicant proposes to encourage members of the community to participate in the selection and provision of programmes to be broadcast.

The *White Paper on Broadcasting Policy* issued by the Department of Communications in 1998 points out that the definition of a community, according to the IBA Act—any group of persons or sector of the public having a specific, ascertainable, common interest—is too open-ended and unlimited. This formulation needs to be changed so that all community broadcasting licenses should be geographically founded in that they should serve the specific community within a determined geographic area:

Community broadcasting must be inclusive. Whatever common interest need is, therefore, expressed by a potential licensee must be catered for in the framework of a geographically founded community within which all of the common or specific needs of the community can be satisfied to the benefit of, and with the participation of, all of the people in the community. The interests identified within the community must be catered for in one license for a given geographic area of local concentration.

Source: http://www.polity.org.za/html/govdocs/white_papers/broadcastin-gwp.html?rebookmark=1

Allocation of Frequency and Technical Parameters

The Department of Communications is the public service arm of the Ministry for Post, Telecommunications and Broadcasting of South Africa and consists of a Broadcasting Policy Development Unit. The IBA (now ICASA) is the regulatory body for community, commercial and public broadcasting. Its central task is to prepare a plan defining and reserving frequencies on all bands for the different categories of broadcasting and determining frequency assignment, footprint and operational prerequisites for every community radio station. The Authority avoids sharing of frequencies but is open to it where the situation requires this, and where broadcasters agree. The White Paper provides that the national strategy for the community sector would especially account for prioritising the licensing of services to those sectors of the South African community that is under- or un-served by the broadcasting system whether assessed by geography, age demographics or social status. This is done in a manner that helps to increase both participation and ownership by the historically disadvantaged. The policy directs the Authority to observe the principles of empowerment when awarding licenses in order to achieve these outcomes. The elements of this strategy would include:

- the setting aside of frequencies specifically for the maintenance and expansion of community broadcasting;
- community broadcasting stations in needy areas will pay less than the normal rates for signal distribution services. The IBA will be required to report to the government on the tariff structure;
- a resource strategy which includes training, human resource development and financing.

Sustainability/Funding

South Africa's broadcasting policy does not impose any restrictions on community radio stations to accessing revenues from advertising, sponsorships, grants and community contributions and donations. Access to local advertising is open while national advertising time is restricted through regulations of the ICASA. The regulator also ensures that the pursuit of advertising revenue does not interfere with the delivery of a truly community service. All surplus funds derived from the running of a community broadcasting station are to be invested for the benefit of the particular community and monitored by ICASA, which has the power to audit the financial records of the services. Community broadcasters can access government assistance for training programmes to develop their broadcasting trainers.

The policy puts the responsibility for funding on the community broadcasting sector itself, but is inclined to act as a catalyst by injecting some modest capital by way of an independently administered Community Development Trust to assist particularly the unserved, needy communities. The trust will provide funds on merit for the establishment and maintenance of community broadcasting stations in areas where communities do not have access to resources and are in need of development. Trustees to be appointed by the government will be eminent people from different walks of life. The government will help the community sector to interact more effectively with other development agencies and facilitate a closer relationship with other government departments, such as agriculture, health and water.

Management and Ownership

This White Paper that pronounces the South African government's policy for broadcasting proclaims that, 'Community broadcasting must be for the community by the community, through the community' (Government of South Africa, 1998). It must truly represent all the people of a community in ownership, control and decision making. The larger broadcasting policy mandate is to increase both participation and ownership by the historically disadvantaged groups.

Programme Content

Programming for community stations, as described by the Broadcasting Act, must promote development of a sense of community while addressing the particular needs of communities as mentioned here:

- provide a distinct broadcasting service, dealing specifically with community issues, which are not normally dealt with, by the broadcasting service covering the same area;
- be informational, educational and entertaining;
- focus on the provision of programmes that highlight grassroots community issues, including, but not limited to, developmental issues, health care, basic information and general education, environmental affairs, local and international, and the reflection of local culture; and
- promote the development of a sense of common purpose with democracy and improved quality of life.

Regulation and Monitoring

The principal functions of ICASA as the regulator include, but are not limited to:

- the conduct of research, including research into community standards, so as to inform its regulatory role;
- the enforcement, where appropriate and necessary, of broadcasting laws and regulatory requirements;
- dealing with complaints about broadcasters' observance of community standards in programming and advertising; and
- the making of regulations necessary to give effect to broadcasting policy through due public processes.

The civil society counterpart to ICASA, the National Community Radio Forum (NCRF) is the umbrella affiliatory body for the South African community radio sector. The NCRF was launched in 1993 as a support service organisation to lobby for the diversification of the airwaves in South Africa, and to foster a dynamic broadcasting environment in the country through the establishment of community radio stations (NCRF Constitution cited in Naidoo, 2002; for more details see Tacchi, 2002). Its aims and objectives include:

- promoting the ideals, principles and role of community radio as an integral part of the broadcasting environment of a democratic South Africa;
- encouraging the participation of historically disadvantaged communities in all levels of community radio;
- facilitating the establishment and development of community radio stations throughout the country;
- encouraging networking and cooperation between community radio stations;
- advocating the role of community radio within institutions responsible for legislating and regulating broadcasting policy, as well as popularise the value of community radio within the reconstruction and development of South Africa;
- encouraging the production of high quality and innovative programming from diverse sources to serve local programming goals; and
- promoting democracy, development and empowerment of communities through community radio.

CANADA

History of Evolution of Community Radio Sector

Public broadcasting in Canada is documented as beginning in 1920. Early public policy initiatives in broadcasting were mostly motivated by a desire to protect Canadian cultural sovereignty against the onslaught of the technologically superior American broadcasting.

The current Canadian Radio-Television and Telecommunications Commission (CRTC) evolved from a series of legislative interventions in 1968 and 1976. It is an independent public authority vested with the authority to license, regulate and supervise all broadcasting and telecommunications within Canada. This was also the period when the importance of community radio was acknowledged, and consequently, Canada has a well-developed community broadcasting sector today. The early 90s saw the revamping of broadcasting policies in Canada and the CRTC now derives its regulatory authority over broadcasting from the Broadcasting Act of 1991. The CRTC relies on informed public participation, through well-established processes, in carrying out its regulatory mandate.

Definition of Community Radio

Community radio is a vital constituent of the Canadian broadcasting system. Section 3(1)(b) of the *Broadcasting Act, 1991* provides for a Canadian broadcasting system organised into public, private and community sectors. On 28 January 2000, the CRTC released a revised policy for community radio stations in its Public Notice 2000–2013. The new policy document defines a community radio station as follows:

> A community radio station is owned and controlled by a not-for-profit organization, the structure of which provides for membership, management, operation and programming primarily by members of the community at large. Programming should reflect the diversity of the market that the station is licensed to serve.

Source: http://www.crtc.gc.ca/

Licensing Procedure

The Department of Canadian Heritage is responsible for national policies relating to broadcasting, culture industries, arts, heritage, official languages, Canadian identity, Canadian symbols, exchanges, multiculturalism and sport. The CRTC is one of its independent regulatory agencies. It regulates Canada's broadcasting and telecommunications systems along with Industry Canada that takes care of the technical aspects (Price-Davis and Tacchi, 2001). Applicants for a community radio license are expected to provide information in their applications regarding their current and/or proposed measures to:

- facilitate community access to programming;
- promote the availability of training throughout the community; and
- provide for the ongoing training and supervision of those within the community wishing to participate in programming.

The Commission distinguishes between Type A and Type B community radio stations. This is done for the purpose of regulating the programming content. A community radio station is a Type A station if, at the time of licensing, no other radio station, other than one owned by the CBC, is operating in the same language in all or part of its market. A Type B community station is a station operating in a competitive market. A community radio station is a Type B station if, when the license is issued, at least one other station, other than a station owned by the CBC, is licensed to operate in the same language in all or any part of the same market. While assessing the applications for licenses, the CRTC takes into consideration how well they further the objectives of the Broadcasting Act, especially with respect to cultural diversity. This refers to section 3(1)(d)(iii), which states that the broadcasting system should reflect the multicultural and multiracial nature of Canadian society and the place of aboriginal peoples. The CRTC evaluates the extent to which community stations fulfil their mandate to provide community access to the airwaves and to offer diversified programming that reflects the needs and interests of the communities they are licensed to serve. The Commission expects community stations to promote local talent, particularly, minority cultural groups and specific commitments by individual stations are assessed on a case-by-case basis. The soundness of the financial base of the applicant is also taken into account.

Allocation of Frequency and Technical Parameters

The governmental body responsible for managing the radio spectrum is the department for industry. Community broadcasters predominantly use the FM waveband and tend to broadcast on relatively low power frequencies. Licenses last for up to seven years. A simplified process for licensing low-power 'developmental' community stations (low-power FM, 5 Watts) for up to three years has been authorised to serve as a training ground for the future establishment of higher power community stations.

Sustainability/Funding

In a bid to give the community broadcasting sector greater scope to broaden its potential revenue sources, the Commission has eliminated all restrictions on the amount of advertising that may be broadcast by stations. It believes that if community stations are to fulfil their intended role and mandate, they must have adequate, secure revenue streams. The new policy states that community radio stations operate with limited financial and other resources and generally achieve lower levels of listenership. Placing limits on advertising is not the most effective way to guarantee that community stations offer programming that differs in style and substance from that provided by other types of stations.

Management and Ownership

Community stations are owned and controlled by not-for-profit organisations. Volunteers from the community participate in all aspects of the programming and operations of these stations. The policy objective for establishing community radio stations in Canada is the provision of public access to the airwaves with the aim of offering a unique type of grassroots local programming as an alternative to what is generally available from other types of radio stations. All community radio licensees are expected to facilitate community access to their programming by clearly informing the public of opportunities for community participation.

Programme Content

The Commission's primary objective for the community radio sector is to provide a local programming service that differs in style and substance from that provided by commercial stations and the Canadian Broadcasting Corporation.

The programming should respond to the requirements and interests of communities served, including official language minorities. The Commission considers that community stations should add diversity to the broadcasting system by increasing programme choice in both music and spoken word. They should contribute to diversity at three levels:

(*a*) community stations should offer programming that is different from and complements the programming of other stations in their market. Their not-for-profit nature and community access policies should assist them in contributing to the achievement of this objective;

(*b*) community stations should be different from other elements of the broadcasting system, including commercial stations and stations operated by the CBC; and
(*c*) the programming broadcast by individual community stations should be varied and provide a wide diversity of music and spoken word.

The primary focus of a community radio station is to provide community access to the airwaves and to offer diverse programming that reflects the needs and interests of the community that the station is licensed to serve, including:

- music by new and local talent and that not generally broadcast by commercial stations;
- spoken word programming; and
- local information.

For Type A stations, the Commission generally expects at least 15 per cent of programme aired in each broadcast week to be spoken word, with an emphasis on community-oriented spoken word whereas for Type B stations, the Commission requires at least 25 per cent of the same.

Regulation and Monitoring

The revised community radio policy streamlines the regulatory requirements to lessen the administrative burden of the community broadcasting sector. The new approach lifts the requirement by community stations to complete a Promise of Performance clause as part of the application process for licenses. Certain programming and other requirements are listed in the community radio application form and the applicants are expected to express their willingness to accept each as a condition of license. They are also given an opportunity to explain why a particular condition may not apply to them. The Commission has powers to monitor the performance of the licensees in relation to objectives set out for the broadcasting of programmes, financial affairs or otherwise relating to the conduct and management of their affairs as the regulations may specify.

UNITED STATES OF AMERICA

History of Evolution of Community Radio Sector

Since 1930, US broadcasting has been predominantly commercial, although coexisting with a besieged public sector. The Federal Communications Commission (FCC) was created by Congress in 1934 for the purpose of 'regulating interstate and foreign commerce in communication by wire and radio so as to make available, so far as possible, to all the people of the United States a rapid, efficient, nation-wide, and world-wide wire and radio communications service' (www.fcc.gov). The modern community radio movement in the US was born in the late 40s, when Lewis Hill, a disillusioned commercial broadcaster, conceived of a new kind of radio and founded KPFA in Berkeley, California. In 1946 Hill and some like-minded intellectuals created the Pacifica Foundation, and in 1949 KPFA went on air. The libertarian pacifists who founded KPFA[2] refused government funds as well as commercial advertising, preferring the then-untried notion of sponsorship from their listeners (Walker, 1997). Several new stations sprung up in the 60s, drawing from the counterculture movement and its do-it-yourself ethic, adopting volunteer management and local focus as their credo. In 1975, 25 of those stations formed the National Federation of Community Broadcasters, an organisation that provides advocacy on the national level and empowers community stations at the local level (Walker, 1997).

The Corporation for Public Broadcasting (CPB) was established in 1967 to promote public, non-commercial broadcasting in the US. After much hesitation in accepting state subsidies, many community stations started receiving CPB funds only in the mid to late 70s. The stringent conditions for funding, such as programming hours and quality, trained staff, equipment standards, listenership volumes, etc., have fostered professionalisation, centralisation, and a certain amount of mainstreaming of programming content. Many small groups interested in broadcasting to local communities have resisted the trend and managed to remain autonomous, often running illegal, low-watt 'micro' radio outlets. Several of these stations are part of a fledgling Grassroots Radio Coalition (Walker, 1997).

As if in answer to the desperation of local communities seeking a place in the broadcasting spectrum, the FCC in January 2000 announced the approval of a new low power FM (LPFM) radio service in the country. The FCC's note on proposed rule making was met by great enthusiasm from many schools, churches, local governments and other community-based organisations. In contrast to existing full power FM radio stations which operate at between 6000 and 100,000 Watts, the LPFM service will consist of 100 Watts and 10 Watts stations.

Definition of Community Radio

Community radio stations are defined by their devotion to local programming and programming outside the mainstream. In 1946, the FCC issued a programming policy statement, known as the Blue Book, which included four programming requirements. Two of the four were 'local live programs' and 'programming devoted to discussion of local public issues'. In 1960, the FCC Program Policy Statement gave a similar emphasis, citing 'opportunity for local self-expression' and 'the development and use of local talent' as programming priorities. This statement also held that the 'principal ingredient' of the public interest standard 'consists of a diligent, positive and continuing effort by the licensee to discover and fulfil the tastes, needs and desires of his service area. If he has accomplished this, he has met this public responsibility' (Taglang, 2000).

The FCC Chairman William E. Kennard declares that 'low power FM radio service open the doors of opportunity to the smaller, community-oriented broadcaster, and will give hundreds, if not thousands, of new voices access to the nation's airwaves'. He further elaborates that low power FM would serve as a forum for discussions of issues relevant to local communities, or to provide job training for young people seeking to make a career in broadcasting. Some also see it as a way to emphasise cultural learning and others as a means for keeping their communities informed of public safety concerns, including weather and traffic conditions.

Licensing Procedure

Non-commercial, educational radio service, community or LPFM licenses are not available to individuals or commercial entities.

Applicants must be based in the community in which they intend to broadcast and points are awarded to those with established local presence and amount of locally originated programming. Eligible applicants would include:

- government or non-profit educational institutions, such as public or private school, or private or state university;
- non-profit organisation, association or entity with educational purposes such as a community group, public service or public health organisation, disability service provider or faith-based organisation; and
- government or non-profit entity providing local public safety or transportation services, such as a volunteer fire department, local government, or state transportation authority.

Existing broadcasters, cable television system operators, or daily newspaper publishers are not eligible for LPFM licenses as it is designed to create opportunities for new voices to be heard on the radio. Applications that request the same frequency are resolved through a selection process which awards applicants one point each for *(a)* showing a community presence of at least two years prior to the application, *(b)* pledging to operate at least 12 hours daily, and *(c)* pledging to locally originate at least eight hours of programming daily. Where the competing applicants have the same number of points, time sharing proposals, in which applicants share a given frequency, are encouraged.

Allocation of Frequency and Technical Parameters

The FCC has developed a computer software program to identify FM frequencies that may be available for LPFM stations in particular locations. This program is available to everyone at the FCC's website. Potential applicants can also consult with broadcast engineers to determine the availability of radio spectrum in their areas.

Sustainability/Funding

Non-commercial educational stations are not allowed to broadcast promotional announcements or commercials on behalf of for-profit entities. They can support themselves by contributions from listeners and may also receive government funding and contributions from for-profit entities. Such contributions or underwriting donations should be acknowledged with announcements naming and generally describing the entity. Most community radio stations also rely on the communities they serve for expertise and labour. The CPB funds help organisations in obtaining grants or loans for the construction of a low power radio station.

Management and Ownership

Community radios depend entirely on volunteers not only for programming but also for administration and support services. Sometimes state and federal sources of funding enable and require stations to develop a core paid staff for station operations ranging from administrative and technical functions to professional programmers. A community radio station is usually licensed to a civic group or an independent foundation formed for the express purpose of operating a station. The essential distinction lies in community radio's local orientation and disdain for professional control. One observer has characterised the difference this way—National Public Radio (NPR) says, 'We know what's good for you.' Community radio says, 'We want to determine ourselves what's good for us' (quoted in Walker, 1997).

Programme Content

The broadcasters and not the FCC or any other government agency are responsible for selecting the material that is aired. Community radio stations are devoted to programming outside the mainstream, particularly local programming. Community radio is truly 'public', in relying on local volunteers for most of its programming, financial support, and day-to-day administration and going out of its way to broadcast material that is unavailable elsewhere on the dial.

Regulation and Monitoring

Community radio stations (like all broadcasters) are required to maintain programming and engineering logs; to comply with FCC regulations governing indecency, equal time, technical standards, etc.; and to periodically apply for license renewal. The LPFM licenses will be renewable at the end of an eight-year license term. The state and federal authorities require the filing of periodic financial reports and tax forms, and require that certain hierarchical forms (Boards of Directors, Chief Engineer, etc.) be observed. They are required to maintain a Public Inspection File containing documents relevant to the station's operation. As stations have an obligation to serve their local community's needs and interests and to comply with certain programming and other rules and as FCC does not monitor a station's programming, viewers and listeners are a vital source of information about the programming and possible rule violations. The documents in each station's public inspection file have information about the station that can assist the public in this important role.

Comparative Analysis

Having laid out in some detail the salient features of community radio legislation in the five countries under discussion, this section offers a comparative analysis of the main aspects of community radio in categories of analysis that we have examined. The aim here is to draw on the provisions which could inform the suggestions/ recommendations that we tender for a community radio policy framework in India in the concluding chapter.

Definition of Community Radio

All five countries examined have clearly defined the key aspects of community radio. The most crucial aspect that comes out in the definition of community radio in all countries is that community radio stations not be run for the purpose of making financial profit. This clearly distinguishes the stations from the commercial sector. Australia identifies community broadcasting services as those that 'are not operated for profit or as part of a profit-making enterprise'. In both Ireland and Canada, community radio must be 'owned and controlled by a not-for-profit organization', while in South Africa community broadcasting service is defined as one which is 'fully controlled by a non-profit entity and carried on for non-profitable purposes'.

Another vital characteristic of the definition of community radio is that this sector, unlike the public and private broadcasting, is intended primarily to serve a particular community and must be identified distinctively with community and voluntary organisations. The Australian Broadcasting Authority stipulates that community broadcasting services are provided for 'community purposes' and its definition of community takes into account 'social, historical and cultural linkages'. The statement of objectives for community stations in Ireland includes a commitment to working for 'social purposes' and 'remaining independent of government or large media corporations'. South Africa defines community radio as one which 'encourages the development of human resources and training, and capacity building within the broadcasting sector especially amongst historically disadvantaged groups'. William E. Kennard, Chairman of the Federal Communications Commission (FCC) in the US declared that the low power FM radio policy would open the doors of opportunity for the community-oriented broadcaster, and 'will give hundreds, if not thousands, of new voices access to the nation's airwaves'.

Another characteristic of the community radio services is that members of the community it serves are given opportunities to participate in the operation of the service. In Ireland, the community radio programming must reflect the special interests and needs of the listenership and be based on community access. The objective of community broadcasting in Australia include providing programming that is locally significant and reflects Australian identity, character and cultural diversity. The South African Broadcasting Act defines such service as one which encourages members of the community or persons associated with the community to participate in 'the selection and provision of programmes to be broadcast in the course of such broadcasting service'. In Canada, community radio station must provide opportunities for 'membership, management, operation and programming primarily by members of the community at large'.

Licensing Procedure

There are some predictable differences among the five countries with regard to the actual procedures of licensing and regulatory mechanism, which reflect their unique administrative and cultural conditions. Nevertheless, all the five countries have single regulators for broadcast media: Australian Broadcasting Authority (ABA), Broadcasting Commission of Ireland (BCI), Independent Communications Authority of South Africa (ICASA), Canadian Radio-Television and Telecommunications Commission (CRTC), and the Federal Communications Commission (FCC) in the USA. In three of the countries, Canada, South Africa and the USA, the regulator is also responsible for telecommunications, which includes the Internet. All countries follow detailed guidelines for the invitation of applications, evaluation of applicants, clearance of licenses, and the fee charged for access to the spectrum.

Given here is a compiled list of criteria from all five countries that are commonly used for deciding whether, and to whom, to allocate a community broadcasting license and to assess the community character of relevant organisations and groups.

(*a*) The extent to which the service proposes to serve the interests of the community in keeping with the ethos or value system which underpins community activity;
(*b*) the nature and diversity of other broadcasting services within the license area;
(*c*) the community presence of the applicant: its capacity to provide the proposed service to be carried on for non-profitable purposes; and
(*d*) the proposed measures to facilitate community access to programming and to promote the availability of training throughout the community.

In South Africa, the object of the *Broadcasting Act* is 'to encourage ownership and control of broadcasting services through participation by persons from historically disadvantaged groups'. The current Act includes two types of community licenses. These licenses are defined as those serving a geographical community and those serving a community of interest. The *White Paper on Broadcasting Policy* issued by the department of communications points out that all community broadcasting licenses should be geographically founded in that they should serve the specific community within a determined geographic area and there are measures likely to be adopted in this direction. The CRTC, while assessing the applications for licenses, takes into consideration how well they reflect the multicultural and multiracial nature of Canadian society and the place of aboriginal peoples. The FCC favours those with established local presence and amount of locally originated programming. Existing broadcasters, cable television system operators, or daily newspaper publishers are not eligible for LPFM licenses as it is designed to create opportunities for new voices to be heard on the radio.

While in Australia there is no cost involved in lodging an application for Community Broadcasting license and there is no spectrum fee to be paid by the community broadcasters, the South African government charges an application fee, which is non-refundable and community services also have to pay an Issue of License Fee and an Annual License Fee. The ICASA can reduce fees to promote community services in needy areas.

Allocation of Frequency and Technical Parameters

Community radio stations in all the five countries broadcast on FM. Only in a situation where FM is totally taken up or unavailable, is AM considered for allocation. The license term for stations in the community strand varies from 12-months in South Africa to seven years in Canada, whereas in Australia, Ireland and the USA, the licenses are awarded for a period of five years. The LPFM licenses in the USA are renewable at the end of an eight-year license term.

The frequency allotment plan (FAP) and the license area plan (LAP) of ABA is based on priorities such as identifying geographical areas least well served by existing services. The nature of licenses is determined by available frequency and perceived public need, and the Broadcasting Act stipulates that the programmes of the community services must be available free to the general public. In Ireland, each license application is individually considered and the most appropriate frequency allocated. The maximum radius for transmission is normally five miles, though there are variations. In certain remote rural areas where the only form of local radio available is the community station, and the broadcast area is geographically dispersed, the transmission area permitted may be larger than five miles.

The ICASA sets aside frequencies specifically for the maintenance and expansion of community broadcasting and the national strategy for the community sector prioritises the licensing of services to those sectors of the South African community that are under or unserved by the broadcasting system whether assessed by geography, age demographics or social status. Canada has authorised a simplified process for licensing low-power 'developmental' community stations (LPFM, 5 Watts) for up to three years to serve as a training ground for the future establishment of higher power community stations.

Sustainability/Funding

Community radio stands out as a sector which is distinctive not only in terms of its mandate and programming content, but also in terms of its sources of revenue and funding. In all the five countries, advertising and/or sponsorship is permitted but confined within specified norms and an emphasis is placed on funding from a diversity of sources to ensure that, primarily, the community served determines the programming. Government funding is non-existent in Ireland and South Africa, but sizeable in Australia. Canada and the USA rely on support from their listeners and on contributions or underwriting donations.

Australia prevents all its community broadcasting licensees from broadcasting advertisements, and allows only up to five minutes of sponsorship announcements and other promotional material in any one hour. Adequate backing to community broadcasters is administered by an independent funding body, the Community Broadcasting Foundation, which receives annual grants from the government departments. The BCI allows community stations in Ireland to broadcast up to six minutes of advertisements and sponsorship announcements per hour, but no more than 50 per cent of income may be secured from commercial activity. South Africa's broadcasting policy does not impose any restrictions on community radio stations to accessing revenues from advertising, sponsorships, grants and community contributions and donations. All surplus funds derived from the running of a community broadcasting station are to be invested for the benefit of the particular community. Canada has eliminated all restrictions on the amount of advertising that may be broadcast by stations. It believes that if community stations are to fulfil their intended role, they must have adequate, secure revenue streams.

The BCI provides support for specific initiatives through the Community Radio Support Scheme developed in consultation with licensed community broadcasters through the Community Radio

Forum. In South Africa, community broadcasters can access government assistance for training programmes to develop their broadcasting trainers. A Community Development Trust for funding broadcasting initiatives in areas where communities do not have access to resources and are in need of development is likely to be facilitated by ICASA in the near future. The CPB funds help organisations in obtaining grants or loans for the construction of a low power radio station in the USA.

Management and Ownership

Ownership and management structures distinguish community radio stations from the conventional broadcasting institutions. Australia has an established community broadcasting code of practice and organisational mechanisms to provide for active participation of the community served in its management, development and operations. The BCI policy states that the stations should be accountable to the community and the community must be in control of, and therefore responsible for, the station. Participation by members of the community in a voluntary capacity to support their station is seen by BCI as a key indicator of the success of that station. South African government's policy for broadcasting proclaims that, 'community broadcasting must be for the community by the community, through the community'. The larger broadcasting policy mandate is to encourage both participation and ownership by the historically disadvantaged groups. Volunteers from the community participate in all aspects of the programming and operations of the stations in Canada and in the USA. All community radio licensees are expected to facilitate community access to their programming by clearly informing the public of opportunities for community participation.

Programme Content

The programming guidelines followed by community radio stations, that seek to maintain passionate involvement of the audiences, clearly differentiate them from the public service or commercial broadcasting in all the five countries. The AMARC Charter states that community stations should promote and protect cultural diversity and inform their listeners on the basis of information drawn from a diversity of sources. The CBAA *Code of Practice* for programming in Australia reflects the principles of community broadcasting to 'provide access to views under-represented by the mainstream media' and aims at encouraging members of the community to participate in 'the operations of the service and the selection and provision of programmes'. The BCI endorses community broadcasting as a form of media with strong roots in the local community in Ireland and, therefore, the programming ought to be based on community access and reflect the special interests and needs of the listeners.

Programming for community stations in South Africa must promote the development of a sense of community and highlight grassroots community issues, which are not normally dealt with by other broadcasting services covering the area. The policy objective for establishing community radio stations in Canada is the provision of public access to the airwaves with the aim of offering a unique type of grassroots local programming as an alternative to what is generally available from other types of radio stations. Community radio stations are devoted to programming outside the mainstream, particularly local programming, and the broadcasters are responsible for selecting the material that is aired in the USA. Community radio stations are defined by their devotion to 'discussion of local public issues', 'opportunity for local self-expression' and 'the development and use of local talent' as programming priorities.

Regulation and Monitoring

The independent broadcast regulators in all the five countries endorse the qualitative approach to audience research for authoritatively evaluating the relationship between a station and the audience. They facilitate conducting of research into community standards, so as to inform its regulatory functions. The regulators have powers to monitor the performance of the licensees in relation to objectives set out for the broadcasting of programmes, financial affairs and management. In the USA, community radio stations (like all broadcasters) are required to maintain programming and engineering logs, to comply with FCC regulations governing indecency, equal time, technical standards and to periodically apply for license renewal.

CONCLUSION

The comparative analysis offered in this chapter has several lessons for community radio broadcasting policy in India. Juxtaposing the policies and practices that have worked in these five countries with the social, economic and cultural contexts as well as the political and grassroots realities of broadcasting in India, we employed this comparative analysis to make suggestions for a community radio policy framework for India in the concluding chapter.

Australia provides us with an example of a well-developed 'third tier of broadcasting' as distinct from commercial and state-funded services. It was in the mid-70s that the community radio sector was created in Australia following persistent campaigns by people for access to airwaves. The independent broadcasting regulator ABA plans allocation of frequencies to ensure diversity of broadcasting services and equity of access for all areas and people. The vast majority of community radio stations in Australia broadcast on FM. There is no cost involved in lodging an application for community radio station and access to spectrum is free. As community broadcasting is not for profit, grants from international organisations or the government to support this sector are routed through the autonomous CBF. The fundamental distinguishing feature of community broadcasting in Australia is a commitment to local access as active participants in core activities such as programme production, marketing, administration and station management.

The Irish *Policy on Community Radio Broadcasting* springs from the report, *A Community Radio Model for Ireland* produced by the Community Radio Forum after careful evaluation of an 18-month pilot project established by the BCI (then IRTC) in 1994. It recognises the important role of community broadcasting sector constituted by community and voluntary organisations in its media environment and provides support for its development through the Community Radio Support Scheme. The sector is characterised by its community nature underlined by the participation of members in ownership, operations, management and programming of the station. The standard license term is five years. Funding and finance norms are open to a variety of sources that may essentially be local. Workshops for community evaluation of projects are encouraged.

Notwithstanding some hiccups in policy implementation, there is much one can learn from the South African case, which is one of the most comprehensive and progressive communication policies in recent times. The community radio sector in South Africa has on the whole been commendably resilient. Some stations have buckled under the financial strain of maintaining the service with limited resources. Most of those who have gone on air have weathered the storm and kept afloat. Income is derived from a variety of sources, including: advertising, sponsorships, grants, donations and membership fees. A number of stations, particularly in the metropolitan areas and environs, have quite effectively tapped the advertising market.

The success of Bush Radio, for instance, is quite well known globally. One of the earliest to be licensed, Bush Radio was started in 1995 by a small group on the outskirts of Bush Flats in Capetown to give the local black and coloured population a voice. Bush Radio broadcasts 24 hours a day, seven days a week serving the local community by broadcasting in English and local languages. Bush Radio gets much of its funding from donor agencies, which help to support the purchase of equipment and training. In an effort to raise the quality of its output, it runs regular training courses for volunteers who want to be involved in radio production.

The community radio sector is well established in Canada as a tier of radio that complements and is distinct from the services provided by the CBC and commercial radio stations. There are simple but effective regulations concerning the content of all radio sectors, including community radio, which help to maintain each sector's distinctiveness from the others. The CRTC also licenses stations for ethnic programming, campus radio and native language programming within the not-for-profit broadcasting sector. Community radio stations are owned or controlled by not-for-profit organisations. Most community stations derive revenues from various sources: grants, advertising and fund-raising activities. Lack of stable funding is often a concern for them. Community stations rely primarily on volunteers for programming and other operations. Some have paid staff members who also train and facilitate the work of volunteers.

Three distinctive models of communications, commercial, public (government-sponsored) and community make up broadcasting in the United States, each characterised by different modes of financing, control, programming and access. Community broadcasting outlets are usually located in the non-commercial band and funded by listener subscriptions. The FCC announced a LPFM radio service that would consist of 100-Watt and 10-Watt stations in January 2000. Non-profit organisations, associations or non-profit educational institutions can apply for non-commercial, educational radio, community or LPFM licenses. Applicants must be based in the community in which they intend to broadcast. Commercials are not allowed though there is no ban on sponsorships and grants from non-profit organisations and loans. Locally originated programming produced by community volunteers and their active participation in station operations are encouraged. Though certain basic FCC norms for all broadcasters are to be adhered to, self-regulation is the approved monitoring device in the community sector.

Notes

1. 'Commons' is used in the sense of any sets of resources that a *community* recognises as being accessible to all members of that community. *The Ecologist* (1993: 8) describes it as including: 'trees, forests, land, minerals, water, fish, animals, language, time, radio wavelengths, silence, seeds, milk, contraception and streets.' Commons are neither private nor public but represent a third option, a space and time for autonomy. They are concerned with continuing sustenance, security and habitat. For an interesting discussion on global communications commons, see Kidd, 1998.
2. KPFA (94.1 FM) is a radio station in Berkeley, California. Launched in 1949, three years after the Pacifica Foundation was created by pacifist Levis Hill, KPFA became the first radio station in the Pacifica Radio network and the first listener-supported radio broadcaster in the United States.

3 MIXED SIGNALS

Radio Broadcasting Policy in India

The principles and practices of broadcasting as they have existed and evolved in India are audibly reflected in the key issues that the media planners and policy makers have sought to resolve at different times in the 80 years of its existence now. The discourses and imperatives at any given time with regard to Indian broadcasting have been quite in conflict with each other. The state's monopoly over broadcasting is under attack, while anxiety is being expressed for regulating the invasion from satellite because of its perceived impact on national culture and cultural identities. While private broadcasters are seeking free market for media, and consumers are demanding the right to choose, there is worry over the increasing commercialisation and homogenisation of media content that is thwarting its public service function.

However, a temporal perspective of the history of broadcasting in India shows that certain vital concerns have been ignored over several eras though they find a consistent mention in the reports of various committees periodically appointed by the Government of India to examine media-related issues. Some such perennial questions relate to people's access to communication technologies and content, audience participation for perpetuating plurality of ideas and facilitating self-representation through popular and community based media. These subjects are discernible in the fascinating debates on the nature of appropriate media policy in India and are conceptualised in documents that should ideally form the underpinnings of the broadcasting scenario in the country.

An analysis of the broadcasting form and functioning in India reveals that the attempts to address such persistent inadequacies or to balance the dilemmas facing broadcasting have been marked by pressures other than those of public service or the pressing demands by civil society. As a result, broadcasting in India continues to be governed by the archaic *Indian Telegraph Act* of 1885 and the *Indian Wireless Telegraphy Act* of 1933 and regulated through an assortment of legislation that have been scripted as expedient populist measures by suave politicians to tackle high priority short-term demands. There exists nothing in the form of a comprehensive policy that takes into account the contradictory pulls of the concerns surrounding broadcasting in India and places its role within the context of new socio-political and techno-economic realities.

An example of how governments appropriate and co-opt fervent concerns and give them an interpretation that is convenient to their political interests is the public policy pronouncement in January 2003 to grant 'community broadcasting' licenses to established universities, colleges and schools. This decision to allow setting up of FM transmitters to run radio stations in the campuses was projected as a move to open up the broadcasting sector for non-profit social sector by allowing community radio stations. While the policy pronouncement was not unwelcome as it diluted somewhat the hegemony of the state and market over broadcasting, but to open it up for an urban, educated, elite coterie in areas that are already well served by media betrays the fundamental philosophy behind community radio as the world understands it today. The historical philosophy of community radio is to use this medium as the voice of the voiceless, the mouthpiece of oppressed people and generally as a tool for development (AMARC, 1998b).

It was mere tokenism to say that these stations would provide space for development and change-oriented content. If radio does not enable the marginalised, rural or poor populace to disseminate their own messages and to challenge the mainstream understanding of social issues, the whole purpose is lost. But the government was content with postponing the critical decision of allowing autonomous broadcasting spaces to communities and the social sector as that entails re-distribution of power and control over media resources and technologies. The history of the broadcasting system in India is witness to the fact that one of the main factors that perpetuates status quo is the desire of the state to retain control. In fact, the attitude of successive governments even after more than half a century of Independence has unmistakable traces of the norms set by the British who introduced organised broadcasting in the country.

The Legacy of Indian Broadcasting

The first regular radio service was inaugurated in India by the Indian Broadcasting Company (IBC) with the opening of the Bombay Station on 23 July 1927.[1] The then Viceroy of India, Lord Irwin inaugurated this 1.5 KW station with an effective range of 30 miles (48 km). This came about seven months after the creation of the British Broadcasting Corporation (BBC) in the UK in January 1927 as a publicly funded organisation with John Reith as its first Director General. Indian broadcasting has borrowed much of its programming pattern, philosophy and even talent for development from the Corporation. However, except for the first two years and eight months, when broadcasting was operated as a commercial venture, it has been under government control in India till recently when it has taken on the avatar of a public corporation.[2]

It is interesting to observe the similarities between the maiden *Report on the Progress of Broadcasting in India* issued from the office of the first Controller of Broadcasting, Government of India, Lionel Fielden on 3 June 1939, and the content categories of statistics in the Annual Report of All India Radio published by Prasar Bharati in 2004. This goes to show that the parameters to validate performance and define what 'puts national broadcasting on a proper footing'[3] do not seem to have undergone any prominent changes even after Independence. The interests of the British government largely guided the expansion of radio during the colonial period and importance was given to the economic, strategic, engineering and administrative aspects. In this report, Fielden included 'a historical survey of broadcasting in India' as 'no separate report on Indian Broadcasting had previously been issued' (Fielden, 1939: i). The prototypes of such reports passed on from our colonisers to the present heads of government are modelled to project the top-down 'reach' of the medium, which is sought to be justified in terms of growth, spread, coverage of area and of population, listenership percentages, programming patterns and the number of languages in which programmes are broadcast.

The IBC started in 1927, and went into liquidation by March 1930. Fielden's report ascribes this failure to high prices of receiving sets at Rs 500 for a four valve set, an undercapitalised company, and to 'Indian conditions and traditions' that were 'by no means as favourable to the rapid growth of broadcasting as those of the west'

(Fielden, 1939: 3). Ironically, he also acknowledges later, that the slow increase of licensed listeners could have been owing to the small coverage radius of the two stations (the second 1.5 KW station was started in Calcutta in August 1927) and successive curtailment of expenditure by the government resulting in low standard of programmes. A decisive factor he says was 'undoubtedly the great difficulty in collecting both the licence fees and the "tribute"' (Fielden, 1939: 3).

In April 1930, the Government of India took over broadcasting following 'universal' representations for action from existing license holders and dealers of wireless equipment who were stuck with stockpiles of broadcasting kits; and broadcasting was placed in the department of industries and labour as 'Indian State Broadcasting Service'. To deal with the alleged evasion of payment of license fee and to monitor possession of wireless gear, the Indian Wireless Telegraphy Act of 1933 was brought into force, which made the possession of radio receivers and wireless equipment without a license an offence.

The Indian Government's current monopoly over radio and television broadcasting derives from this Act together with the Indian Telegraph Act, 1885 (and its subsequent amendments) which gives exclusive privileges of the establishment, maintenance and working of wireless apparatus to the Central Government. With these two laws and some other means of obtaining sufficient revenue in place, broadcasting turned into a profitable venture by 1934, and the 'government felt justified in embarking on a policy of development' (Fielden, 1939: 6). The years 1931–34 had seen an increase in the listenership of radio, although there were no new stations added and no improvements in programming. Fielden attributes this spurt to the starting of the Empire service of the BBC in December 1932 and 'the consequent purchase of sets by a large number of Europeans in India' (Fielden, 1939: 2).

Fielden himself arrived in India in the year 1935 with the brief to work out the development scheme for Indian broadcasting for which Rs 20 lakh (later raised to Rs 40 lakh) were allotted. He and H.L. Kirke, technical expert from BBC, felt that the amount was disproportionately inadequate for a country like India.

> In Europe which may be compared with India from point of view of size and coverage, there are over 100 high and medium power stations, representing

> a total cost of 10 crore rupees. From this it is clear that the service, which can be given to India for a sum of 40 lakhs, will be poor (Fielden, 1939: 11).

Their report made recommendations for expansion of broadcasting to rural areas, stating that though Indian State Broadcasting Service was more a commercial than social service, 'the idea of self-supporting service was wrong and government should devote the limited funds available to "unremunerative" stations in rural areas.' The emphasis on planning they felt would initially bring funds 'only from the sophisticated listeners who can pay for their entertainment', but there was a possibility to 'provide a service both for the towns and for the villages; which has within it the seed of development on a self-supporting basis' (Fielden, 1939: 13).

On 1 January 1936, a 20 KW Delhi station was set up at 18, Alipur Road as the first new centre under the new scheme of expansion and development of Indian Broadcasting.[4] On 8 June 1936, the nomenclature of the Indian State Broadcasting Service was changed to All India Radio (AIR).[5] Ahmed Shah Bokhari joined AIR as Station Director in March 1936 on deputation from the Government College Lahore and became the Deputy Controller of Broadcasting in June 1936[6] and C.W. Goyder, another expert from BBC, became AIR's first chief engineer in August 1936. Goyder, who differed with Kirke's plan for medium-wave transmitters, is remembered for the short-wave coverage of the entire country, which he achieved with Fielden's backing by 1938 (Luthra, 1986; Baruah, 1983). Walter Kaufman, Director of Western Music programmes in Bombay, composed AIR's signature tune in the year 1936 (MIB, 1978).

Broadcasting began in India as a private amateur venture, but even after it rolled into the hands of the British Government the Indian princely states were given the right to install and use transmitters and to collect fees for receiving sets as stipulated in the Government of India Act 1935. This is an amusing historical nugget because after Independence, though the Indian government has emulated British rules, guidelines and planned approaches to broadcasting, it has kept broadcasting firmly in the hands of the government at the Centre (Ninan, 1998). Bokhari succeeded Fielden as the Controller in 1940 and was at the helm of AIR till almost the end of World War II. With the declaration of the War, all expansion plans were stayed but urgent steps were taken to increase the hours of transmission of centralised news bulletins in various Indian languages (totalling 27 in a day) to counter Nazi propaganda and to promote the allied cause[7] (Luthra, 1986; MIB, 1978).

In 1937, AIR was transferred from the department of labour and industries to the department of communications. It was relocated to the department of information and broadcasting, set up in 1941, which, after Independence, became the Ministry of Information and Broadcasting (MIB) in 1947. All India Radio moved to its new Broadcasting House in Parliament Street in February 1943 and in the same year, the Controller of Broadcasting designation was changed to Director General (Baruah, 1983; Chatterji, 1991). On 3 June 1947, Viceroy Lord Mountbatten, Jawaharlal Nehru and Mohammad Ali Jinnah made their historic broadcasts on the Partition of India. The transfer of power on the midnight of 14–15 August 1947 was broadcast live with Jawaharlal Nehru's famous speech 'Tryst with Destiny' which is preserved in the archives of AIR (Baruah, 1983). The first and the only time Gandhiji visited the Broadcasting House in Delhi was on Diwali in 1947 when he addressed refugees at the Kurukshetra camp (Luthra, 1986).

The responsibility of broadcasting to 'serve' the public through programmes that 'inform, educate and entertain' (http://www.allindiaradio.org/about1.html accessed on 26 April 2007) was part of the paternalistic Reithean legacy. All India Radio set out after independence to 'benefit' the masses by giving them not what they sought to hear but what they ought to hear. As affirmed by all the ensuing *Annual Reports* of AIR and also posted on its website, the objective of broadcasting in India was to 'provide information, education and wholesome entertainment, keeping in view the motto, *Bahujan Hitaya; Bahujan Sukhaya*, i.e., the benefit and happiness of large sections of the people', and strive to 'produce and transmit varied programmes designed to awaken, inform, enlighten, educate, entertain and enrich all sections of the people, with due regard to the fact that the national broadcast audience consists of a whole series of public' (http://www.allindiaradio.org/index.html).

With a view to realise these objectives, a regime of planned development of broadcasting to cover the country, as kicked off by Fielden and reworked by Goyder, was brought back to life. Over the years, with allocation of funds made in all subsequent Five Year Plans (FYPs), AIR, claimed to be 'one of the largest media networks in the world, boasts today of a network of 215 broadcasting centres (which include 115 regional and 77 local radio stations) and 144 medium wave, 54 high frequency (SW) and 139 FM transmitters. The broadcast coverage of 91.42 per cent by area is received by 99.13 per cent of the people in 24 languages and 146 dialects in home service. All India Radio broadcasts in 26 (10 Indian and 16 foreign) languages in its external services. As against a mere 2,75,955 receiving sets[8] in 1947, now there are about 13.2 crore (7.8 crore with FM band) radio sets in about 11.7 crore radio households in the country with the number of average actual listeners of AIR on any day estimated at 53 crore (Prasar Bharati, 2004).

Planned Growth of Infrastructure

The history of the growth of broadcasting network and expansion of its coverage is chronicled in the AIR annual reports, in books[9], almost all of which have been written by former AIR officials, and in a couple of government publications. The reports of committees set up from time to time to review the status of broadcasting in India also recount major landmarks in its progress. The first formal review of the working of the official media in India[10] came about with the appointment by MIB in 1964 of a committee under the chairmanship of Asok K. Chanda, former Auditor General, Government of India, to, among other things, 'examine and evaluate the operations, policies, programmes and production of the various media units of the ministry'. It was a time when there 'had been persistent criticism both in Parliament and the press of the deficiencies of AIR,' and also 'a belated realization in official quarters that the media of mass communication had largely failed to inform, educate and entertain the people and to enlist their co-operation in fulfilling the plans of social and economic development' (MIB, 1966: 2).

At the time when the Chanda Committee submitted its report on Radio and Television (18 April 1966), AIR had acquired a fairly extensive set-up with the MIB embarking on a two-phase plan for expansion of broadcasting service. In the initial phase, with Sardar Vallabhbhai Patel,[11] the first and ostensibly the most influential minister for information and broadcasting, at the helm of affairs, a scheme to build up 'pilot' stations with one KW medium wave transmitters was taken up to expand radio broadcasting infrastructure in state capitals and in border areas and to include the linguistic and cultural areas that had remained without coverage.

At the time of Independence, the AIR network had six stations located at Delhi, Bombay, Calcutta, Madras, Lucknow and Tiruchirapalli. While the Baroda station was taken over in 1948, in 1950, all the other four 'native' stations belonging to former princely states, Hyderabad, Aurangabad, Mysore and Trivandrum were integrated with AIR. By 1950, the number of stations had risen from 11 to 25 and the AIR network was in a position to serve listeners in all regional languages but could embrace only 21 per cent of the country's population and 12 per cent of its area (Baruah, 1983). The Staff Training Institute was started in July 1948 to impart in-service training to various cadres of the programme and administrative staff of AIR and Doordarshan. Broadcasting along with post, telegraphs, telephones and wireless was placed in the Union List of the Seventh Schedule on 26 January 1950 under the newly effective Constitution of India.

In the second phase of AIR network expansion, which became part of the Five Year Plan (FYP), the existing stations were upgraded or replaced by stations of higher power (MIB, 1966). It is interesting to note that during the first FYP period, six new radio stations were opened and a few stations closed down[12] keeping the number of broadcasting centres almost constant at 26, by the end of the plan. Several low-power transmitters were upgraded, although no new transmitters were set up. Though the numbers remained unchanged, the reach of broadcasting swelled manifold covering 46 per cent of the population and 31 per cent in terms of area (Prasar Bharati, 2002). Several high power medium and short wave transmitters were installed during the second FYP and the third FYP undertook to execute an ambitious medium wave expansion scheme with the primary objective to extend the AIR network to the whole country.

In the years subsequent to Independence, India had ventured out to become developed and industrialised in keeping with the West-inspired dominant paradigm of modernisation of the 50s through 70s. Mass media were seen as instruments to change the mind-set of the people and to create a climate for modernisation and development through centralised economic planning, large-scale industrialisation and the expansion of basic communication infrastructure (Lerner, 1958; Schramm, 1964; Rogers, 1976). The Chanda Committee endorsed this view and expressed its dissatisfaction with the place given to the development of mass communication in India. It felt that the media had not been adequately harnessed for informing, educating and enthusing people to participate actively in the social and economic development programmes. The Committee observed that radio had not been accorded priority with respect to the allocations made in successive plans:

> ... despite its own evaluation that the plans have failed to evoke the expected response in the country, the Planning Commission has persistently overlooked the potentiality of radio in enlisting public cooperation in implementing plans and programmes designed to bring progress and prosperity to the community. In continuing to regard broadcasting as a routine function of the state and giving it routine treatment, the Commission has also ignored the experience of other countries, which have accelerated the pace of development by imaginative use of radio and television (MIB, 1966: 10).[13]

Commenting on the policies and plans of the technical coverage of AIR, the Committee reiterated the need for additional measures to facilitate wider coverage and stressed the need for a 'reasoned' review of the direction of quantitative expansion, in order to ensure a balanced growth of AIR network, selection of ideal locations and procurement of standardised equipment which may even be indigenously produced.

> We have found that neither the location of the transmitters nor their procurement is always determined on technical considerations. Regional pressures for transmitters have often lead to the choice of unsuitable locations for the coverage intended. Similarly, political considerations have intervened in the selection of sources of supply (MIB, 1966: 33).

The report pointed out that lack of funds and faulty orientation were factors inhibiting the potential of AIR's rural broadcasts and the impact of its external services.

> Its transmitters and studio equipment are insufficient, largely obsolete or obsolescent, its broadcasts cannot even reach the sensitive areas of North East Frontier, let alone project the correct image of India overseas or counteract unfriendly propaganda, and its planning and administrative staff are lacking in vision and imagination (MIB, 1966: 12).

The Chanda Committee pointed out that deficiencies, both of the instruments of transmission and reception, were rendering rural services ineffective. Community listening was suffering on account of maintenance of receiving sets. It suggested that to make coverage of rural areas meaningful mass production of low cost transistorised sets and their distribution was essential.[14] The report emphasised that for qualitative improvement of coverage, at least two-channel transmission be provided in all regions. The report recommended that low-power transmitters be installed in each compact agricultural area that would primarily deliver services for the ministries of health, agriculture and education. It suggested that such local transmitters could operate on frequency modulation (FM), which AIR was proposing to introduce only in the metros, and that a plan to manufacture FM receiving sets also be drawn up simultaneously.

> In countries so large and varied as India, most states have groups with different cultures, customs and traditions. The stations should be placed to cater to their divergent needs and requirements. Yet, for example, the Ranchi Station located at the centre of the tribal belt of Chhota Nagpur can provide only snippets of song and drama for tribal community. The Commissioner of Scheduled Castes and Scheduled Tribes has complained that All India Radio has not given much time and attention to the tribal people (MIB, 1966:29).

It was only in July 1977 that the first FM service started from Madras and it was not until 30 October 1984 that the first local station was established at Nagercoil in Tamil Nadu. The lacuna observed in the working of the planning and development unit of AIR was that, on the one hand, advice of technical staff was overlooked by higher officials to accommodate political factors, while on the other, no programme official was associated with the structuring of a broadcasting centre. Hence the stations were built without any insight into the scope and objectives of its programmes leaving very little flexibility for programme planners who had to fit their content to the available facilities.

National, Commercial and Rural Broadcasts

The Chanda Committee castigated AIR's programme policy in the two decades of its functioning after Independence on the grounds that the government was overlooking development imperatives and that a technical infrastructure built with public resources was being misused for propaganda of public policy and as a vehicle for setting political agendas. Centralisation and bureaucratisation were resulting in improper selection of talent, curbing of staff enterprise for adventurous programmes, inadequate remuneration to artistes and indifference in content, quality and presentation of programmes. The inquiries by the Committee brought to the forefront what listeners long knew, that AIR programmes were dull and drab and low on variety. They did not engage with contentious political matters or even those of civic consequence. A 'psychology of conformity' prevailed in AIR as recruitment of directing staff ensured unquestioning compliance, influential people monopolised talks and discussions and, even among them, eminent people critical of administrative policies were avoided (MIB, 1966).

Other visible trends during this period were the remodelling of programmes towards a new nationalist image, a countrywide broadcast of national programmes and the promotion of Hindi as the national language. In July 1952, the first national programme of music went on air. In October, the same year, the National Orchestra (*Vadya Vrinda*) was set up in Delhi under the conductorship of Pandit Ravi Shankar. The Carnatic violin-player T.K. Jairam later joined the orchestra as the second conductor (Baruah, 1983). The National Programme of talks (English) went on air in April 1953. Regional news bulletins were started from Lucknow (Hindi) and Nagpur (Marathi) on 15 April 1953. National programmes of operas, plays and features were started in 1956 and AIR came to be known as *Akashvani*[15] from 1957 (Prasar Bharati, 2002). On 25 January 1958, an unusual but short-lived experiment in the use of folk media for social communication was launched as an annual festival. 'Songs of Nation Builders' in which folk musicians and dancers from different parts of India presented songs with a developmental content (Baruah, 1983).

B.V. Keskar, the country's longest serving minister of information and broadcasting for 10 years from 1952, patronised Indian classical and folk music and harboured an unconcealed aversion for 'cheap and vulgar' film music.[16] As AIR's classical music content rose to nearly 50 per cent, Indians switched to Radio Ceylon's commercial service that played all the film songs that AIR's holier-than-thou dignity and conformity to 'good taste' and serious purpose did not permit (Page and Crawley, 2001). The Indian government was slow in responding to the challenges of foreign competition posed by

Radio Ceylon (a phenomenon repeated with television in the 90s) but eventually did launch an entertainment channel, Vividh Bharati, broadcasting Indian film music and other entertainment fare on 3 October 1957. Commercial advertising was introduced in the Bombay–Pune–Nagpur chain of Vividh Bharati stations 10 years later, in 1967 (Baruah, 1983). This had been one of the major recommendations of the Chanda Committee. At present there are 36 Vividh Bharati and commercial broadcasting stations operating in the country (Prasar Bharati, 2002).

Chanda Committee attributed the lack of popularity of AIR programmes also to the absence of any system for audience research to gauge the extent and quality of listening of each programme that should ideally form the basis of policy decisions.

> Listener's research is an integral part of most broadcasting systems. Without a continuous and intimate touch with its audience a broadcasting system cannot fulfil the purpose for which it exists nor can it ensure maximum listening to its programmes in preference to others. Without a review, money and effort might be wasted in producing programmes, which do not attract listening. There is also the attendant risk of listeners tuning into other broadcasts, which have undesirable features both morally and politically (MIB, 1966: 58).

This lack of systematic survey of preferences of listeners or of the impact of broadcasts was even more pronounced in case of rural services. The Committee ascertained that absence of news, views and feedback along with undue publicity of government policies had made rural programmes unattractive and villagers were unable to identify with them owing to pedantic and stilted language and references to peculiar agricultural inputs and chemicals.

The earliest attempts at rural broadcasting go back to 1935, when private stations in North-West Frontier Province and the United Provinces started programmes for rural audiences. All India Radio incorporated these stations into its network and rural programmes were started at Delhi, Madras and Lucknow stations in 1936, 1938 and 1939 respectively (Mathur and Neurath, 1959). Rural service became an integral component of all AIR stations from 1965 when, in line with the emerging agricultural extension philosophy, farm and home units were also established in 10 AIR stations to provide suitable technical support to farmers. Now all regional stations house these units and rural broadcasts are a crucial output of AIR (Baruah, 1983; Chatterji, 1991).

All India Radio's broadcasting to rural areas was designed essentially to garner support for the national enterprise of all-round development, to carry information of practical use to villagers, widen knowledge of national ideals and to provide entertainment (Mathur and Neurath, 1959). The broadcasts used regional languages and local dialects and were meant for community rather than individual listening. Provision was also made in the FYPs to provide community listening sets in villages. Though the number of receiving sets had escalated to 150,000 by 1965–66, this scheme did not thrive because of problems of replacement of batteries and maintenance of receiving sets. By the 70s the transistor revolution had taken over and the scheme was withdrawn (Chatterji, 1991).

Although the use of radio for development was a cornerstone of public service broadcasting policy in India, no attempt to solicit people's participation, even in the form of feedback, was made till 1956 when an experiment in farm radio forums was conducted with the assistance of UNESCO in 150 villages across five districts of Maharashtra. It was based on a Canadian model and was designed to establish two-way communication between village audiences and programme producers of the radio station. The theme of the rural radio forums was 'Listen, Discuss, Act!' (Singhal and Rogers, 2001: 70). A pioneering effort for its time, 'radio farm forum as an agent for transmission of knowledge proved to be a success beyond expectation' (Mathur and Neurath, 1959: 105) and was 'very successful in communicating knowledge of agricultural techniques and encouraging participation in decision making' (Page and Crawley, 2001: 328).

Between 1959 and 1964, the movement gained strength and it was claimed that there were 7,500 forums in 30 odd radio stations in the country in 1964 after which nothing is heard about them (Chatterji, 1991). All India Radio failed to capitalise on lessons learnt from the farm forums project and it remained just an experiment (like the SITE and Kheda projects in case of television later) in development communication with community involvement in media. However, the Chanda Committee evokes the success of farm radio forums to institute faith in radio's enormous potential to carry developmental messages to poor, rural Indian households and that 'given the right approach and the opportunity to discuss and find solutions to local problems, the farmer is receptive to new ideas and techniques' (MIB, 1966: 11).

These observations were validated in the 60s when AIR played a pivotal role in disseminating information of new techniques and practices to propel the Green Revolution. Its experimental broadcasts from Trichinopoly station in 1966 launched in the fertile rice growing areas of Tamil Nadu helped persuade farmers to adopt high yielding varieties of rice. It led to the new variety becoming known as 'Radio Paddy' (Page and Crawley, 2001).

Media Misuse and Quest for Autonomy

The Chanda Committee attributed the failure of AIR to give 'purpose and substance' to the programmes and to reflect the development imperatives of national reconstruction to organisational deficiencies, inadequate financial resources and over-centralisation.

> ...it is not possible in the Indian context for a creative medium like broadcasting to flourish under a regiment [*sic*] of departmental rules and regulations. It is only through an institutional change that AIR can be liberated from the present rigid financial and administrative procedures of Government (MIB, 1966: 177).

The Committee recommended the setting up of two separate autonomous public corporations for radio and television. The attempt was to reconcile autonomy with control by endowing AIR (and Doordarshan) with sufficient liberty in financial and managerial matters, while retaining clearly defined areas of regulation by the state. The Committee was averse to AIR being employed as an instrument of the government and also to it being entrusted into private hands. It is notable that the Committee was in favour of allowing universities, municipal corporations, and state governments to install transmitters. All these proposals were 'carefully considered' in 1970 by the government, but it was declared that, 'the present is not an opportune time to consider the conversion of AIR into an autonomous corporation'.[17] However, TV was separated from AIR under the name, 'Doordarshan' on 1 April 1976 (MIB, 1978).

All India Radio was blatantly misused as 'a government organ'[18] during the national emergency in 1975. In her address to the AIR station directors on 9 September 1975, Prime Minister Indira Gandhi said,

> ...while anybody is in government service, they are bound to obey the orders of the government. If they feel that the government policy is not right, they are unable to obey, they have some other views which they want to express, nobody is stopping them from resigning and joining any organization where they will have that freedom (GOI, 1977: 8).

Several constraints were imposed on radio and television, the 'AIR Code' (for broadcasters) was declared obsolete and there was a clampdown on oppositional views. The then minister of information and broadcasting, V.C. Shukla, instructed AIR station directors that AIR was not a forum run by the government to debate on the conflicting ideologies but to make people 'understand' government policies. Further, as governments were run by parties, media must reflect the policies of the party in power. Credibility took a backseat, as AIR became a propaganda tool for the prime minister and her policies, but proved counter-productive during the elections as it further precipitated the existing demand for autonomy for the government-run media.

After the termination of Emergency, the country's first non-Congress government pledged 'genuine autonomy' to the electronic media. The *White Paper on the Misuse of the Mass Media* was commissioned, followed by the constitution of a Working Group headed by former newspaper editor, B.G. Verghese, in August 1977 to look into autonomy for the electronic media. The group was mandated:

> To examine the functional, financial and legal aspects of the proposal to give full autonomy to Akashvani and Doordarshan, consistent with accountability to Parliament, keeping in mind the different forms of autonomous organizations existing in other democratic countries in the matters of broadcasting (MIB, 1978: 7, 37).

The Working Group proposed the formation of an autonomous National Broadcasting Trust, *Akash Bharati*, 'a non-profit making body, an essential public service licensed to operate under a Parliamentary Charter and accountable to the Parliament' (MIB, 1978: 21). The apex of the Trust was to consist of a board of trustees (*nyasis*), between 12 and 21 in number, drawn from eminent men and women sensitive towards the role of the media.

Attributing the haphazard growth of broadcast media to the absence of a well-defined national communication policy, the Group observed that the commitment to 'open government', 'a dialogue with the people', the thrust towards participative development from below, and decentralisation in political and economic decision making imply the need for democratising communications through a 'transfer of power' (MIB, 1978: 18).

> As mass media, radio and television must fit into a wider perception of a national communication policy or philosophy. Such a policy would be presumed to envisage a web of vertical and lateral communication designed to facilitate the transmission of informational, educational, and cultural messages not merely from government to people but from people to government. People to people, masses to decision-makers, rural to urban, the young to the rest and so on, at all levels and as a circular flow with switches for cross-cultural exchange. Dissenting voices and minority voices must be heard to complete the true harmony of national debate and expression (MIB, 1978:18).

The Working Group was not in favour of two separate trusts for radio and TV though it urged for a distinctive identity for the two mass media under an integrated charter of *Akash Bharati*. Among the specific aims of the trust, the Group included the task to produce and transmit varied programmes designed for all sections of the people. It emphasised that 'mass' does not necessarily imply a 'monolithic or homogeneous' national audience and that the trend in the world was towards catering to area-and-culture specific minority audiences (MIB, 1978). The Group also identified that the trust should be authorised to grant licenses to franchise stations through a board for education and extension broadcasts. These educational stations would not broadcast news bulletins of their own and not take up any commercial broadcasting.

The misuse of media as a publicity vehicle had not ceased even during the tenure of a government that had promoted autonomy for broadcast media. However, in terms of opening up the media, it did introduce party election broadcasts in May 1977, 15 years after the Election Commission had recommended their transmission (Thomas, 1990). A watered down Akash Bharati Bill was introduced in Parliament, but it lapsed after the dissolution of the Lok Sabha in 1979 when the Government fell. When the Congress government returned to power in 1980, it decided against freeing the media from government control, and instead, heralded an era of commercialisation even before the satellite invasion of the 90s. With the ninth Asian Games held in Delhi in 1982, began a move to set up transmitters and to switch to colour on television. The expansion of television in the country entered a new phase as the multinationals and Indian monopolies started dictating terms.

This period witnessed more directives from the government in the form of policy guidelines. In 1980, an advisory committee headed by G. Parthasarathi was created for restructuring media organisations to facilitate a more professional outlook. *News Policy for Broadcast Media* released in May 1982 was one of the products of this committee and the guidelines therein are followed to this day (Ninan, 1998). These cover wide-ranging topics related to news coverage particularly those considered crucial for national development, national integration and maintenance of communal peace (MIB, 1982). The document outlines some themes that require special coverage, one of them being the achievements and problems of development and lays emphasis on the use of AIR and Doordarshan newsgathering apparatus 'to make a deliberate effort to explore new areas of development and nation building news. People's participation in such activities should be duly highlighted as also the significant work being done by voluntary agencies' (MIB, 1982: 3).

> In December 1982, a Working Group on software for Doordarshan headed by P.C. Joshi was appointed to 'prepare a software plan for Doordarshan, taking into consideration the main objectives of television in assisting in the process of social and economic development of the country and to act as an effective medium for providing information, education and entertainment' (MIB, 1985, vol. 1: 7).

Besides suggesting several steps for restoring the development function of television, the Working Group's report, *An Indian Personality for Television*, drew attention to the frequent use of national communication framework to present 'a Delhi-centric view of India' (Ibid.: 27). It offered insights into opportunities and dangers of the technology-led communication revolution and emphasised the need to evolve 'our own version of communication revolution'.[19] The report commented extensively on how 'communication should help to create a participatory model of development, a participatory rural community in which information flows not only downwards, from governments to the people but also upwards from people to the government' (MIB 1985, vol. 2: 30). The report refers to Brecht's statement about radio being equally relevant for television and urges for changing television to 'receive as well to transmit', and 'to let the listener speak as well as to hear' with a view to 'turning the audience not only into pupils but into teachers' (MIB, 1985, vol. 1: 13).

Annotating McLuhan, the report says, 'any software which does not evolve out of some form of public participation is weak in authenticity and appeal', and hence the need for incorporating 'an intimate, participatory down-upwards orientation' in television and for encouraging 'people to be participants in the process of generating software' (MIB, 1985, vol. 1: 13). The counsels of the working group hold good for radio too, but copies of this public document are not available easily for reference in the departments concerned. Neither the recommendations of the Verghese Committee nor those of the Joshi Committee to render radio and television independent and to discourage their misuse by the government were implemented.

Prasar Bharati Bill versus Political Will

Nothing was done to facilitate autonomy till about 1989 when a non-Congress government, in order to keep its campaign promise of autonomy for state media, opened Akash Bharati for reconsideration. The bill that was produced in Parliament was called Prasar Bharati. It differed in significant ways from the exercise undertaken 11 years earlier by the Verghese Committee and illustrating how thinking on the subject of autonomy for the government media had evolved. The first was envisaged as a trust, the second as a corporation. Akash Bharati provided for trustees, Prasar Bharati for a board of governors (Ninan, 1998).

The Akash Bharati Bill recommended granting broadcast franchise licenses to universities and other educational institutions through its Licensing Board, while the Prasar Bharati Bill does not. Both the drafts were similar in terms of the objectives of serving the rural, illiterate, underprivileged populations, providing adequate coverage to languages of various regions of the country, informing and stimulating national consciousness with regard to the status and problems of women, and keeping in mind the needs and interests of young, social and cultural minorities, and the tribal population (Thomas, 1990). The autonomy granted by the Bill that was finally passed in 1990 was watered down by, among other things, the supplementary provision for incorporation of a parliamentary committee to oversee the functioning of the Corporation. Parliament passed this Bill, but the Government fell before it could be notified. This Act was then kept in cold storage for seven years till it was notified in 1997.

On the autonomy front, no advancement was made by the Congress government to execute Prasar Bharati, as amendments to the Act were still not complete. The ministry that had been avoiding putting its own house in order with respect to granting autonomy sprang into action as cable-delivered foreign satellite channels started making rapid inroads into the country in the 90s. The exigency for autonomy was expressed for becoming competitive and commercially upmarket as also the need for monitoring the use of airwaves (discussed in the ensuing section of the chapter). The government abruptly laid down the Cable Television Networks (Regulation) Act in March 1995 to regulate cable television and to influence cable distribution in favour of Doordarshan. Though AIR was not facing competition from private broadcasters, these developments were sending loud and clear signals that it was time to sit up and take notice.

Meanwhile, a high-power committee that had been appointed in 1995 to remodel the role, organisation, and functions of Prasar Bharati in the context of the influx of foreign satellite channels in the 90s furnished its report. This committee (MIB, 1996a) headed by Nitish Sengupta, put forward a provision, to be included in the Prasar Bharati Act, for an Independent Radio and Television Authority of India to grant licenses to domestic or foreign satellite channels and permit them to uplink from Indian soil (Ninan, 1998). The Committee's recommendations with respect to Prasar Bharati sought to dispense with the changes introduced in the 1989 draft before the bill was finalised in 1990. In order to cope with unprecedented reduction in budgetary support from the government, the MIB decided to refurbish the system for marketing commercial time on Doordarshan and All India Radio. A Committee headed by Siddhartha Sen set out to examine the needs of both advertisers and viewers and the adaptations that were warranted to make the prevailing system in Doordarshan and AIR commercially effectual (MIB, 1996b).

In July 1997, the United Front Government decided to notify Prasar Bharati, which had been languishing since August 1990. The Sengupta Committee recommendations were overlooked and what came about was diluted autonomy. The Act (MIB, 1996c) was brought into force on 15 September 1997 and Prasar Bharati (Broadcasting Corporation of India) was established on 23 November 1997.

Amendments to augment autonomy conferred by it were made in October 1997 by introducing some of the changes suggested by the Sengupta Committee.

Hostilities with the MIB, controversies, conflicts at the top-level, dearth of funds, unframed rules and regulations for recruitments, and control by government cadre have marked the period following the setting up of Prasar Bharati. With just over half of the members nominated to its Board, it is being looked at 'as a signboard more than a board'.[20] No significant changes are visible in the working pattern of AIR, except an elongation in the chain of command. It still continues to be centralised and bureaucratic in its functioning, and retains its role and reputation as a propaganda tool for the government.

Both AIR and Doordarshan support an enormous structure that keeps growing endlessly as a medium, but in terms of messages, there is minimal manoeuvrability and negligible scope for innovative programming as 'big people continue to address small people'.[21] They are unable to meet with the diverse expectations of different sections of society or play a constructive role in social change or nation building efforts. With the macro-level media environment increasingly becoming challenging and competitive owing to the effects of globalisation and commercialisation, the role of Prasar Bharati as a public service broadcaster becomes even more relevant. But the lack of political will and faulty application appears to be killing an otherwise workable proposition.

An attempt to revitalise the role of Prasar Bharati as a public service broadcaster was made by setting up the Prasar Bharati Review Committee[22] that submitted its report on 20 May 2000. The Committee was of the opinion that:

> The public service broadcaster plays a key role in any society, especially, in a large and thriving democracy. It must be a part of 'civil society', independent of and distinct from the government. In fact, the public service broadcaster must act as one of the bedrocks of society, and seek to continuously enlarge the so-called 'public sphere. It must play host to informed debate, provide space for alternative and dissenting viewpoints, be a voice of the voiceless and give substance to the phrase 'participatory democracy' (MIB, 2000a: 16).

The Committee reiterated that market forces cannot be expected to take care of these objectives and for Prasar Bharati, as the public broadcaster, revenue maximisation need not be an immediate goal and advertising revenue earned should not be the only yardstick for judging its performance. 'Alternative indices—related to audience size and share programme content and impact, channel reach and loyalty—are more meaningful and must be used' (MIB, 2000a: 81).

The Committee suggested several amendments to the Prasar Bharati Act 1990 to enable it to survive in a highly competitive environment created by global media technology and to create public service content of highest quality. The Committee reiterated its faith in decentralisation and devolution and in its recommendations, and emphasised that the local stations must involve local groups and voluntary organisations in programme production. It also recommended giving serious consideration to:

> ... the franchising of local radio stations by Prasar Bharati to selected local community and voluntary groups on an experimental basis. Now that FM radio has been privatised, we do hope that the long-standing opposition and aversion to such a worthwhile step will fade away (MIB, 2000a: 37).

Liberalisation, Privatisation and Regulation of Media

The broadcasting debate assumed an altogether new dimension with the advent of cable operators and the beaming of satellite channels by Hong Kong-based STAR TV into India in the year 1991. Conditions for broadcasting changed radically (Pavarala and Kumar, 2001b). Faced with the eventuality of private sector competition, autonomy, genuine or otherwise, for state-owned media, seemed inevitable. At the same time, the governments were faced with a new set of questions, which they were quite ill-equipped to resolve. What should be the structure of regulatory system to take account of the invasion via satellites, and of the new media technologies? What was to be the fate of national (read political) objectives? Competition in programming as well as commerce or advertising was another unfamiliar territory. All these concerns coupled with a few other landmark developments saw the revival of some of the critical issues concerning broadcasting in India after three decades of unimplemented good intentions.

In February 1995, the Supreme Court delivered a historic judgement in *Ministry of Information and Broadcasting v. Cricket Association of Bengal*. The Court ruled that: 'Airwaves constitute public property and must be utilized for advancing public good' (operative part of judgement available on MIB website).

The spirit of the judgement was to spell the end of the government monopoly of broadcasting. But it was not in favour of deregulation of airwaves for use by the private business firms. It stated that, 'no individual had a right to utilise them (airwaves) at his choice and pleasure and for purposes of his choice including profit.' In two separate concurring judgements, the Court said the right of free speech guaranteed by Article 19(1)(a) did not include the right to use airwaves which were public property.

> From the standpoint of Article 19(1)(a) what is paramount is the right of the listeners and viewers and not the right of the broadcaster—whether the broadcaster is the State, public corporation or a private individual or body.
>
> While the freedom guaranteed by Article 19(1(a) does include the right to receive and impart information, no one can claim the fundamental right to do so by using or employing public property. Only where the statute permits him to use the public property, then only—and subject to such conditions and restrictions as the law may impose—he can use the public property, viz., airwaves. In other words, Article 19(1)(a) does not enable a citizen to impart his information, views and opinion by using the airwaves. He can do so without using the airwaves (MIB, 1996d cited as Appendix B in Price and Verhulst, 1998: 227–28).

Broadcasting media as a whole should promote freedom of expression and speech and, therefore, should be able to enjoy freedom from government monopoly and control subject to regulation by a public body. In this connection, the Court decreed: 'The broadcasting media should be under the control of the public as distinct from government. This is the command implicit in Article 19(1)(a). It should be operated by a public statutory corporation or corporations…' (see Appendix-I).

The judgement did not, however, endorse dismantling of controls. Private broadcasting, if permitted, cannot be left to the market forces. It needs to be regulated in the larger public interest. The observations of the Supreme Court in this regard are as follows: 'The airwaves or frequencies are a public property. Their use has to be controlled and regulated by a public authority in the interests of the public and to prevent the invasion of their rights' (see Appendix-I).

The judgement ordered the central government to 'take immediate steps to establish an autonomous public authority to control and regulate the use of the airwaves'. The Ministry of Information and Broadcasting sets about drafting broadcasting legislation that would establish a broadcast authority and open up the airwaves to private parties, individuals and public bodies wishing to enter the field of broadcasting and telecasting.

While this exercise to place the role of Broadcasting Authority of India in the context of a comprehensive law on broadcasting was still being carried out, a parliamentary subcommittee formulated a working paper on national media policy in March 1996. The objectives of this draft media policy included several of those that have been asserted in earlier laws and reports (MIB, 1996e). The newer concerns mentioned related to those that warned against permitting growth of monopoly in any media, and expressed themselves in favour of restricting cross-media ownership. The working paper took a stand against permitting direct or indirect foreign equity participation in private broadcasting companies (Ninan, 1998). The subcommittee laid emphasis on the setting up of non-commercial broadcasting stations to be run by universities, educational institutions, panchayats, local bodies, state governments, etc. It was in favour of allowing state and local governments and NGOs to enter the field of broadcasting.

It was only in 1997 that some urgency was expressed for a broadcasting law for India, 'in view of the impending start of the much more powerful digital Direct to Home (DTH) services any time by the next year' (MIB, 1997). In May 1997, the Broadcast Bill for setting up a Broadcasting Authority of India was introduced in Parliament. It corroborated the fundamental principles of all the earlier efforts to reposition broadcasting in India. The Broadcasting Bill 1997 may in fact be seen as a confluence of the major imperatives derived from constitutional clauses, committee reports, judgements, and policy statements concerning broadcasting in India. But, the government fell again and the draft of the Broadcasting Bill along with the Working Paper on Media Policy remains a major piece of unfinished business till today.

On the radio front, in July 1999, it was announced that private companies registered in India would be allowed to set up 101 independent FM stations in 40 cities. Of the 148 frequencies identified for 40 centres, 40 have been reserved for educational channels to be operated by the Human Resource Development Ministry without payment of any license fee (MIB, 2002a). The auction of FM frequencies in favour of the open-market lobby is a perverted interpretation of the Supreme Court judgement. None of the recommendations favouring alternative media practices in the country seem to be materialising in the near future, as the government has now decided to tackle the issue of convergence of telecommunications, information technology and electronic media before announcing a comprehensive policy that will cover the entire communications sector.

The Draft Convergence Bill proposes the setting up of a Communications Commission of India on the lines of the Federal Communications Commission (FCC) in the US to manage, plan and monitor spectrum for non-strategic and commercial usage of communication infrastructure. The Commission would also grant licenses while exercising some (among several other) of the following principles:

> - that communication services are made available at affordable cost to all uncovered areas including the rural, remote, hilly and tribal areas;
> - that there is increasing access to information for greater empowerment of citizens and towards economic development;
> - that quality, plurality, diversity and choice of services are promoted.
>
> (MIB, 2000b: Clause 19)

As the country still awaits a comprehensive media policy and a broadcast law to enable the democratisation of media, efforts are on for carving out an alternative media sector in India, which would neither be state-run nor market-driven. The groups advocating community radio as part of the movement for an alternative public realm can only hope that the right to use radio for development goals at the community level and to represent the priorities of the vulnerable would be granted soon.

Conclusion

Radio broadcasting in free India endeavoured to shape up in the mould of Public Service Broadcasting. According to communication scholar Dennis McQuail, the idea of 'public service' broadcasting encompasses eight principles:

> Geographical universality of provision and reception; the aim of providing for all tastes and interests; catering for minorities; having a concern for

> national identity and community; keeping broadcasting independent from government and vested interests; having some element of direct funding from the public (thus not only from advertisers); encouraging competition in programmes and not just for audiences; and encouraging the freedom of broadcasters (McQuail 1994:126).

However, the state-controlled broadcasting in India ended up following what Herman and Chomsky (1988) sketch out as 'the propaganda model' where media serve 'to mobilize support for the special interests that dominate the state and private activity', becoming a propaganda tool for government policies and actions. 'In countries where the levers of power are in the hands of a state bureaucracy, the monopolistic control over media, often supplemented by official censorship, makes it clear that the media serve the ends of a dominant elite' (Herman and Chomsky, 1988: 1).

With liberalisation of the economy in India, broadcasting witnessed backdoor and reluctant privatisation, but eventually, as Kiran Karnik, long-time observer of India's media scene and currently President, NASSCOM, opines, forces of commercialisation prevailed, leading to a shift towards empty entertainment (Sen, 2000). As Barnard points out,

> The classical argument against commercialisation of mass communication media is that pursuit of advertising revenues encourages programming assumed to appeal to the greatest number, thereby marginalizing less popular tastes and interests. It creates an environment most conducive to reception of advertising message, leading to programming that is undemanding, unchallenging and pacifying (2000: 51).

Technology-led globalisation of media did not do anything to change the order of things for broadcasting in India. It led to the concentration of ownership in a handful of transnational media conglomerates, further diminishing the freedom and diversity of information. As cultural homogenisation became the order of the day, the uniformity of the content rendered meaningless the increase in the number of information sources (Pavarala and Kumar, 2002). As a result, the shrinking of democratic spaces has weakened civil society, allowing the state and the market to have unfettered control over the minds of the people.

These concerns have been articulated in several reports of committees set up to examine the status of broadcasting in India and also in numerous policy documents. In spite of plainly stated objectives, little has been done to re-orient broadcasting to produce meaningful content that dovetails rather than emulates current practices of commercial radio, and addresses the developmental, social, cultural, communal and democratic imperatives of the country. No effort has been made to ensure that the weakest and the vulnerable are empowered through access and control of media-technologies.

For instance, All India Radio's 77 Local Radio Stations (LRS) were mandated to produce field-based programmes with accent on local problems, news and views, and local talent. The organisation's annual report states:

> What distinguishes the Local Radio from the regional network is its down to earth, intimate approach. The programmes of the local radio are area specific. They are flexible and spontaneous enough to enable the station to function as the mouthpiece of the local community (Prasar Bharati, 2002).

In reality, however, owing to inherent deficiencies of a bureaucratic system these stations only replicate the style of working and even the programming patterns of a regional station. Their staff is ill equipped to run them in a manner that is democratic and participatory.

Even as the well-intentioned state broadcaster is frozen into inaction, commercial broadcasting has revived a plummeting medium. But the latter's agenda to accumulate profits renders it incapable of exploiting the potential of the medium for social change. This has propelled a number of civil society organisations to articulate the need for alternatives in the form of popular and community-based media. The community radio initiatives by several groups across India for a share of the airwaves, which are 'public property', are one significant indication of this popular demand.

The major barrier in ushering a vibrant community radio sector in India appears to be the perception that it poses a threat to the power structure. This perception is based on what White (1994) calls a zero-sum notion of 'distributive' power. If, as she suggests, power is understood as 'generative', whereby different groups can generate their own sources of power necessary to accomplish social, cultural and community objectives, this fear about loss of control could be seen as misplaced. Radio must, therefore, be looked at as a tool for empowerment, an appropriate technology to conscientise and build capacities of communities to become active participants in development.

NOTES

1. According to the Akash Bharati report, the inauguration of IBC's Bombay station was reported in the *Times of India* in a banner headline, reading 'Viceroy Inaugurates a Wireless Era for India'.
2. According to H.R. Luthra, Nehru, in 1948, had favoured a set-up approximating the BBC public corporation model. Letters of appointment of Akashvani staff have always included the stipulation that they are liable to transfer at any time to the service under a Public Corporation.
3. An expression borrowed from the Chanda Committee report.
4. According to H.R. Luthra and the Akash Bharati Report, on the same day, the programme journal *Indian Radio Time* was redesigned and named *The Indian Listener*. It remained unchanged for the next 22 years, when it became *Akashvani*.
5. The story of how the name 'All India Radio' came to be coined is related by Fielden in his autobiography, *The Natural Bent* (1960).
6. With A.S. Bokhari's brother Z.A. Bokhari becoming the station director, critics could not resist labelling AIR, the Bokhari Brothers Corporation (BBC) (Luthra, 1986).
7. External Services broadcasts started at this time, the first broadcast commencing on 1 October 1939.
8. According to the Chanda Committee report, the number of radio licences had doubled from 2,75,955 in 1947 to 5,46,319 in 1950.
9. These include, *Broadcasting in India* by G.C. Awasthy (1965), *All about AIR* and *Broadcasting and the People* by Mehra Masani (1985), *Tangled Tapes* by K.S. Mullick (1974), *Radio Programmes of All India Radio* by Pamela Philipose, *What Ails Indian Broadcasting* by K.S. Duggal (1980).
10. Chanda Committee report points out that many countries, including the UK and Canada, have found it necessary to institute periodic reviews of their broadcasting systems by independent committees but it has not been so in India. H.R. Luthra cites it as a case in point that the BBC during its 40 years had been reported upon by four expert commissions: Crawford Committee (1925), Ullswater Committee (1935), Beveridge Committee (1950) and Pilkington Committee.
11. In his book, *My Reminiscences of Sardar Patel,* V. Shanker, his private secretary, mentions that one of the first steps taken by Sardar Patel to 'clean up' radio was to prohibit musicians 'whose private lives were a public scandal'. Some regarded this as a measure directed against Muslim women artists.
12. These included the Shillong, Baroda, Amritsar and Mysore stations.
13. The Committee observes that, in both the first and the second FYP, allocation to broadcasting was about one-tenth of one per cent of the total resources while it was reduced to one-eighth of the total resources in the third plan.
14. Also see Sanjay (1991), for an account of the problems that arose for rural listeners as manufacture of reception sets was left entirely to market forces.

15. Dr Keskar is said to have explained that *Akashvani* was a kind of an all-India name and trademark for All India Radio and the word had been taken from Kannada where it was originally used for the Mysore station during the British days.
16. Also see David Lelyveld (1996) on how under Patel and even more so under Keskar, measures were taken to assure that the 'Hindu' side would prevail in music on AIR, by systematically marginalising influences of Muslim *gharana* music.
17. Cited in Thomas, 1990: 4.
18. As stated in the Extracts of Prime Minister Indira Gandhi's address to the Conference of AIR Station Directors on 9 September 1975. See Appendix 6, Page 13 in MIB, 1977.
19. The report attributes this expression to Yashpal (1983).
20. B.G. Verghese in an interview with the authors.
21. Ibid.
22. Ministry of Information and Broadcasting, Government of India constituted a Committee on 22 November 1999 comprising N.R. Narayanamurthy, Chairman and Chief Executive, Infosys; Kiran Karnik, Managing Director, Discovery Communications India; Shunu, Chairman and Chief Executive, Quadra Advisory, Marketing Consultant; R.C. Mishra, Jt. Secretary (Broadcasting, Ministry of Information and Broadcasting); Rajeeva Ratna Shah, Chief Executive, Prasar Bharati, Special Invitee; to carry out a comprehensive review of Prasar Bharati.

4 FACILITATING COMMUNITY RADIO IN INDIA

Profiles of NGOs and their Community Radio Initiatives

Several non-profit and development organisations as well as media activists in India have campaigned to get communities the right to set up low-cost local radio broadcasting facilities. Even as the government was diffident about legislation to facilitate the functioning of community radio in India, some grassroots organisations had initiated radio projects to support their community development work. This chapter outlines the history of the presence of NGOs in the region where their community radio projects are located and also their philosophy of development work. The lobbying efforts of the NGOs and their ideas about the role community radio can play in strengthening an internal democratic process in their villages are discussed. The socio-economic and cultural profile of the region and the political context in which the community radio initiatives have emerged are also explained in the chapter. The chapter highlights the level of community based organisation in existence in the community radio projects that formed a part of this study and the basic norms that guided the setting up of these projects. The community radio initiatives that are profiled in the chapter include:

(*a*) Alternative for India Development (AID) project in Daltonganj (Jharkhand);
(*b*) Kutch Mahila Vikas Sangathan (KMVS) project in Bhuj (Gujarat);
(*c*) VOICES project in Budhikote (Karnataka); and
(*d*) Deccan Development Society (DDS) project in Pastapur (Andhra Pradesh).

Chala Ho Gaon Mein: The Community Radio Project of NFI/AID

Alternative for India Development (AID), a grassroots NGO, with the strategic and financial backing of the National Foundation for India (NFI) and in technical collaboration with *Manthan Yuva Sansthan* started airing a community radio programme on the local AIR–Daltonganj station in the Palamau district of Jharkhand from 5 August 2001. The 30-minute programme, *Chala Ho Gaon Mein* (come, let's go to the village) was broadcast on FM band every Sunday at 7.20 p.m. and covered 45 villages of the Lesliganj and Panki blocks. The radio programme was put together with the help of village reporters and digital post-production work was carried out in the state capital Ranchi (165 km from Daltonganj).

Today, *Chala Ho Gaon Mein* is broadcast twice a week, on every Sunday and Wednesday, from 7.15 p.m. to 7.45 p.m. and covers more than 160 villages of Palamau, Latehar and Garwah districts of Jharkhand. All post-production inputs like dubbing, recording and editing take place in the new studio set up in the Loknayak Jayaprakash Narayan Community Technical College of AID in Garwah, 50 km away from Daltonganj, where the programmes are fully produced by the local volunteers without any external assistance.

The Region

The state of Jharkhand became a functioning reality on 15 November 2000 after almost half a century of people's movements around Jharkhandi identity, which disadvantaged societal groups articulated in order to augment political resources and influence the policy process in their favour. Even at present, the dynamics of resources and the politics of development largely influence the socio-economic structures in Jharkhand, which has been carved out of the relatively 'backward' southern part of undivided Bihar. Jharkhand is the leading producer of mineral wealth in the country, endowed as it is with vast variety of minerals like iron ore, coal, copper ore, mica, bauxite, graphite, limestone, and uranium. Jharkhand is also known for its vast forest resources.

This paradoxical development profile of Jharkhand is combined with the fact that distortions in distribution and access to resources have made little difference to the lives of ordinary people and the state is nationally well known for the lowest levels in terms of social indicators including literacy, health, infrastructure, skill development, sustainable livelihoods, etc. (Prakash, 2001). However, the people of the region are politically mobilised and self-conscious and are actively seeking better bargains for the state. The people in Jharkhand have the advantage of being culturally vibrant, as reflected in the diversity of languages spoken, festivals celebrated, and variety of folk music, dances, and other traditions of performing arts in the region.

The Palamau district, where the AID's community radio project is located, is one of the most neglected parts of Jharkhand. It has a population mix of *adivasi* (tribal) and non-*adivasi* rural communities, of about 15 lakh (15 per cent SC and 10 per cent ST). Rampant deforestation has led to ecological changes, which have adversely affected the natural wealth of the region and also made it drought prone. People living in the district earn their livelihood out of minor forest produce and grow basic crops like paddy, wheat and lentils. Most live on the edge of poverty.

Less than a third of the women folk know how to read and write and a sizable number of men depend on migratory labour opportunities to earn their living. Poverty, however, has not hampered their aptitude for song-writing, musical compositions, folk theatre and other non-formal styles of information dissemination. Developmental infrastructure in Palamau needs drastic improvement: roads are in poor condition; access to electricity supply is either missing or erratic; the public distribution system is irregular; telephone lines are yet to roll out; and hand-pumps are the only source of water both for agriculture and household usage. The administration at best is ineffective and at its worst defunct. Socially too, the continuing prevalence of feudal system has perpetuated practices such as bonded and child labour, child or early marriage, dowry, debt, superstitions and guerrilla activities. Palamau is by and large underserved by the media, but one of AIR's 77 local FM radio stations is located in the district headquarters, Daltonganj. The local communities in the region are familiar with its programmes.

The NGOs

Alternative for India Development (AID) has its origins in the state of Bihar, now bifurcated into Jharkhand. Many of the community-based groups and individuals who became part of AID were involved in mass struggles against injustice, corruption, illiteracy, poverty, exploitation, and unemployment led by Jayaprakash Narayan (JP) in the mid-70s. Students, inspired by JP formed the *Chatra Yuva Sangarsh Vahini* (Student Youth Struggle Force) initially in Bihar and later in other parts of India. Ramraj, who was an activist in that movement and currently the coordinator for the Palamau chapter of AID-Jharkhand, observes that AID was founded in the year 1982 by a group of *Vahini* activists and social scientists, who felt the need to have an organisation that could provide institutional and technical support to volunteers and other grassroots movements working for transformation.

According to Suresh Kumar, project coordinator of the Palamau chapter of AID-Jharkhand, the volunteers of the movement faced constant threats and intimidation from the local landlords, politicians, and corrupt government officials. It is in this situation that many of the activists felt that they needed external social, financial, and legal support. AID was established in response to this need. The ideological basis of AID, as stated in its documents and website, are as follows:

> Alternative for India Development (AID) is committed to the total development of the poor, socially, economically and politically. The organization believes people's participation in their development process is the key to the success. This is the vision of AID.
>
> Sustainable development of people ensuring everyone, even the most deprived, can progress towards achieving basic education, health provision & an adequate livelihood. This is the mission of AID.
>
> Enabling the more disadvantaged to analyse and deal with their problems themselves. To enable them to gain access to basic education, health provision & an increased livelihood. This is the goal of AID.
>
> To bring about total transformation and create a just society. We believe in grassroots democracy, decentralisation, equality, respect for women's rights, an end to caste discrimination and non-violence. This is AID's philosophy (http://www.aidindia.net/aboutus.htm).

AID-Jharkhand, a subsidiary of Alternative for India Development, has been involved in grassroots development for the past 16 years in villages spread over eight districts in the Jharkhand region. It works through youth groups, women's groups, and community organisations. Their head office is at Ranchi and the regional offices are located at Jamshedpur, Palamau, and Garwah. The organisation with more than 200 local community workers has been actively involved in several projects, including education, micro-credit for women, basic health programmes, campaign against child marriage, reproductive health and water management. AID's local office in Palamau is situated in Lesliganj.

National Foundation for India (NFI), a national level grant-making and fund-raising non-governmental organisation, supports development activities, focusing especially on issues of poverty, illiteracy, and health. It also has a programme area for development communication, which recognises the significance of media in facilitating grassroots level work for social change and community empowerment. Following the Supreme Court judgement in 1995, which emphasised people's right to the airwaves, NFI got interested in promoting initiatives with direct participation of the communities in the use of media, with the belief that access to media could empower marginalised groups. The NFI decided to avail the state infrastructure for experimenting with community radio for development at the grassroots level. It identified AID as a partner for implementing the project and a media activist group from Ranchi, *Manthan Yuva Sansthan*, was invited to join the project as the technical associate.

The Project: Overview

AID preferred to start its community radio pilot project in Palamau because it is an area with poor communication infrastructure and lack of electricity. For most of the villages their only contact with the outside world is through radio. With a majority of the population illiterate, the print media has negligible presence. Television and video are yet to make inroads into the region, most of which is still without electricity. Even on radio, barring a very few regional programmes, hardly any programming caters to the rural population. The main aims of the community radio programme of AID are:

- to enable people to produce programmes locally;
- to build expertise among rural people to speak about issues affecting their lives;
- to do the above in their own language; and
- to rejuvenate local art forms and culture.

Interviews with AID representatives suggest that the organisation views community radio primarily as a pedagogical tool to extend the development goals of AID and to use this as a mass medium to highlight local issues, through local language and culture. During one of our focus group discussions in a village, Suresh Kumar, the community radio coordinator of AID, offered the following explanation to an elderly woman who wanted to know why the radio project was started and by whom:

> AID, which has its office in Lesliganj, wants more and more people in the villages to be educated. AID desires that all villages and villagers develop equally, that people give up bad habits and work hard, that government officials come and help in solving your problems, and that every person leads a happy and peaceful life. For this purpose, AID, along with NFI of Delhi has started the programme *Chala Ho Gaon Mein*.

To initiate the community radio project, a content development workshop was held at Lesliganj in February 2001. AID gathered volunteers from villages across Lesliganj and Panki blocks, who had been associated with one or the other AID projects in the past. Out of these, 16 community representatives, including four women, were identified to form the core group of the project. Each volunteer was asked to identify two more villages in addition to their native village for which he/she could act as local reporter cum project motivator. At the end of the workshop, 45 villages were identified as the target area for the first phase. By this time, AID also appointed a project coordinator who was aware of the problems of the area and was familiar with its ideology. The Lesliganj workshop was also devoted to identify focal issues for the radio programme. Both NFI and AID decided that the issues to be highlighted in the community radio programme would be those chosen by the community. The core issues identified by the community volunteers were: adult illiteracy, education for the girl child, child marriage, practice of dowry and related domestic violence, health and hygiene issues, and information on rural development and livelihood schemes. The volunteers also arrived at *Chala Ho Gaon Mein* as a suitable title for the programme (NFI, 2001).

These 16 volunteers were then divided into four groups, according to their choice of villages. Each group was asked to choose one central issue and make recordings in the field using portable cassette recorders. *Manthan* provided the initial operational training for field recording. These field recordings were then used as basic study material at the five-day long training workshop conducted by *Manthan* in Ranchi. At this workshop the volunteers were acquainted with the techniques of audio presentation and production. The field recordings of the four groups and studio exercises conducted at the workshop formed the basic raw material for the first set of four 30-minute programmes of the project. These four programmes were taken by AID to selected villages for narrowcasting. This process helped in assessing the acceptability of the programmes, testing the impact on local communities, and in designing advance publicity for the community radio initiative. After a month of narrowcasting, another two-day workshop was held in Lesliganj to integrate the community radio initiative with the ground level work of AID. The project coordinators suggested that the period of narrowcasting be limited to three months as the novelty of the initiative lies in broadcasting. Title music for the programme was composed by some of the villagers who came to see the progress of the project at the workshop.

During the various narrowcasting sessions in the villages, many villagers expressed their desire to participate in the community radio initiative and utilise it for social education. Eventually NFI requested AIR Daltonganj for a 30-minute commercial slot on Sundays at 7.20 p.m. for *Chala Ho Gaon Mein* and the first episode went on air from 5 August 2001.

Sudhir Pal, *Manthan Yuva Sansthan*, Ranchi, explains that the structure of the programme was influenced by the feedback obtained during the narrowcasting sessions as also by the technical requirements. As an example, he states that people rejected the narrators of the programme who were professionals from AIR, and then the characters of 'Phulwa behen' and 'Raju bhaiya' were introduced as presenters. They have now become so popular that kids frequently play act the two roles. The structure of the episodes is as follows: drama (10 minutes), folk songs (5–6 minutes), *Chaupal*, i.e., discussion (5 minutes), *vikas ke saathi*, i.e., rural news or *lok katha*, i.e., folk tales alternately (3–4 minutes), and letters from listeners (2 minutes). Earlier episodes also had interviews with professional experts on various subjects.

The Project: in Progress

At present, *Chala Ho Gaon Mein*, broadcast in the local *Maghi* dialect, can be heard every Sunday and Wednesday as the frequency of the programme was increased, on popular demand, to two episodes a week from 1 May 2003. It reaches a population of over 70 lakh covering Palamau, Garwah and Latehar districts in Jharkhand, and some of the bordering regions in Chhattisgarh, Bihar and UP. The technical team—reporters, scriptwriters, actors, musicians and their instruments—are all from the local region. The issues covered in the programme get regular coverage in the local print media. It receives 200 to 250 letters every week from a region with low literacy rates. *Ab hawaon mein gunjtee hain daliton, sositon ki awaz* (Now the voice of excluded and exploited is ringing in the air), was the headline for a series of six articles carried in a popular newspaper, *Prabhat Khabar* that gave details of the impact of this programme on the region.

As the major task of editing the programme has been taken over by AID, current and contextual information and latest updates are being added to the programmes. Single issue-based episodes tackling a subject in-depth using various formats and those carrying reactions of the Block Development Officials to the issues raised by the people in the villages are also aired from time to time. With a view to increase listenership, 400 FM radio sets have been provided to women self-help groups (SHGs) and in remote villages and also to the *Gram Sabhas*. Also, programme development, message gathering and analysis and pre-editing listening sessions are carried out every month during the creative workshops.

Our Case Study

This case study was carried out in the Palamau district (Daltonganj is the district headquarters) of Jharkhand. Following discussions with the project coordinator and the community reporters, the sample villages for focus group discussions were selected on the basis of geographic and demographic variations. This was done to ensure representation of the different communities in the 45 villages of the two blocks of Lesliganj and Panki covered by the community radio project. Of these 45 villages where the radio reporters work, it was decided to select at least one village each from among those chosen by the 12 (who were present for a meeting with us) out of the 14 reporters working in the project.

Keeping in mind the ratio of villages in the two blocks, it was decided to select nine villages in Lesliganj and three in Panki. Selection of villages in Panki ensured that perceptions of listeners who are farthest from the radio station were also included. The research team covered villages, which were located about 20 km–60 km away from the Daltonganj radio station. Since there was a mixture of tribal and non-tribal (Dalit) villages, it was decided to include both types of villages in the sample. The composition of the focus groups was then decided along variables of tribe, caste, gender and age. Since literacy was not very high in the region, it was not considered as a major variable. Similarly, as most of the members of the focus groups belonged to a lower socio-economic status, class was not considered a variable. Table 4.1 gives details of the selected villages, along with the description of the nature of focus groups:

Table 4.1: ***Focus Groups for AID Community Radio Case Study***

No.	*Village/Block*	*Description of Group*
1.	Goradih Khas (Lesliganj)	Mixed Gender Group
2.	Rajhara (Lesliganj)	Older tribal men
3.	Purushotampur (Panki)	Tribal men
4.	Mahe Dema (Panki)	Backward Caste men
5.	Bhalmanda (Lesliganj)	Women's group
6.	Kundari (Lesliganj)	Older women
7.	Harsangra (Lesliganj)	Young men's group
8.	Chainegir (Lesliganj)	Self-help group
9.	Nawadih (Lesliganj)	Young girls' group
10.	Cheri/Chaparna (Lesliganj)	Listening session
11.	Barunahi (Panki)	Tribal men
12.	Pipra (Lesliganj)	Men's group

There were in all 77 people who participated across 12 focus group discussions. In addition, in each village we interacted informally with scores of others who formed curious spectators for the focus group discussions. In order to understand the internal dynamics of the production and implementation of the community radio project, we also conducted in-depth, open-ended interviews and discussions with the 12 community radio reporters, the AID project coordinator, the AID-Jharkhand (Palamau) project manager, station director of AIR Daltonganj, and the *Manthan* production coordinator. These interviews and discussions were also recorded and transcribed. In addition, the study analysed relevant documents, feedback forms and letters from listeners.

Ujjas Radio: The Community Radio Project of KMVS

Kutch Mahila Vikas Sangathan (KMVS), an independent organisation working in the largest district of Gujarat state in western India for the empowerment of rural women in Kutchi society, regularly produces, in technical and creative collaboration with Drishti Media Collective of Ahmedabad, a series of participatory, local-language radio programmes. The programmes reflect the concerns, needs, priorities and issues of the women in the region and use the local folklore, music and Kutch culture to disseminate important information and developmental messages. Since December 1999, KMVS has been airing these programmes through sponsored Kutchi language slots on AM frequency of AIR's Radio Bhuj.

The KMVS radio team was conferred the prestigious Chameli Devi Jain Award, 2000 by the Media Foundation in New Delhi on 29 March 2001 for its first string of radio programmes entitled *Kunjal Paanje Kutch Ji* (KPKJ)—Saras Crane of our Kutch. After completing 53 episodes of KPKJ in December 2000, KMVS launched a bi-weekly 15-minute radio programme *Tu Jiyaro Ain* (To Be Alive) in March 2001, which was aimed at addressing the needs of the earthquake-devastated people of Kutch. KMVS continued its intervention in radio by producing *Kutch Lok Ji Bani* (KLJB)—Voice of the People of Kutch—entirely handled by the media unit of KMVS comprising local rural reporters from the different villages of Kutch.

The Region

Kutch is the second largest district in the country with 950 villages in its nine *talukas*. The name Kutch apparently comes from the shape of the area, which is formed like a tortoise (*Kaachbo* in Kutchi language). The district possesses unique geographical features as it is bound by the Arabian Sea and the Gulf of Kutch in the west and the south respectively, and by the salt desert (*Rann*) towards the northern and eastern parts. A range of hills runs east–west, parallel to the Gulf of Kutch. The administrative headquarters of Kutch district is Bhuj. The *Rann* covers 51 per cent of land and because the rains are inadequate and erratic, Kutch is under constant threat of drought—out of five years, three are drought years and seven out of the nine *talukas* are identified as drought prone. This makes the issue of water scarcity a source of major concern and struggle in the lives of the people of Kutch. In the absence of perennial water sources, and due to the saline soil, the region is arid and unproductive. The grazing land and the indigenous grasslands (*Banni*) have been devastated by the unchecked spread of a fuel wood species, *Proposis Juliflora*, originally introduced by the government to stall the increasing soil salinity.

The traditional sources of income generation for the communities in Kutch have been animal breeding and herding, rain-fed agriculture, wage labour and handicrafts. The 10-year stocktaking report of KMVS explains how a distinct division of labour along the lines of caste and religion marks the rather heterogeneous population of 1.25 million in Kutch. While the Muslims and the tribal *Rabaris* are engaged in cattle breeding and animal husbandry, the *Ahirs* and the upper caste *Darbars* are agriculturists; the Dalits are engaged in crafts and the marginalised *Kolis* subsist on fishing and collection of minor forest produce (Ramachandran and Saihjee, 2000). Kutch has been beleaguered by natural calamities such as cyclones and earthquakes along with recurrent droughts. These ecological setbacks, environmental degradation and the shift in traditional agricultural and livestock rearing practices have adversely affected the livelihoods and food security among Kutch population. This has led to male migration and other far-reaching changes in mutual cohesion among communities and the economic structures of the households further precipitating domestic and social tensions (Soni and Stalin, 2004).

In the absence of income from agriculture and livestock, women are compelled to take up embroidery and handicrafts to make a living and feed their families. This however, does little towards enhancing the status of women by virtue of being the principal earners of the household. Lack of knowledge about marketing and the innumerable restrictions on their mobility encourages the entry of home-grown middlemen and results in blatant economic exploitation of women. During annual droughts, people depend on embroidery and drought-relief work for income. A woman in rural Kutch, on an average, has a 19-hour work schedule out of which 3–4 hours are devoted to accessing water for domestic use (Ramachandran and Saihjee, 2000).

Literacy levels among women are very low and there are areas where there is no literacy. Lack of access to information and resources, inadequate nutrition, early marriage and frequent child bearing, the dual burden of household tasks and income generation are the causes of women's subjugation in Kutch. This is compounded by the spiteful forms that patriarchal norms and behaviour take in the face of economic pressures leading to a rise in the incidents of mental and physical violence against women (Soni, 2004). The annual reports and official documents of KMVS record that the organisation was set up in June 1989 in response to the miserable situation faced by the women during the droughts of 1985–88.

The NGOs

KMVS entered the region within the larger socio-cultural context explained above with the objective of working towards 'the social, economic and political empowerment of rural women in Kutchi society and to help them gain control over resources and decision-making regarding their lives, families, work and environment' (KMVS, 2003: Slide 7). A report capturing its 10-year journey explains that KMVS was conceived as 'an independent organization of poor rural women that would work towards developing women's ability and confidence to address issues of their concern and develop their self-image, self-esteem, human, educational and financial resources through its collective strength' (Ramachandran and Saihjee, 2000: 8). The organisation has more than 10,000 women members in 180 villages of five *talukas* of Kutch (see Table 4.2).

Preeti Soni, the coordinator for the media unit of KMVS, explained that the core group makes its initial forays into the villages through direct contact with the women and works in tandem with them on their expressed issues. Women are not treated as an undifferentiated cluster, and are instead viewed as being stratified along lines of caste, class, ethnicity and religion. A mutual educational process between KMVS and rural women leads to the formation of *mahila mandals* (women's groups), a shared space for women to come together to express their own and communities' needs, to analyse their own situations and take ownership of various activities. The average size of these *mandals* is 30–50 members. Every *mandal* elects a leader or *Agewan* and a core team with some members taking on designated tasks for the village.

Table 4.2: ***Community Radio Initiatives—Geographical Location***

	State	*District (Location)*	*Mandals/Blocks/ Divisions/Talukas (Covered by reporters)*	*Villages Covered (Nos.) (a) By reporters (b) By programme*
Chala Ho Gaon Mein	Jharkhand	Palamau	Lesliganj Panki	(*a*) 45 (*b*) 160 (where AID works including Latehar and Garwah districts)
KMVS Community Radio	Gujarat	Bhuj	Mundra, Pachham, Nakhatrana, Abdasa, Rapar-Bachau	(*a*)/(*b*) 180 (where KMVS works)
Namma Dhwani	Karnataka	Kolar	Bangarpet	(*a*) 35 (Budhikote sector) (*b*) One (Budhikote)
DDS Community Radio	Andhra Pradesh (Telangana region)	Medak	Zaheerabad Jharasangam Raikode Nyalkal	(*a*)/(*b*) 75 (DDS *sangam* villages)

The *mahila mandals* in the villages are organised and federated into the *taluka sangathans* (block-level groups). Preeti Soni observes that all these *taluka sangathans* federate into KMVS. According to her, KMVS aims at building local leadership and developing the women's capabilities for harnessing their collective strength. It concentrates primarily in the remote and less accessible villages along the border areas of Kutch. Today, *sangathans* in two *talukas* are functioning autonomously and manage their own grants, resources and programmes with technical support from the KMVS units that operate as support cells.

Over the years, KMVS has evolved a multiple yet integrated foci and set up issue-based units for education, health, savings and credit, marketing and design support, legal aid, panchayati raj and communication. It also takes on environmental issues and works on natural resource management. These units provide training in organisational leadership to the *taluka sangathan* members and also render specialised inputs including, information, planning, monitoring and research for implementing various village level activities. The KMVS core group works with national financial resources and does not maintain a foreign exchange authorisation (FCRA) number. In order to strengthen the notion of basic accountabilities and sensitivities, KMVS believes that the less privileged have a right to access support from the state and from the more privileged (Ramachandran and Saihjee, 2000).

For KMVS, the state is an important actor in the development process and a significant proportion of the KMVS funds come from the government. It has a balanced relationship with the government, based on dialogue, lobbying, liaison and if required, distancing. The self-empowerment efforts embarked upon by KMVS through the conscientisation, organisation and mobilisation of rural women into a network of local collectives have enabled women progressively to address several issues related to development and gender inequities in the region. This prompted women to articulate the need to equip themselves with more practical information and skills in order to participate in the larger social and political process.

The educational interventions initiated by KMVS in 1992 with functional and customised literacy camps for adolescent girls and *sangathan* members paved way for the *Ujjas Mahiti Kendra* (*Ujjas* Information Centre) set up by the Mundra village *sangathan* in 1994. The women in the *mahiti kendra* started publishing a newsletter, '*Ujjas*' (meaning light) that served as a platform for them to practice their newly acquired literacy and to document and exchange experiences, information and knowledge. The newsletter is written, illustrated and screen-printed by rural women themselves and the language used is simple Kutchi and Gujarati.

In 1998, the *Ujjas Kendra* felt the need to extend its links with the non-literate women collectives formed in far-flung villages. A survey carried out in 1998–99 to assess the media use among rural Kutchis indicated that radio is the most popular medium in the region. Poverty and low literacy levels make it difficult for the villagers to take full advantage of newspaper and television (Soni and Stalin, 2004). A decision was taken to use radio for expansion of the knowledge base in the region and to build an information network. The *Ujjas* initiative thus diversified from print into radio and launched a weekly radio programme *Kunjal Paanje Kutch Ji*.

The Project: Overview

Kunjal Paanje Kutch Ji (KPKJ), the first programme of the *Ujjas* community radio project was produced by KMVS with directorial inputs from Drishti Media Collective, a media NGO based in Ahmedabad with firm faith in the ability of media to give expression to voices on the margins and belief that 'social communication need not be dry, boring, pedantic or depressing' (Virmani, 2000). The radio series was written by Paresh Naik, an Ahmedabad based writer and filmmaker. The financial back-up, including the cost of commercial airtime came from UNDP.

The village-based survey carried out by KMVS to assess the media habits of Kutchis revealed that there was a palpable demand from people for Kutchi language programmes, but AIR Bhuj preferred the state language Gujarati for the bulk of its broadcasts. The Kutchi dialect, which has no written form, was chosen as the basic language for KPKJ as it served as a point of emotional identification for most of the local people. Having started its broadcast as a 30-minute sponsored weekly serial from AIR, Bhuj station on 16 December 1999 KPKJ was on air every Thursday at 8 p.m. (Virmani, 2000). Preeti Soni explains that the central focus of the serial conceived in docu-drama format, is participation of women in political processes, specifically panchayats at the village level:

> This is represented through the character of Rani, the woman *sarpanch* located in the fabled village *Ujjas* where the Saras crane (*Kunjal*)—she is also the *sutradhaar* (storyteller)—comes to live once a year. With the government making provision for 33 per cent reservation for women in panchayat bodies, there was an invariable demand from the *mahila sarpanchs* for training to enable them to function effectively. This demand is the pivotal theme for the serial (interview).

By exploring the entry of women from the private to the public domain, KPKJ was able to generate a debate on gender issues on the one hand, and *swaraj* (democratic self-governance) on the other. Gradually, other issues got interwoven into the central theme using the intrinsic qualities of Saras as she offers a bird's-eye view of the happenings and forms her own relationship with the characters of *Ujjas* (Virmani, 2000). Some of the issues projected are:

- women's leadership and governance;
- girl's right to education;
- female foeticide;
- harassment of brides for dowry;
- unnatural deaths and suicides of women;

- pressure on women to produce boys;
- maternal mortality;
- disregard for natural environment;
- cyclical drought; and
- lack of water resources.

Though scripted and directed with outside professional support, KPKJ sought to reinforce Kutchi identity and provide a platform for local expression and dialogue through participation by communities in the drama, song and news-reporting. The programme ensured a committed space for the voices of people from Kutch by incorporating a seven-minute documentary module *Kutch Kochhanto* (Kutch Speaks) within the serial. Those interviewed include rural women and men, *sarpanchs* and panchayat members, village opinion leaders, religious heads, government officials and village midwives. A team of 12 village-based men and women reporters trained by KMVS and Drishti conducts the interviews in the field or the studio.

The Centre for Alternatives in Education, Indian Institute of Management, Ahmedabad supported KMVS in conducting village-based surveys to assess the impact of the radio programme. The first survey conducted three months after broadcast indicated a dedicated listenership of 6 per cent. After 10 months of broadcast, this figure had grown to 50 per cent of surveyed Kutchis and 80 per cent of the radio-owning population of Kutch. The publicity efforts for KPKJ and the radio programmes that are being produced by KMVS at present include posters plastered on buses, panchayat buildings and bus stands; radio promos; word-of-mouth promotion through the network of field reporters and through road shows in some villages. A re-broadcast of KPKJ started from January 2002 along with the *Kutch Lok Ji Bani* (KLJB), which was launched in July 2002.

Before KLJB and after completion of 53 episodes of KPKJ in December 2000, KMVS continued its involvement with radio by producing, in partnership with Drishti, a 15-minute programme called *Tu Jiyaro Ain* (*Tu Zinda Hai* in Hindi) broadcast twice a week from March 2001. The programme was conceived in an interview format as a platform for those affected by the earthquake to share their concerns about rehabilitation and to keep alive the Kutchi spirit of self-help, dignity and pride.

The next weekly programme produced by KMVS for broadcast on AIR was a 45-minute magazine KLJB. The commitment of KMVS to the participatory nature of the radio project is reflected by KJLB. In the course of the rehabilitation drive after the earthquake, corruption had become rampant and the common people were feeling disappointed. The spirit of *kutchiyat*—to fight against odds under all circumstances had to be reasserted (Soni and Stalin, 2004). The programme design included three capsules that sought to revive the faith of the people in their culture and to also provide a forum to question government malfunctioning.

Pardafash (Exposé) is the investigative journalism segment marked by its distinct title song, 'Darkness veils light, Clouds veil the sky, Picture over picture, and buried lies the truth' sung by the local singers. The investigative reportage aims to unearth social and political scams, irregularities and corruption in rehabilitation works, to highlight culpability of government and the vested interests of people with power (KMVS, 2003). *Musafari* (Travelogue) seeks to resurrect history, culture, music and legends of Kutch and to reinterpret them in the contemporary context. Localised research was a key approach in developing this drama capsule of the magazine. Through many visits to far-flung villages and interaction with elders and poet-historians, views about a particular legend or folktale were collected and songs, proverbs and anecdotes identified for the programme. In each episode, a different set of reporters is taken to journey Kutch by three imaginary characters namely *Vyaro* (the wind), *Dharti* (the earth) and *Kala Dungar* (the Black Hill of Kutch). These characters take reporters back in time where they meet historical characters and experience cultural events to unearth tales of the land of Kutch. A debate between modernity and tradition is also generated through dialogues and arguments between the reporters and the characters (Soni and Stalin, 2004). *Lokvani* (people's voice) is made up of several formats that are used as tools to obtain direct community participation, including, first-hand information by the reporters, *Lok Mat* (opinion poll), *Charcha* (studio debate), village voice, interviews and *Farmaish* (song requests).

The Project: in Progress

Greater autonomy for the dedicated media team of KMVS comprising 14 reporters has been brought by KLJB. The reporters' team consists of village youth, both women and men educated on an average till class eight. The reporters work in conjunction with the *taluka sangathans*. Along with the support of Drishti Media Collective, KMVS provided training in journalism techniques, technical radio production skills (narration, scripting editing, mixing, mastering), interviewing, drama direction, investigative journalism and confidence building. They were also oriented towards developmental concerns, social justice, gender issues and methods of reading history/culture.

The media team now handles the post-production work in the studio set up in the KMVS Bhuj office. Preeti Soni explains that the sense of ownership among the media team and the women leaders of *mahila mandals* towards the radio experiment has grown over time. They have recognised the significance of radio as a medium of self-expression in oral, non-literate cultures and how highly localised programming can be used to generate productive debate on local priorities and issues and enhance their cultural identities.

Our Case Study

Through interaction with one of the core members of Drishti Media Collective, Ahmedabad, who is closely involved in the community radio project and other activities of KMVS, and with the help of preliminary readings, we gathered the first round of information about KMVS, their community radio project and their focus on women empowerment. We were also introduced to some aspects of the programme KLJB, being produced by the media unit of KMVS in Bhuj as part of their community radio initiative, and briefed about how it is different from *Kunjal Paanje Kutch Ji* (KPKJ) and *Tu Zinda Hai* that had been produced earlier. At the KMVS office in Bhuj we met and interacted for several hours with the coordinator and technical executive of the KMVS media unit and several community reporters present in the office.

After getting a grasp of the history of the media unit of KMVS, its structure, thrust areas, approach and philosophy, we interacted informally with the reporters to find out the working pattern of the KMVS rural reporters of the media (radio) team and get an idea about the demographic profile of their coverage area. A schedule for conducting focus groups in the areas where the programme reaches and for visiting the *talukas* assigned to the reporters was worked out in consultation with them. It was decided that we try and include as far as possible all important categories of audiences like nomads (*maldharies*), fishermen, dalits, Muslims, peasants and tribal people in addition to taking into account some factors like age and gender (not so much, literacy). While this was being worked out, we got the opportunity to listen to some CDs of the programmes, KLJB and KPKJ.

The focus group consisting of all reporters and the discussions during long hours of travel to the designated villages brought out details about the composition of the community radio programmes, the process involved in the production, how the schedules were worked out for reporters, issues covered, how issues were decided, criteria for selection of reporters and their training. The reporters also gave us an idea about the post-production work, all of which is carried out in Bhuj and in the KMVS office. The schedule that was finally worked out is given here in Table 4.3. There were minor changes that had to be made in case of some groups/villages but we managed to interact with people in nine villages of six districts of Kutch and conduct focus groups in seven villages.

Table 4.3: ***Focus Groups for KMVS Community Radio Case Study***

No.	*Village (Taluka)*	*Description of Group*
1.	Mudhva (Mandvi)	Fishermen
2.	Hajipir (Lakhpat)	KMVS School girls and teacher
3.	Jhumara (Lakhpat)	Women–Muslim farming
4.	Valka (Nakhatrana)	Young Women–Dalit
5.	Mohaldi (Abdasa)	Women–Jat-nomadic-animal husbandry
6.	Kalatalav (Abdasa)	Men-*Darbar* farming + one artist
7.	Chapar (Bachau)	*Bhil* Tribe men
8.	Mundra (Mundra)	Women *Ujjas* Group (FGD not conducted)
9.	Dhoravar (Bhuj)	Muslim/Dalit men
10.	Bhuj (Bhuj)	All Reporters

People spoke a mix of Kutchi/Gujarati/Hindi during the discussions. The reporters helped us understand the responses. The visits extended till late evening but we would attempt to transcribe as much of the discussions as possible on reaching back to headquarters. We also got a chance to observe the production schedule meeting and to collect relevant documents and other material that would help in gaining a better understanding of the project. A major disappointment was the fact that due to some last-minute change in the travel plans of the women handling the *Ujjas* newspaper (from where the idea of starting a community radio programme had actually originated), we could not interact with them.

Namma Dhwani: The Community Radio Project of VOICES/MYRADA

In September 2001, *Namma Dhwani* (Our Voice) community radio production centre was inaugurated at Budhikote village, 95 km from Bangalore, in the Kolar district of Karnataka. *Namma Dhwani* is the audio studio component of the Community Multi Media Centre set up in Budhikote by VOICES, a Bangalore-based development communication group working for marginalised sections of society, and Mysore Resettlement and Development Agency (MYRADA), a non-profit organisation that has been working in the Budhikote sector for nearly a decade. This information and communication hub was established by VOICES and MYRADA in partnership with women's self-help groups (SHGs) of the Budhikote village and as part of the UNESCO-funded *Assessing Impact of ICTs for Poverty Reduction* project. *Namma Dhwani* has a well-equipped recording station and three trained local persons to run the audio production centre. Volunteers from Budhikote and adjoining villages help in the production of radio programmes. As the broadcast license to operate community radio was not forthcoming, the women's groups managing the centre decided in March 2003 to cablecast the programmes being produced by them to the village households. Now, 250 television-owning families, the village school and those who have bought radio sets with cable jacks made available at subsidised prices by VOICES tune into *Namma Dhwani* in Budhikote.

The Region

The *Namma Dhwani* project is located at Budhikote village in Kolar district of Karnataka, 95 km from the state capital, Bangalore. Budhikote is a panchayat headquarter for eight villages. The nearest town Bangarpet is about 14 km away and the Kolar district headquarters is at a distance of 30 km. Kolar district lies in the semi-arid drought prone region of Karnataka. In spite of being close to a metropolis (Bangalore city), the region skirts the southern border of the Rayalaseema desert belt and shares the same language, culture and social structure, as also the stark poverty that afflicts southern Andhra Pradesh. The major sources of employment are agriculture, dairy and sericulture, and coolie labour. For irrigation and drinking water, the farmers in the district are totally dependent upon bore wells drilled to more than 100 metres depth due to low water table. As the rainfall is erratic and spatial, even these dry up in the summer months and seasonal migration by agricultural labourers is an annual occurrence during this period. Among other things, this district is famous for the Kolar gold mines. Most of the gold mines in Kolar Gold Fields were closed during the 90s due to reducing deposits and increasing costs.

Budhikote village has a population of 3,020 people in about 650 households. There are 10 community-owned (MYRADA-facilitated) and three government-facilitated SHGs. The overall literacy level in the village is 55 per cent while the female literacy levels are lower at 35 per cent (VOICES, 2002). The spoken language is a mix of Kannada and Telugu. The village has only one tarred road connecting it to Bangarpet town, and the condition of the road is quite dismal. Budhikote has a telephone exchange and there is electricity in the village, but the high frequency of power cuts in summer and low voltage make it inappropriate for effective use of electronic equipment. There is no local radio station in the area and the village primarily receives programmes of AIR Bangalore, which is situated 120 km from Kolar. The project document of VOICES puts the number of radio set owners in Budhikote as 184. Local cable TV service has made inroads and there are at present 250 cable connected households.

The NGOs

VOICES was set up in 1991 as a development communications organisation working towards the empowerment of the disadvantaged and marginalised sections of society. According to Ashish Sen, the director of VOICES, this media advocacy group strongly believes that the denial of information aggravates the poverty gap in a country like India. 'We visualise a world where people are empowered to make informed choices and live with dignity and we believe that media has a catalytic role in making this a reality.' It seeks to promote communication for change through production and dissemination of developmental messages, communication training, action research, networking and consultancy. Sen adds that in his view, appropriate media and their role have not been efficiently constructed and exploited in our country and 'the gap between the information rich and the information poor therefore has grown. We believe that the marginalised communities, with whom we work, have been denied access to information, and importantly, also to communication' (interview).

Following the Supreme Court judgement of February 1995 that declared the airwaves to be public property, VOICES convened a gathering of radio broadcasters, policy planners, media professionals and not-for-profit associations in September 1996 to study how community radio could be relevant to India, and to deliberate on policies appropriate for such an action. A declaration calling for the establishment of community broadcasting was signed. Alongside maintaining a robust lobbying for licenses to set up community radio, VOICES started working on a pilot capacity building project at Kolar in 1998 by training women's credit and savings groups to produce and narrowcast radio programmes. The Budhikote intervention was executed from early 2000 based on a needs-assessment study carried out by a community-based organisation, MYRADA in 1999. Between April 2000 and September 2001, volunteers from villages in the Budhikote sector were trained in radio programming and production, in collaboration with AIR. These programmes were broadcast on AIR and narrowcast at community meetings. In September 2001, an analogue audio production centre was set up at Budhikote in partnership with MYRADA and with support from UNESCO.

Describing the role of MYRADA as that of a mediator between VOICES and the Budhikote community, Balakrishna (Balu), the Resource Centre Manager for MYRADA, explains that their experience in organising and mobilising self-help people's institutions at the grassroots level made VOICES collaborate with MYRADA for the Budhikote initiative. Mysore Resettlement and Development Agency was started in 1968 and was involved entirely in the resettlement of Tibetan Refugees. In the second phase of its history commencing in 1978–79, MYRADA has been involved with the rural poor and is at present managing 22 projects in the backward border districts of Karnataka, Andhra Pradesh and Tamil Nadu. Balu revealed that MYRADA has been a pioneer in implementing the concept of SHGs where 'people themselves take up the responsibility of forming into groups, earn, learn, analyse their own issues and find solutions.' They also provide consultancy services to organisations in other parts of India and abroad for which they have gained recognition and acclaim from the Government of India.

Mysore Resettlement and Development Agency has been working in the Budhikote area for over 10 years and has consistently identified the root cause of marginalisation and poverty as the lack of 'regular mechanisms of appropriate information dissemination or viable local communication channels.' Its strategies for rural development, including setting up of Resource Centres, have been adapted to meet these needs, leading to collaboration with VOICES in community radio and other local communication strategies. Balu explains the functions of the MYRADA Resource Centre as that of a 'local service institution' providing services such as training, information on development schemes, conflict resolution counselling, computer-based services like bookkeeping, bank linkages, monitoring, evaluation, etc., to SHGs, organisations and individuals. By integrating the *Namma Dhwani* local Information and Communication Technology (ICT) network into the Resource Centre model, MYRADA seeks to accelerate the development through a process that combines information dissemination with community participation to generate locally relevant content.

The Project: Overview

The Budhikote project is among the seven sites selected by UNESCO to assess the impact of ICTs on poverty reduction. Budhikote sector was considered 'appropriate for an ICTs project given the fact it was a neglected border area and there exists a strong culture of community participation in the development,' affirms Balakrishna of MYRADA. The goals of the project as spelt out on the VOICES website are:

- to bring the voices of the marginalised from the periphery of information and awareness to the centre and give them the opportunity to make informed choices and decisions;
- to foster a sense of ownership and enthusiastic participation by the community;
- to be able to encourage a casteless, women-empowering, value-based environment;
- to make technology accessible and relevant to rural settings;

- to act as a legitimate case to make way for legislation conducive to the opening up of community radio in India; and
- to investigate whether Information and Communication Technologies can help reduce poverty gaps.

In 1999, VOICES and MYRADA began work in Budhikote with a survey that clearly identified 'the inapplicability and irrelevance of available media due to issues of context and language and that the community did want an information centre, which would give them timely and locally relevant information' (Sen, interview). The survey also highlighted that the community wanted locally relevant information on crops, market prices, health, particularly women's health, etc., preferably in their own dialect which is a mix of Kannada and Telugu. Between April 2000 and September 2001, training sessions in radio programming and production were organised in collaboration with AIR for volunteers from 35 villages in the Budhikote sector following which they began to make programmes on topics such as sericulture, organic farming techniques, insurance, crop patterns, local electricity, water problems, health issues, etc. These programmes were narrowcast through tape playback during weekly group listening sessions in the SHG meetings.

With the setting up of the analogue audio production centre *Namma Dhwani* in September 2001, the programme production became more systematic and regular. The centre gained popularity through a special feature of loudspeaker narrowcast done during the weekly market day, when people from the surrounding villages would also visit Budhikote. Short-term training workshops in audio programming were conducted periodically to enhance community participation. Special workshops for children increased the number of volunteers manifold.

In April 2002, computers were brought into the production centre. With technical and financial assistance from AIR and UNESCO and in conjunction with the local cable operator, VOICES and MYRADA launched the first phase of its cable audio initiative and cablecast its first programme through the TV cable on 28 March 2003. This enabled residents of 250 households in Budhikote to listen to two hours of *Namma Dhwani* programming daily from 6.30 to 7.30 in the morning and 6.30 to 7.30 or 7.00 to 8.00 in the evening on their TV sets, subject to the restrictions imposed by the power supply timings.

Three volunteers of the first batch of training by VOICES—Mangala Gowri, Surya Prakash and Amaresh are now employed as studio managers and steer the entire production process. With the initiation of cablecasting, the narrowcasting of programmes in the SHGs of Budhikote sector was stopped. This has not discouraged the flow of volunteers from these 35 villages to *Namma Dhwani* studio for recording programmes and to acquire training in audio production as well as basic computer usage. With technical and research-based support provided by studio managers, programmes with plenty of local-flavour entertainment, live debates on current issues, folk songs, discussions among youth, dramas and children's programmes are being produced on a regular basis. Mangala Gowri says:

> The *Namma Dhwani* studio has a kitty of 408 programmes on agriculture, health, indigenous medicine, devotional songs, cookery, widow pension, government schemes, interviews with doctors and bank managers, besides songs, dramas and live debates. On the basis of the decision taken in the management committee meeting, we put up a chart on the notice board outside the studio every week displaying the schedule and topics of the programmes to be broadcast on each day during the week (interview).

The programme content and format is decided by the Management Committee, explains Seema Nair, the project coordinator from VOICES, 'which comprises 19 members—10 women members who represent their SHGs, two volunteers each from Budhikote village/sector, three studio managers and one representative each from MYRADA and VOICES.' The committee meets every fifth and 25th of the month to evaluate programming, provide feedback and discuss management issues. A programme committee has also been created and consists of a panel of local experts such as a lawyer, an *anganavadi* worker, panchayat secretary, two doctors (one male and one female), who can be contacted to talk on programmes or to suggest resource persons who may be approached for comments. 'Sometimes the members of the programming committee conduct meetings to advise us about the kind of programmes to produce. Teachers also come,' says Amaresh.

Children form a significant chunk of volunteers in the *Namma Dhwani* scheme of programming. An audio cable connection was laid in July 2002 between *Namma Dhwani* and the Budhikote Government High School with the cooperation of the Block Education Officer, school staff and parents. Around 350 students in the age group of 12–15 now listen to two hours of programmes twice a week. Students are encouraged to make their own programmes that include newspaper reading, local news, general knowledge, music, model lessons, and issues like dowry, environment preservation, etc., which are then cablecast into the classrooms.

There is a children's club, *Hosa Belaku* (New Light) of about 60 children from Budhikote and the neighbouring villages. They assemble every Saturday in the studio to produce programmes and are fast learning audio production techniques. A programme 'Rural Dreams' produced by children was broadcast on AIR on Children's Day. Another success of the *Namma Dhwani* is the formation of a 'Disabilities Club' wherein the physically and mentally challenged people meet weekly and make their own audio programmes to spread awareness about opportunities and schemes for the disabled.

The Project: in Progress

The MYRADA Resource Centre and *Namma Dhwani* together have become the nodal focal point of all information and communication activity of the Budhikote sector. People identify *Namma Dhwani* as a site 'where I can listen to my own voice'. A VOICES document reveals that during their stocktaking and five-year vision building exercise, the management committee came up with a wish list and efforts are thus on to accomplish those objectives which include:

- to cable the entire village so that everyone could listen to *Namma Dhwani* programmes;
- to make sure that every eligible child attends school;
- to educate every household about indigenous medicine;
- to make sure that every household has contributed to the making of at least one programme; and
- to work towards making the youth of Budhikote computer-literate.

Our Case Study

The VOICES/MYRADA community radio project is located in Budhikote village in Kolar district of Karnataka, about 95 km from Bangalore. This Panchayat headquarters has 10 community-owned

(MYRADA-facilitated) SHGs and three government-owned SHGs. The languages spoken in the area are Kannada and Telugu.

The community radio initiative is named *Namma Dhwani* (Our Voice) and is one vital component of a partnership between the farmer community, VOICES, MYRADA and UNESCO to establish a community-owned information and communication centre in Budhikote. Adequate documentation about the project had been provided by VOICES' office. However, we chose to personally interview all the people involved in the implementation of the project and those managing it. These included interviews with the director of VOICES, project coordinators for VOICES and the project-coordinator for MYRADA. The studio managers for the radio in Budhikote were also interviewed in long sessions.

Focus groups were conducted to include the views of the management committee of the project. As the reception of the programmes and participation is limited to the Budhikote village and more so to the families of the members of the SHGs, the selection criteria for other focus groups was limited. The focus groups mentioned in Table 4.4 were organised.

Table 4.4: ***Focus Groups for VOICES Community Radio Case Study***

No.	*Village (District)*	*Description of Group*
1.	Budhikote (Kolar)	Children Volunteers
2.	Budhikote (Kolar)	Adult Volunteers(Men)
3.	Budhikote (Kolar)	Management Committee
4.	Budhikote (Kolar)	Purnima Mahila SHG (Government-owned)
5.	Budhikote (Kolar)	Navjyothi Mahila SHG
6.	Budhikote (Kolar)	Laxmi Mahila SHG
7.	Budhikote (Kolar)	Shalini Mahila SHG

Women Speak to Women: The Community Radio Project of DDS

In Machnoor village of Zaheerabad *mandal* (block) in the Medak district of Andhra Pradesh, a UNESCO-supported community FM radio centre was set up in 1998 with a recording studio, control room, two transmitters, one transmitting tower and all other related facilities to function as a radio station. This station managed and run by rural Dalit women, who are members of a local NGO, the Deccan Development Society (DDS), is awaiting license to broadcast. For the women who are equipped with remarkable oral narrative skills, radio is a natural medium. The women feel that the rich cultural traditions of the Telangana region could be better sustained through a radio station that caters specially to the needs of the region. The women record programmes on numerous issues related to women's empowerment and regional problems and those that promote indigenous knowledge and local cultures through the folk traditions of song and drama. These programmes are then edited on their editing equipment in the studio, and played back on tape recorders at village *sangams*.

The Region

The four *mandals* of Medak district—Zaheerabad, Jharasangam, Raikode and Nyalkal—where the DDS works, fall in one of the least developed regions of the country, Telangana, which is also the most neglected province in the state of Andhra Pradesh. Telangana is a border area contiguous with the least developed districts of north Karnataka. It is a semi-arid tract where the land is extremely degraded and offers limited livelihood opportunities in agriculture to people. Telangana is drought-prone and the problem is made worse as irrigation is underdeveloped. As most of the agriculture is rain-fed, very little institutional finance is available for investment in agriculture. There is hardly any industrialisation and no skill development has taken place in the region, as development schemes do not reach the targeted populations because of power relationships between different castes within the villages, between the poorest social groups and the more affluent sections. Capital inflows into this region are therefore slim. Majority of the people, the poor and the landless are at the mercy of nature and there is a lot of seasonal out-migration to look for wage labour outside.

Poverty, illiteracy, malnourishment among children, child labour, farmer suicides, unemployment, water scarcity and electricity shortage are some of the problems of this region. It is in this geo-political and developmental context that the efforts of DDS are centred. The DDS works with about 100 poor and Dalit women's groups (*sangams*) consisting of nearly 5,000 members in 75 villages. These women form the poorest sections of the rural community with an average family income (mostly from farm labour work) ranging from Rs 600 to Rs 1,200 per month. Wage levels in some places are still as low as Rs 10–15 for a 6–8 hours working day (http://www.ddsindia.com/www/def_main.htm).

The NGO

Deccan Development Society is a grassroots organisation working since 1983 with *sangams* (voluntary village level groups) of poor women, most of whom are Dalits. The DDS head office is located in Pastapur village of its project area, Zaheerabad, 100 km away from Hyderabad, the capital of Andhra Pradesh. DDS has a vision of 'consolidating these village groups into vibrant organs of primary local governance and federate them into a strong pressure lobby for women, the poor and dalits' (DDS, 2005). The society facilitates regular dialogues and debates with the public, and organises educational and training programmes along with other activities to translate this vision into reality.

According to P.V Satheesh, Director of DDS:

> In the beginning the idea was that we would try and transfer technology to rural people. It was heavily influenced by the barefoot theory. We thought that we would create a lot of bare footers here—bare foot bankers, bare foot foresters, something like that. But still it was quite biased towards what was called in those days, appropriate technologies. Soon we understood that any technology brought from outside and administered by outside people does not work. Our faith in peoples' own knowledge and technology grew. We understood that that people have the best technologies available for their regions, very area specific technologies, the ones which are related to peoples' knowledge systems, the ones in which people have long years of experience (interview).

DDS thus recognises that people have more knowledge than we have credited them with and their own appropriate technologies, which can yield solutions to their own problems. Within this framework, the DDS programmes have evolved three principles: gender justice, environmental-soundness and people's knowledge. Over the years, the initiatives have advanced from fulfilling the basic sustenance needs of the *sangam* members to enabling them to address issues such as food security, natural resource enhancement, education and health needs of the region. The various activities of DDS have helped in retrieving for women their natural leadership positions and dignity in their communities through their new-found access and control over their own resources.

Satheesh explains further that at the heart of all activities of DDS is the fundamental principle of ensuring access and control, which leads to the autonomy of local communities. Control and autonomy becomes far more important in a globalising world with shrinking national boundaries and disappearing national sovereignties. In this context, it is crucial for local communities to take over certain spheres of autonomies to protect themselves from being trampled over by invisible globalising forces. 'The questions of gender, of marginalisation, of poverty, all come within this control and autonomy structure. More the autonomy of the community, more they can write their own destiny' (interview).

DDS *sangams* have worked towards the following autonomies:

- autonomy over food production;
- autonomy over agriculture;
- autonomy over seeds;
- autonomy over natural resources management;
- autonomous market;
- autonomy over their health; and
- autonomous media.

In trying to reverse the historical process of degradation of the environment and people's livelihood systems in this area and for retrieving a strong agro biodiversity on their farms, DDS women have taken up a variety of land-related activities like *permaculture* (a system of ecological agriculture), Community Grain Funds (for PDS), Community Gene Banks (by growing diverse crops, which had been obliterated by modern agricultural practices) and collective cultivation through land lease. Since 1996, they have designed and managed a radical, path-breaking alternative Public Distribution System (PDS), based on the principles of local production, local storage and local distribution, thereby demolishing the myth of the need for permanent government patronage for their food security. Education at all levels is a fundamental component for DDS starting with *balwadies* (childcare centres) to provide a creative learning environment for young children to *Pacha Saale* (Green School) that redefines formal education by linking it to areas and skills of relevance for rural children. Several workshops for adult women and village night schools for out-of-school children also form part of the effort to provide educational opportunities to the most deprived.

DDS women have also been revitalising the traditional healthcare systems by growing over 60 different species of medicinal plants on patches of village common lands. They are advocating the principles of ecologically produced safe food among the urban consumers, who are slowly shifting to organic foods produced by DDS *sangams*. DDS women have published a millet cookbook and opened 'Café Ethnic', a millet restaurant to widen the circle of consumers for marginalised foods. Efforts are also on to understand, document and promote people's knowledge of farming systems and practices. An organisation that values people's knowledge and builds its work on the confidence of the people, must explore various tools of expression with which people can communicate among themselves as well as with the outside world. The DDS adopts a participatory communication approach to strengthen its initiatives in the region. (For a comparison of the areas of work of the four NGOs in the study, see Table 4.5.)

The organisation uses a wide range of horizontal communication techniques. These include:

- *sangam* meetings;
- *jathras*;
- social audits;
- Participatory Rural Appraisals (PRAs); and
- interface sessions with government agencies and other NGOs.

These strategies have been essentially interpersonal in nature with all its inherent strengths and limitations. However, in the new environment of decentralisation and optimal use of new information and communication technologies, DDS is exploring ways and means by which its communication potential can be enhanced. For DDS, the possibility of providing video and audio technologies as a means of expression and an alternative to literacy for the disadvantaged rural women was an exciting idea. To crystallise this idea, DDS contemplated a community radio station.

The Project: Overview

On 2 October 1996, Mr James Bentley, Regional Communication Adviser (Asia), UNESCO had a consultation with about 35 women

Table 4.5: *Subject Areas of Work of NGOs*

AID	*KMVS*	*VOICES/ MYRADA*	*DDS*
Education for Working Children	Education Literacy	Development Communication	Food security
Adult Education	Legal Issues	Media Advocacy	Ecological agriculture
Education for Deprived Children	Environment	NGO Networking	Community Grain Bank (New PDS methods)
Special Schools for Adolescent	Self-Governance	Media Training	Community Gene Fund (Seeds sovereignty)
Non-Starters	*Panchayats*		
Health for All	Health	e-governance	Watersheds
Reproductive Health Programmes	Savings and Credit Programme (SCP)	Rural Development	Cultivation through Land Lease
Micro-Credit Women Groups	Handicrafts	Livelihood Strategies	*Balwadi* (Childcare centre)
Women Empowerment	Water	Rural Banking	Night schools
Campaign against Child Marriage	Natural Resource Management	Watershed Management	*Pacha Saale* (Green School)
Watershed Management	Media Advocacy	Health	*Krishi Vigyana Kendras*
Community Technical College	Research and Development	Self-Help Groups	Health Medicinal Commons
Livelihood Initiatives	Drought Relief	Resource Centres	Biodiversity Festivals
Forest Produce Training	Gender Issues	Community Radio	Women *sangams*
Employment Generation	Community Radio		Shelter for Single Women
Empowering Excluded Communities			Community Radio Station
Agricultural Research			Video Women
Community Radio			Media Trust

from the *sangams* of the DDS. The women gave their reasons to want their own radio. They suggested that a radio of their own would provide more effectively a medium for articulating locally relevant issues, in their own language, and in their own time. UNESCO also recognised the presence and services rendered by DDS in the region with regard to empowerment and education of the poorest of the poor women, and thus identified DDS women as suitable partners for UNESCO's 'Women Speak to Women' project under its larger 'Learning without Frontiers' programme. It was proposed to operationalise a low-cost radio station, subject to issuance of a license by the Government of India, and DDS initiated the necessary steps for establishing a radio station in Machnoor village.

The DDS station, which received partial funding from UNESCO, cost a total of Rs 22 lakh. This is only for the building, acoustics treatment, equipment including recorders, mixers, microphones, cables and installation. The building for the FM radio station was constructed using locally available material. It has dome-type roofing and three octagonal shaped blocks consisting of the studio, transmitting-cum-control room, the dubbing section, the director's cabin and the reception area. The FM station is designed to work on the audiocassette technology. It has two FM transmitters and a 100-metre tall transmission tower, which has a capacity to broadcast to a radius of 30 km, roughly the coverage area of DDS. With this installation and the nominal amounts paid to community members who are compensated for the time they spend in the studio, the programme costs currently amount to about Rs 500 per hour. It is estimated that if and when the station goes on air, it may be able to operate at Rs 1,000–1,500 per hour.

As is clear, this control over media technology did not happen overnight. It was preceded by a long process of sustained awareness, capacity building and training in the areas of people's agriculture, health, education and indigenous knowledge and value systems and establishment of community's control over their food, health and natural resources. Three DDS women, 'General' Narsamma, Algole Narsamma and Sukkamma, were trained to manage and operate the radio station. Once the station gets permission to broadcast, more and more Dalit and poor women from villages are expected to bring their form and content into it and make it a tool for horizontal communication.

The programming content of the station is a reflection of the activities of the DDS women and seeks to serve the information, education, and cultural needs of the region. As General Narsamma explains,

> We have done programmes on nearly 50–60 topics, even more. Generally, we think what topic is important to all the people this month. If it is time to start sowing seeds, we will record programme about seed sowing, when to sow, how to sow? After the sowing of seeds, we will make the programme about weeding, how to weed different types of crops, we will prepare songs on that, the songs which the people have forgotten. During rainy season, we will record programmes about the precautions to be taken for different crops in the absence of rains or if there is excess rain (interview).

Some of the issues on which programmes have been recorded include: seed sowing, ploughing of lands, public health and hygiene, diseases of women, children's diseases, animal diseases, diseases of summer season, Vision 2020 of Andhra Pradesh Government[1], education (both formal and non-formal), elementary school, night school, balwadis (day-care centres), summer camps, adult literacy, land tenancy, crop insurance, watershed, PDS, biodiversity, food security, old crops, preservation of seeds, gender justice, women empowerment, local knowledge, festivals and folk songs.

The Project: in Progress

The DDS Women's radio, in spite of its long-time readiness to go on air, is still awaiting a community-broadcasting license as the Central Government is still finalising the regulations of the new broadcasting legislation. In the meantime, the studio facilities are being used to produce audio cassettes with programmes in various formats including discussions, interviews, drama, local songs and *burra katha* (a folk form indigenous to Andhra Pradesh). There are already over 400 hours of recorded programmes in the studio, some of which are being edited into half-hour and one-hour magazine modules. The women have recently started developing a signature tune to identify their programmes. The programmes are then narrowcast in *sangam* meetings held periodically in all the project villages of DDS. Feedback from the *sangams* is recorded by field workers and brought back to the station. This feedback is used to improve upon and decide further programming. Local shops and tea-stalls have also shown a keen interest in playing these cassettes in their outlets. Once they get a license, the community radio team has plans for a short-duration broadcast initially, which will be expanded later.

DDS inaugurated its Community Media Centre on 15 October (the International Rural Women's Day) 2001. The facility has three edit suites, one dubbing booth, and a storage space alongside one rehearsal/discussion room and one computer room. The equipment installed in the Media Centre consists of eight video cameras, five mini DV edit recorders, one computer edit unit, one edit recorder and one eight track audio mixer. On the same day, a Community Media Trust has also been launched, formally transferring the ownership of the media facilities of the DDS to a body consisting of women members of the rural community.

Our Case Study

Methodologically speaking, this was probably the most satisfying case study as we could apply all the lessons learnt from our earlier work. We could also go much better prepared as we were familiar with the place, the project and the people, having visited DDS villages several times in the past. We had also interacted with the radio and video women of DDS in conferences and workshops and so we were not strangers for most of the people there. Several relevant documents had been collected in the earlier visits and were studied before the visit. The information collected earlier and consultations with the DDS media coordinator yielded the criteria for selecting the sample villages for focus groups (Table 4.6).

Villages were selected keeping in mind their distance from the station and whether the village members have participated in the

Table 4.6: ***Focus Groups for DDS Community Radio Case Study***

No.	*Village (Distance from Station)*	*Description of Group*
1.	Zaheerabad/Humnapur (5 km)	Mixed-Video women (DDS Staff)
2.	Pastapur (5 km)	Seniors (Participated)
3.	Machnoor (zero)	Mixed-Radio Committee (DDS Staff)
4.	Raipally (13 km)	Middle Age Not (Not Participated)
5.	Pyalaram (20 km)	Seniors (Not Participated)
6.	Bidekane (9 km)	Middle age (Participated/Autonomous)
7.	Kalemela (25 km)	Young (Participated)

radio programmes or not. Age was used as a factor and it was also ensured that at least one village out of the few where the *sangams* now operate autonomously was represented. The three women from these villages who manage the radio studio and the director of DDS were interviewed and discussions held with the participatory video production team as they form an important component of the DDS community mediascape.

NOTE

1. Vision 2020 is the name given to the comprehensive plan for development of Andhra Pradesh put forward by the then Chief Minister, N. Chandrababu Naidu. The plan visualised by international consulting firms came under fire from activists, NGOs and small formers' organisations for what was perceived as its pro-globalisation and anti-people vision.

5 NARROWCASTING DEVELOPMENT

Community Radio and Participatory Communication

Communication for development should not be technology driven. It should be based on social issues and concerns. Technology is at best a facilitator and tool.

—Jan Servaes quoting August 2003WSIS Declaration

It was after the Second World War and as a consequence of the liberation movements of many former colonies that the pivotal role communication plays in development became more acknowledged and defined. The dominant paradigm of development communication that emerged in the 60s and 70s identified development as something governments deliver for or to people. It promoted a top–down approach to planning and growth that treated people as objects and did not incorporate self-reliance and popular participation in its agenda. Mass media were used as persuasion agents for making people listen to what was being planned for them and for 'domesticating' people through information, therapy and manipulation (Deshler and Sock, 1985). The language reflected the bureaucratic approach—'objectives', 'targets', 'strategies', 'beneficiary' and 'capability'. There was little involvement of those undergoing this makeover termed as 'modernisation' or 'development'. Vertical decision-making, little involvement of communities and a lack of understanding of local cultures were among the causes of the failure of such 'development' in combating poverty or in improving the standards of living of the people in the Third World countries.

Participatory approaches to development arose as a reaction to the realisation of this failure and were popularised by the growing number of social movements and non-governmental organisations. Participatory communication advocates that media technology can become a full partner in the development process only when the ownership of both the message and the medium—the content and the process—resides with the communities. The new communication approaches seek to deploy participatory media as a tool for facilitating a self-propelled and self-sustained social change at the grassroots and a more democratic development process. This chapter, through case studies of ongoing experiments with community radio by civil society organisations, seeks to examine the potential of community radio as a medium for generating an autonomous, democratic, community-based communication environment with opportunities for articulating localised and people-centred development needs. The chapter also investigates how the participatory message development process of community radio by itself becomes a training ground for participation in the broader issues of development at the community level.

The first part of the chapter elucidates how the thinking in the field of Communication and Development has evolved over the years and outlines the critiques and discourses that contributed to what we now understand as participatory communication for social change. While simultaneously highlighting the complex nature of participation in diverse social, economic and cultural circumstances and pinpointing important related concepts such as conscientisation and knowledge sharing, the second section of the chapter examines patterns of reception of the various community radio programmes under study.

The third section uses the conceptual framework developed by Nair and White (1994) to establish the nature and levels of community participation discernible at various stages of the content development and distribution process of community radio in the different initiatives. An attempt is made to assess the extent to which grassroots expression is given primacy in programme-production and whether people's issues and indigenous ideas get transformed into radio programmes. The fourth and closing section of the chapter addresses the crucial questions related to whether or not the democratic, dialogical and participatory process of community radio has helped in raising the consciousness and understanding of the community about social reality, problems and solutions in addition to playing a constructive role in enabling rural people to manage their own development.

Towards Participatory Communication for Social Change

Development Communication as a sub-field of mass communication emerged in the years subsequent to the Second World War as newly independent Asian, African, and Latin American countries ventured out to become progressive, self-sustaining and industrialised. The use of the term 'development' became associated with themes like modernisation, nationwide economic growth and technological diffusion leading to centralised planning, large-scale industrialisation, and the expansion of basic communication infrastructure (Nair and White, 1993; White, Nair and Ascroft, 1994; Servaes, Jacobson and White, 1996; Servaes, 2002). A powerful development discourse was established through the institutional mechanism of so-called development decades sponsored by multilateral organisations, donor agencies and aid packages devised for planned development. This dominant paradigm promoted a top-down approach and the 'one size fits all' policy prescriptions by the World Bank, IMF and WTO for development. Nations started imagining their underdevelopment. Their physical and social realities were produced and reproduced in the dialectic of development and underdevelopment, 'marginalizing and precluding other ways of seeing things' (Escobar, 1995). The Third World was invented through this discourse.

The theories of development that constituted the dominant paradigm, both liberal-capitalist and socialist, shared the assumption that development necessitates the replacement of traditional structures by modern economic and social organisation (Mowlana and Wilson, 1988). While capitalist modernisation projected industrialisation, individual freedom of choice, free markets, vast consumption and laissez faire economy as the desirable route, the Marxists preferred to confine the dimensions of bureaucratic planned technological growth within state control. These 'unilinear perspectives and evolutionary characteristics' got suitably reflected in the various approaches to communication and development during that period, and much academic research continued to be based upon the social and political values of the Western societies (Servaes, 2002).

The mainstream empirical social scientists in the Euro-American tradition whose works influenced the communication and development wisdom during the 50s and 60s were Daniel Lerner (*The Passing of Traditional Society*), Everett M. Rogers (*Diffusion of Innovations*) and Wilbur Schramm (*Mass Media and National Development)* (Kumar, 1994). They talked of mass media as instruments to change the mindset of the people and to create a climate for modernisation and development, which will eventually produce higher levels of living. Lerner (1958) believed that development meant change from a traditional to a modern society. He postulated that development was fundamentally a communication process; the way to 'modernise' was to invest in large-scale projects in building up the modern development communication infrastructure. The role of mass media was to motivate change in attitudes, beliefs and behaviours. Lerner argued that modernisation was a prerequisite for making literacy widespread. Mass media exposure and literacy were seen as related to economic and political maturity.

Rogers made a mark in the area of agricultural extension through his *Diffusion of Innovations* model. Describing 'innovation' as an 'idea' or a 'practice' (and in the later editions of his book as a 'technology') perceived as new by an individual, Rogers defines development as 'a type of social change in which new ideas are introduced into a social system in order to produce higher per capita incomes and levels of living through more modern production methods and improved social organization' (Rogers, 1962). He believed in the ability of communication channels and opinion leaders to disseminate knowledge about new practices and ideas and to convince target groups to adopt the exogenously introduced innovations (Rogers and Shoemaker, 1971). To Schramm (1964), the mass media were 'agents of social change'—marvellous 'Magic Multipliers' in their potential to bring about change. Schramm argued that the mass media could help accomplish the transition to new customs and practices (the innovations of Rogers) in order to widen horizons, to raise aspirations and to create a climate for development.

The mid-70s saw disenchantment with the postulates underlying the modernisation and economic growth oriented theories of development including diffusion of innovations approaches, as they did not correspond to the social realities and cultural milieu in the Third World countries. Evaluation reports of extension programmes indicated that the main beneficiaries of the little success that was visible in agricultural, health, nutrition and educational extension programmes, were the better-off sections of society. The hope that development benefits would eventually trickle down to the neediest was belied as rural social structures thwarted all attempts to reach the poor. At the international level also, the main beneficiaries were the multinational industrial firms and the financing banks and institutions (Kumar, 1994). The extensive mass media networks degenerated into being tools of government propaganda or a source of superfluous entertainment for the urban middle-class. The emphasis was on media exposure rather than its use for development, leading to a revolution of rising frustrations in the developing countries (Melkote, 1991). The few attempts to use mass media for development were rendered ineffective by the elitist bureaucracies and the existing social hierarchies.

Dependency approach came to the fore in the early 70s when modernisation and innovations perspective on development was challenged by Latin American social scientists and the neo-Marxists (proponents of structuralism). It was Paul Baran (1957) who first articulated the thesis that development and underdevelopment are 'interrelated processes' and uncompromisingly designated Western monopoly capitalism as the main cause of the chronic backwardness of the developing countries. Other scholars within the dependency school worked on multiple variables to infer that underdevelopment was the result of the same historical process by which the 'developed' countries became economically advanced. This consciousness resulted in the new nations disassociating themselves from the super powers and moving to form the non-aligned nations for political, economic and cultural self-determination within the international community of nations. The New International Economic Order is an example of an attempt toward this end.

At the macro-level, the dependency debate played an important role in the movement for a New World Information and Communication Order from the late 60s to the early 80s. Third World news networks were established and people from developing countries wrote articles about themselves from their own perspectives. Mass communicators made serious efforts at redirecting information flows away from the conventional gate-keeping junctions located in London, Paris, Madrid and New York (Yoon, 2004). The 'dependency' economists emphasised self-reliant development through industrialisation and import-substitution, though under the aegis of foreign investment. The outcome of this approach was a bigger dependence on advanced countries for finance, marketing, capital goods, and design and led to mounting foreign debt and dumping of obsolete equipment and technologies in recipient countries (Kumar, 1994). It was because of this that McAnany (1983: 4) denotes dependency theory as '... good on diagnosis of the problem ... but poor on prescription of the cure.'

The Third World response to the modernisation and the dependency models of development came not so much as a well-defined, coherent and clearly mapped approach. It was more a critique by scholars in the 80s who disapproved universal application of development models and pointed out that development must be conceived as an integral, multidimensional and dialectic process which can differ from one society to another (Servaes, 2002). The one common standpoint that the newer approaches on development shared was that the orientation of social change must be 'bottom-up' and aimed at self-development of the local community. These alternative approaches were stimulated by Freire's (1970) influential work on the 'pedagogy of the oppressed' through conscientisation, and Schumacher's advocacy of appropriate technologies (Schumacher, 1973). This thinking was also related to the rise of new social movements that focused on ecology, gender equity, sustainable and people-centred development, world peace, and self-determination of ethnic minorities, indigenous people and peasant groups.

The terms 'another development' and 'multiplicity in one world' that came into play can be traced back to the 70s when former United Nations Secretary General Dag Hammarskjold urged that development should have more than just economic dimensions. 'Another development' favours a multiplicity of approaches based on the context and the basic, felt needs, and the empowerment of the most oppressed sectors of various societies at divergent levels (Jacobson, 1994; Servaes, 1996). Participation and cultural identity are vital elements of such alternative approaches to development. Several other factors provided impetus to the emergence of the participatory development approach:

(*a*) evidence in World Bank projects in rural and population/health areas of positive impact of community participation and bottom-up approach on project efficiency;

(*b*) local and national governments finding it increasingly difficult to manage adequately the innumerable development projects and programmes thus paving way for a more prominent role of non-governmental and community organisations; and (*c*) non-governmental organisations making it their developmental objective to empower the underprivileged populations by giving them greater control over resources and decisions in the projects and programmes affecting their lives (Bamberger, 1988: 2).

With this shift in focus of development approaches, the participatory communication model that emerged sought to transform the elitist, vertical and top-down character of the diffusion model of communication (congruent with the modernisation theories) and incorporate democratisation and participation at all levels in the planning and production of media content. New approaches to communication brought a greater knowledge of and respect for forms of people's communication, which were consonant with the cultural identity of the community (Servaes, 2002). 'Another' communication favoured 'multiplicity, smallness of scale, locality, de-institutionalisation, interchange of sender-receiver roles (and) horizontality of communication links at all levels of society' (McQuail, 1983: 97). It emphasised the need to establish decentralised media systems with a more 'receiver-centric' rather than 'communicator' orientation and accent on an exchange of information and 'meanings' rather than on persuasion. Community-based independent media, such as community radio, participatory video and popular theatre are now perceived by media activists and grassroots organisations as a means of enabling rural people to manage their own development and to acquire a sense of control over its course through self-management. The following sections discuss the role of community radio in furthering alternative thinking on development issues and its ability to address the issues of 'access', 'participation' and 'representation' of marginalised voices.

Radio and the Community: Listeners' Context

As illustrated in the NGO profiles given earlier, the community radio programmes of Alternative for India Development (AID) in Jharkhand and those of Kutch Mahila Vikas Sangathan (KMVS) in the Kutch are broadcast on sponsored slots of All India Radio (AIR). DDS women in Andhra Pradesh narrowcast their programmes through cassettes in the *sangam* meetings of their villages. The community radio programmes of VOICES/MYRADA (Mysore

Resettlement and Development Agency) are cablecast mainly to TV owning households of the members of self-help groups (SHGs) in the village of Budhikote in Karnataka. In the first two case studies, the focus groups we conducted consisted of people selected from among the receivers of the programmes in the villages where the NGOs have a presence. For the DDS and VOICES/MYRADA case studies, discussions were carried out only with members of the women SHGs and others who were directly involved in the activities of these grassroots organisations. An attempt was first made to find out whether or not radio as a medium was popular among the villagers. How did differences like age, class, education, gender (analysed in Chapter 7), mobilisation and participation affect the reception within the community of the programmes rooted in local issues and culture being produced by their own people?

Most of the villages in the Lesliganj and Panki blocks of Palamau district of Jharkhand do not have electricity. Roads and other basic infrastructure are noticeably substandard. Widespread illiteracy means that newspapers hardly play a role in the lives of the people. Some of the younger, literate men who travel to nearby towns, occasionally bring back regional or local newspapers with them. Television, although negligible, has made its appearance in the region, with some young men who have migrated to Punjab and UP for employment returning home with television sets that are battery-operated. So radio, as a post-literate and inexpensive medium, becomes the only link to the outside world for the poor and deprived communities. In fact, it is obvious that in regions such as these, which are under-served by other media, local or community radio serves as a lifeline.

In a survey conducted by KMVS during 1998–99, to ascertain the media habits of the people of this geographically dispersed region, it was found that the long distances between villages, poverty and low literacy make access of media like the newspapers and television unfeasible for villagers. It indicated that radio is the main medium being used in the region. Mohd. Hussain Haroon, a fisherman of a village in Mandvi, Kutch listens to radio at home. 'We also carry it on the boat when we go into the sea,' he comments. He adds,

> Men, young or old listen to radio regularly. If we had two radio sets, we would keep one in the boat and one at home. We tune in to AIR Bhuj, AIR Rajkot and BBC essentially for the sake of information and news and also for entertainment, including sports (Focus Group Discussion—FGD).

Access to their 'own' media and its outreach among members of the community is essential for promoting the popular use of such technologies to a point where the people can operate these independently. Organisations experimenting with participatory communication for social change across the world have found radio to be the most important medium for development and social change. Radio broadcasting leaps the barriers of isolation and illiteracy and it is the most economic electronic medium to broadcast and receive (Fraser and Estrada, 2002). A Rockefeller Foundation report asserts that community radio is 'one of the best ways to reach excluded or marginalized communities in targeted, useful ways,' and in giving them a 'voice' that matters most in development communication (Dagron, 2001).

Radio reaches communities at the very end of the development road—people who live in areas with no phones and no electricity. Radio reaches people who can't read or write. Radio is a relatively economical medium, and even in very poor communities, radio penetration is vast. It is portable and has made its way into regions where television has not yet reached. Radio has the advantage of adaptability for localised coverage of news, events, and community-based programmes. In fact, media theorist and critic, McLuhan (1964) described radio as 'the tribal drum'. Radio for him is an earthy medium with the native power to involve people in one another and resonating a web of kinship. He argued that radio revives the primordial 'acoustic space' of oral societies and thus creates an environment of simultaneous experiences and sensory unification.

In Jharkhand too, there seems to be a culture of radio listening, as was evident from the sight of farmers returning from or going to their fields, with radio sets slung on their shoulders. Twenty-eight-year-old Nandakishore of Harsangra village in Jharkhand spoke of how radio provides *'manoranjan'* (entertainment) as they work, while a blacksmith in Pipra village said that the radio was always on when he was at work, although he could not recollect much of the content. However, another man in the predominantly Dalit village of Goradih Khas in Jharkhand complained that many times the choice may be between buying batteries for the radio or paying school fee for the child.

Residents of all the villages of Jharkhand and Kutch who participated in the focus group discussions reported that the signal of the Daltonganj FM and the Bhuj AM station respectively were quite clear, although there were occasional glitches during broadcast. This was true of even the farthest village, Barunahi, in Palamau district, which is a predominantly tribal village, about 60 km from the radio station. The farthest village that the researchers visited in Kutch was Chapar, 250 km from the Bhuj radio station. The women of the Bhil tribe we met there were regular listeners of radio programmes from Bhuj as well as Rajkot AIR stations and did not report any problems related to quality of broadcasts.

People are happy with the Sunday evening time slot for the *Chala Ho Gaon Mein* as well as *Kutch Lok Ji Bani* (KLJB) programmes in Jharkhand and Kutch, respectively. The programmes are slotted at a time when both men and women are relatively free from work. Some women said they listen to the programme while cooking and many men stated that they listen to the programme over dinner—'*khana khate khate sunte hain*'. Listeners in many villages expressed their disappointment that if they missed any broadcast, there was no other opportunity to catch it again. 'If we miss the programme for any reason, we feel bad.' Amin, a shop owner in the Dhoravar village of Kutch where there is no television but almost 40–50 radio sets in the village, insisted that the time of broadcast was suitable except that during the *Ramzan* month, they are likely to miss five episodes because of *Namaz*. A resident of Rajhara in Jharkhand felt that 'repetition has its value' while the young *adivasi* men in Barunahi felt that the duration of the programme should be increased.

The primary issue in participation is the facilitation of dialogue and debate among members of a community so that they become the ultimate arbiters and negotiators of the development norms suitable for them. Participatory communication must be transactional in nature wherein sender and receiver of messages interact over a period of time 'to arrive at shared meanings' (Nair and White, 1987; White, 1999). Thus the context in which the community radio programmes are received is significant to determine whether or not an interactive process has been established. It is also important to ascertain if the interactive process initiated opens up avenues for both conflict and cooperation and prompts people not only to express their viewpoints and share their knowledge but also moves them to participate in programmes. Moore (1986: 586–623) pointed out that 'access to messages provides a basis for knowledge and social transformation through enculturation, socialization and participation' and that the major obstacles to participatory communication are 'the anti-participatory, often inflexible structures and ideologies, either at local or national government levels'.

In KMVS and AID community radio initiatives, organised group listening sessions are not a regular feature and are arranged sporadically to create awareness only to elicit feedback, and to invite participation in programme production. Much is left to the prevailing radio listening habits. The existing hierarchies in the household, socio-economic position, division of labour and fulfilment of basic needs come into play and affect not only the listening patterns but also inhibit discussions that community radio programmes are mandated to trigger. Women, older men, poor, illiterate and the less articulate often tend to be excluded from active listening. The feedback from listeners is left to the conventional methods of writing letters to the radio station and to evaluation exercises carried out by internal or external agencies.

Those who own a radio set or a 'two-in-one' (radio-cum-tape player) in Jharkhand and Kutch tend to listen to radio mostly at home. A few men listen to the programmes with family members but frequently, the radio set is taken out of the house by the men folk and they listen to it along with friends and others in the neighbourhood. Men who have occupations that require working at home (e.g., blacksmith) or in small shops, as well as women who are homemakers or engaged in embroidery do their work with the radio playing in the background. A young fisherman, Suleman of Mudhva village in Bhuj likes to listen to the Kutchi language broadcasts with family or collectively in a small group. 'If a friend or a visitor is there, we invite them to listen also. Women would sit inside and listen if there are visitors.' Twenty-five-year-old Ibrahim, a farm labourer of the Saeed community in Dhoravar village in Paccham region disclosed, 'We listen to all the episodes of *Kunjal* and KLJB. Children remind us about the programme. Women in our families do not listen to radio much.' The argument of men is that women are not interested in listening to radio as they are illiterate and cannot make much sense of the issues discussed in the programme.

Most of the men who owned radio sets in Jharkhand reported that they listen to radio regularly, especially *Chala Ho Gaon Mein*. The frequency of listening as well as the degree to which they listen attentively to the programme varied according to age, literacy and socio-economic position. Chandrika Bhuinya, a 35-year-old Dalit labourer in Goradih Khas village shouted at the research team angrily: 'Can we eat radio? Nothing will come out of all this. People here don't have land, water, or electricity while all the upper caste villages around us enjoy all these facilities' (FGD).

Similarly, the case of Nanhu Bhuinya, a 65-year-old man of Rajhara village, reinforces the observation during the field trip that radio listening and enthusiasm for any particular programme are less evident among those struggling to meet the basic needs. When asked if he listens to radio, he replied: 'We have nothing to eat or drink. There are no wells or roads. Kids are going hungry. What do we gain from listening to radio? Can a radio drama reduce our hunger? It's another matter if listening to radio can solve these problems' (FGD).

In the distant, drought-affected Mohaldi village in Kutch, the members of the *maldhari* (engaged in animal husbandry), nomadic *Jat* community struggling to keep their cattle alive or seeking alternative employment and the tribal men in the focus group discussion held at Barunahi village in Panki block of Jharkhand did not own a radio set. Even those who did, said that their work pressures do not allow them to listen regularly or attentively. Walking long distances searching for cattle-feed or daily work leaves them little time to 'indulge' in radio listening.

It is only by creating a listening environment in which everyone from the community gets access to community radio programmes and enters into a dialogue that they will be in a position to participate in discussion about their concerns. This would give them an opportunity to collectively analyse their problems, decide on the changes that affect their lives, and become active in implementing these changes. The International Commission for the Study of Communication Problems (popularly referred to as the MacBride Commission) argued that 'this calls for a new attitude for overcoming stereotyped thinking and to promote more understanding of diversity and plurality, with full respect for the dignity and equality of peoples living in different conditions and acting in different ways' (MacBride, 1980: 254). This model stresses reciprocal collaboration throughout all levels of participation.

For the practitioners of participatory communication, media and communicators are no longer neutral movers of information. They respond actively to the change in the ideologies and philosophies behind media practices especially those that seek to encourage people's participation. The question of who initiated a communication, how decisions leading up to the communication were made, have become crucial (Yoon, 1996). Community radio points towards this changed strategy, not merely inclusive of, but largely emanating from, the traditional 'receivers'. Freire refers to this as the right of all people individually and collectively to speak their word:

> This is not the privilege of some few men, but the right of every man. Consequently, no one can say a true word alone—nor can he say it for another, in a prescriptive act, which robs others of their words (1983: 76).

It was observed that among the male listeners in our study, those who are younger and relatively more literate seem to listen to the programme more regularly. Many of the elderly men, even those who said they listen fairly regularly, seem to be alienated from the programme as could be seen from their poor recall of the content. In striking contrast to the older tribal men, 37-year-old Surajdev Prasad Yadav of Rajhara village, who has completed his B.A. and has participated in radio productions on AIR, is an avid listener of *Chala Ho Gaon Mein*. Mohammad Yakuf of Jhumara village of Lakhpat *vistaar* (sub-block) and Lakhiarji of Valka village in Nakhatrana block of Kutch are young literate men who have been given radio by KMVS with the purpose of motivating people, especially women, to listen to the radio programme. They read *Kutch Mitra*, the popular local newspaper, listen to radio regularly and exuded a great deal of enthusiasm for the KPKJ and KLJB programmes. They were aware of the community radio process put in place by the *sangathan* and seemed to be involved with the activities of the radio reporter assigned to their villages.

The younger men, nearly half of whom were literate, in the focus group at Harsangra village in Jharkhand were keen listeners and demonstrated very good recall of programme content. Their palpable enthusiasm is also related to the fact that the village and some of its residents figured in at least four different episodes of *Chala Ho Gaon Mein*. From this as well as examples of villages such as Kalatalav and Valka in Kutch, one could draw the conclusion that the more a village participates in programme production, the more its residents would listen and pay attention to the programme.

According to Dagron (2001), communication until recently, rarely formed part of the core of any developmental process and was the fifth (spare) wheel in the car of social change. It is this lack of communication and its basic principle—dialogue—that prevented many projects from succeeding. Experiments with alternative development the world over have affirmed that people's participation in communication is vital to the success of any given project. Conscious effort to involve people in their own development through street theatre, folk songs, group activities, traditional media, community radio and participatory video are becoming commonplace. The success of 'participatory' approaches, however, needs to be seen against the interpretation and notion of participation adopted by NGOs and governments (Yoon, 1996). Despite its widespread use, the concept of participatory communication is subject to loose interpretation that appears at best to be variable and contested and at worst misused and distorted (Arnst, 1996; Jacobson and Servaes, 1999).

Deshler and Sock (1985) conducted a critical review of participatory communication literature and found it lacking in rigorous measures and indicators. Their research did yield a useful delineation of two levels of participation (White, 1994)—

(*a*) pseudo-participation categorised as

- domestication: involving information therapy and manipulation;
- assistencialism: including placation and consultation.

(*b*) genuine participation constituted by

- cooperation: points towards partnership and delegation of power;
- citizen control/member control: means of empowerment.

Participation that looks at people as receivers of benefits and decisions taken by planners, administrators and community elites and an audience to what is being planned for them and what would be done unto them is pseudo-participation. When development agency, the local elite and the people work in tandem throughout the decision-making process and people are empowered to direct the action being taken, only then it is genuine participation (White, 1994). In projects where a culture of popular, local participation in development efforts has been integrated over the years, as in the case of DDS in Andhra Pradesh and VOICES/MYRADA in Karnataka, community radio plays an important role in enhancing and nurturing people's opportunities to participate in the programme planning and production process. Even where media ownership is low, the community mechanism ensures that people are enthusiastic and active receivers of community radio.

Almost all the members in the DDS *sangams* (village level collectives of women) and those who participated in our focus groups were Hindu or Christian Dalits or Muslims and were either marginal farmers or worked as farm labour. Out of the 54 women we talked to in the focus groups, only 10 (18.5 per cent) had a radio set at home and five (9.3 per cent) said they were owners of black-and-white television sets. Thirteen (24.1 per cent) women said they had a tape recorder at home. All of the women confessed that because of the pressure of work, they would hardly spend time watching television or listening to radio, and the tape recorder would generally be playing in the background when the children would 'put in' one or two cassettes that are lying at home. Forty-three (79.6 per cent) out of the 54 women with whom we conducted our discussions were illiterate. Their exposure to the print medium was clearly negligible. According to 'General' Narsamma, who manages the DDS radio station:

> Today the situation is better for us. Twenty years before there were no TVs or tape recorders with us, nothing was there. There was no news paper circulation. If it was there also, it will come to some *zamindars'* (landlords) houses only. We didn't even see that. There used to be just one radio that too in the rich people's—who are known as wise people—house only (interview, Machnoor).

The DDS community radio station in Machnoor village in the Medak district of Andhra Pradesh is in all readiness to go 'on air' but the licence for broadcast has not been forthcoming. Therefore, the women of DDS produce cassettes of their programmes on a regular basis, which are then carried to the weekly meetings of the *sangams* and played using a tape recorder. The *sangam* supervisor and the radio women then solicit feedback about the cassette, seek suggestions for future programming and also motivate women to volunteer as participants. When asked about the radio programmes that were played in their *sangam* meetings, all women across focus groups immediately responded by acknowledging the fact that their supervisor brings tape recorder and the cassettes of programmes that are played in their weekly meetings. Some women said that this was done once in a month while others said the frequency was once in two months.

The recall of the subjects of programmes played in the last few meetings was immediate as also of the songs related to the old crops, but the women could not list out all the programmes that they had heard so far, which, in the last one year were between five in some *sangams* to 12 in others. Although the recall of the issues was not very encouraging among the older women, but women (*a*) who were formally a part of the DDS activities; (*b*) those who had participated in one or the other radio programmes; or (*c*) the middle-aged ones who were active *sangam* members (*karyakartas*), were keen to discuss the various subjects taken up in the 'cassettes'. All the women said that the supervisor would carefully make note of any feedback that they would give about the programmes in the listening sessions. Algole Narsamma who is also a station manager explained that in addition to the organised listening that is carried out during the *sangam* meetings the radio station was 'open to all and any one can listen to the cassettes. If they have interest they will come to the radio station and listen to the cassettes.'

In Budhikote, the adult and children volunteers motivated by the women SHGs participate in and produce programmes and also the members themselves some of whom are on the management committee that decides all the programming. The cablecast programmes can be received on TV sets on a particular channel depending on the frequency set by the village cable operator. The screen is blank, but the sound quality was found to be good. Among the 47 persons who participated in the discussions, 24 (51 per cent) had television sets at home, while only 15 (32 per cent) had radio sets. Most of the literate respondents were regular readers of the popular Karnataka language newspapers. Everyone who was part of the discussion claimed to be keen listeners of the programmes. 'If *Namma Dhwani* programme is coming we leave all our work and listen to it,' a middle-aged *anganwadi* teacher, Uma affirms. According to Mangala Gowri, the studio manager:

> If they had given us licence, we could have broadcast on FM band, over 30 km and could have covered the villages of the Budhikote sector. Now we have provided a special jack that can be connected to both television and radio. If people want to listen on TV they can, otherwise they can use radio also. But, radio cannot be carried as mobile sets and the reception is only for those who have cable connection in this (Budhikote) village (interview).

Namma Dhwani is an important component of the *sangha* (self-help group) activities and their representatives are involved in the decision-making process at every stage. The women in the management committee exchange feedback and programme ideas in the *sangha* meetings and also motivate their members to participate. Most of the women in the focus group were aware of the content and its format. They said that children were enthusiastic listeners as they participate regularly in the programme-making but men also listen to the programmes. 'The songs can be listened to anytime. But *Namma Dhwani* is about our own problems. So, they listen with interest,' declared 26-year-old vegetable vendor Triveni. She added, 'Here, the work is only of the ear. If I am cooking also, I can listen to the programmes.' Pushpa, a young homemaker and an articulate member of the Purnima *Sangha* was quick to point out:

> We listen to *Namma Dhwani* in our homes on TV. We all sit together and listen. Not just that. We force others—our neighbours, to listen also. We tell them that *Namma Dhwani* has come to Budhikote and people from our *Sangha* have spoken in that, so come and listen. Even if a serial is coming we switch it off and listen to *Namma Dhwani*. We have given programmes, so if there is power failure we curse it—why should this wretched power go off now only? It would have been nice if it were on radio, because even if current goes off we can use the cells (FGD).

As evident in the responses earlier, community radio, in the ideal situation, is the by-product of participatory processes of consultations, reflection, discussions and action that form part of the wide-ranging development activities within the community. Freire (1983) first introduced the concept of 'dialogic action' as a dialectical interplay of action with reflection, which constitutes the process of 'conscientisation'. Freire contends that conscientisation is imperative for any participatory action and comes into play through a self-sustained effort to activate the community's consciousness and critical understanding of one's situation, environment, identity, and one's alternatives for liberty of action. He uses the term 'praxis', which for him is a process beginning with reflection and continuing with action and returning to reflection in a continual, circular manner (Thomas, 1994; White, 1994).

According to Servaes (2002), the dialogical pedagogy of Freire is one of the two major normative approaches to participatory communication that form the basis for every development project that works on the principles of democratic communication. The second involves the ideas of access, participation and self-management articulated in the UNESCO debates in the late 1970s. Going by the UNESCO discourse, community radio means a radio station that is self-managed by those participating in it. The final report of the 1977 meeting of UNESCO in Belgrade, Yugoslavia (as quoted in Servaes, 1996: 18) defines the terms as mentioned here:

1. Access refers to the use of media for public service. It may be defined in terms of the opportunities available to the public to choose varied and relevant programs and to have a means of feedback to transmit its reactions and demands to production organisations.
2. Participation implies a higher level of public involvement in communication systems. It includes the involvement of the public in the production process, and also in the management and planning of communication systems.
3. Participation may be no more than representation and consultation of the public in decision-making. On the other hand, self-management is the most advanced form of participation. In this case, the public exercises the power of decision-making within communication enterprises and is also fully involved in the formulation of communication policies and plans.

As discussed earlier, DDS works primarily with non-literate people. The more and more they used participatory processes for their developmental work, the kind of analysis women brought into their programmes was 'absolutely revealing for us', says P.V. Satheesh, Director, DDS:

> On the one hand our respect for their knowledge and our respect for their capacities grew. And on the other hand, we started looking at the tremendous amount of limitation that a literacy-based emphasis in development had. A kind of oppression on non-literate people, especially people from marginalized sections like dalits and women. They also start believing that if we don't have literacy we can't do anything (interview, Pastapur).

This made DDS look out for tools, which could be used by people who may not be in a position to equip themselves with enough 'formal literacy' to strongly negotiate with the outside world. Satheesh adds, 'After all what is literacy? It's a kind of a tool for negotiation with the outside world.' This was the reason DDS thought that electronic media 'which doesn't demand literacy' and can be a part of the strong oral culture of the people can prove to be a big advantage for the poor, illiterate, Dalit women. The belief was that once people understand a simple technology like radio, then there is no need for anybody from outside to be present there constantly to facilitate that whole process. This is borne out by the women who are working in DDS radio. They are all from the community and produce programmes that are 'beneficial for the community' with the participation of the people of the DDS villages.

Extent of Participation in Message Development Process

Awareness among the listeners about the process involved in implementing AID and KMVS community radio projects is varied. While most of the listeners seem to be knowledgeable about the fact that the programme is made by recording interviews, discussions, songs, etc., right in their villages (rather than in distant studios), this knowledge seems to vary according to the degree to which the reporters are active in their assigned villages. If the reporters frequent their assigned villages, people develop a sense of familiarity with him or her and tend to come forward with *mahiti* (information), programme ideas and suggestions. KMVS has been engaging with the concerns of rural women by making direct interventions in villages to set up *mahila mandals* that work towards self-managed *sangathans* (rural women's groups) at *taluka* (block) level. The women who are members of KMVS *mandals* and *sangathans* are aware of all stages of the production process of community radio programme. The reporters are answerable to the *sangathans* of the respective blocks they cover. Interaction with women of the block *samitis* (managing committee of a *sangathan*) is a regular feature for finalisation of content.

Most of the reporters selected by AID in Jharkhand work quite hard to cover about three to four villages each, motivating people to participate in programme production, developing story ideas and scripts, and recording. Many of these villages are not well connected by roads and public transport. As a result, although these may not be too many villages for each reporter, the distance between them and the difficult terrain make it a tough job, especially for the women reporters. According to the reporters in Kutch, the first tough task that they accomplished with success was to make contact with the people in the areas other than their own village that they cover, so that people recognise them and have faith in them. Now that they have a '*pahchan*' (recognition)—people recognise them as '*Kunjal wale*' or '*KLJB wale*'—it is easier to gather information and discuss the concerns of the area. Some of them recall being shunned and thrown out before they could establish a rapport with the villagers.

Very few of those who participated in the focus group discussions displayed any awareness of the post-production process. In Palamau, some thought the recorded tapes are sent to Delhi or Patna for broadcast, while a handful of literate youth said that they knew the programme is 'cut' suitably and broadcast from Daltonganj. In Bhuj everyone knew that 'our reporters and *mahila mandal* women make this programme' but could not describe the process of production. 'We are not educated, so we do not understand much!' some reacted. Except for a couple of people, who had gone to the audio studio of the AID or KMVS to participate in some recording of folk songs, or for a discussion or interview, none of them has ever seen any radio production equipment or visited the AIR station at Daltonganj or Bhuj. There is still a fair amount of awe about the medium and we did not get the impression that the two projects had gained much in terms of demystifying the technology for the listeners in general.

If the overall process involved in a participatory media project could be divided into three phases, viz., definition of problems, production and post-production, the coordinators of *Chala Ho Gaon Mein* programme in Jharkhand themselves admit that none of the phases are yet marked by full participation of the people. It is evident that the focal areas for the broadcast were not identified through any specific participatory assessment of needs. AID's own programmatic agenda, and the experiences of field workers seemed to have generated the priority issues for the radio programme. With the content parameters already set by the programme, the community members do, from time to time, offer new suggestions directly to their respective reporters or through letters to the programme.

People are actively encouraged by AID to submit scripts, songs, or drama plots, etc., and participate in issue-based discussions or perform in cultural items. However, as already discussed earlier, there has been a mixed response to this invitation, with women and the non-literate still quite reluctant. As individuals with their own cultural talents for singing and other performances, the reporters end up taking a lead role in producing many of these programmes.

KMVS awareness of issues at grassroots level gets reflected in the programme *Kunjal Paanje Kutch Ji* (KPKJ—Sarus Crane of Our Kutch), its first community radio programme, which also sought to augment the ongoing efforts in thrust areas of KMVS. The demand for a programme to cater to the information needs of the women of Kutch came from the *Ujjas* (rural women's newsletter) women, those involved in the various activities of the organisation and women *sarpanchs* of the village panchayats. *Kunjal* was produced with crucial inputs coming from professionals including a media production NGO, a scriptwriter and a music composer. Local talent and narrators were selected through auditions.

At present, the programme on air is *Kutch Log Ji Bani* (KLJB—Voices of the People of Kutch), handled wholly by the media unit of KMVS at Bhuj with reporters from different villages of Kutch. Gradually, the programme has reduced dependence on professionals and increased direct involvement of the villagers in the form of participation and information inputs. The reporters made several trips to villages and carried out research on the history and legends of the region and located local talent and forgotten artists. They regularly interact with the people to find out the concerns of different areas. Table 5.1 brings out the positive shift in the extent of direct community participation from *Kunjal* to KLJB, especially in the production and post-production stages, as the KMVS media team became more and more self-reliant.

Let us examine this in the context of Nair and White's (1994) conceptual framework for participatory message development. The authors argue that participation must not be interpreted as 'villagers' behavioural response to persuasive stimuli' and that the so-called 'followers' of the diffusion model of communication 'need to be transformed into self-sufficient actors in participatory development'. This calls for transactional communication that is looked upon as a 'two-way persuasion process' where the 'development communicator' and the 'intended receiver' give and take, talk over their differences and arrive at common goals. Such communication is aimed at making people participate meaningfully in development programmes. Genuine participation results in strengthening people's thinking, reflection, acting and problem-solving abilities and inculcates a sense of control over their own destinies. Transactional communication process acknowledges the contribution of 'indigenous knowledge, local solutions and context-specific solutions'.

Table 5.1: ***Participation Levels in KMVS Community Radio Programmes***

Kunjal Paanje Kutch Ji	*Kutch Log Ji Bani*
Planning and Design:	
As KMVS had not worked with the media before, a professional media production NGO, Drishti Media Collective, was involved for designing the format.	The format was worked out with the help of Drishti, in consultation with the KMVS programme executive.
Content derived from suggestions of *Ujjas* women, experience of KMVS, information needs of women *sarpanchs*, and research taken up on culture.	The content is decided through a monthly meeting of the programme executive, reporters, and *samiti* women where information gathered about problems and *mudde* (issues) is exchanged and prioritised.
Production:	
At AIR Studio	In KMVS media unit office at Bhuj
Direct involvement was in the form of: (*a*) Inputs from programme executive and six reporters who were simultaneously being trained for production work.	*Musafari* is presented in drama format and involves the reporters as characters. Information discovered through interaction with rural men and women, especially elders.
(*b*) Women selected as characters and local talent.	*Lokvan*i goes to people directly. *Pardafash* is in direct interview format.
Post-Production:	
Drishti Media Collective office at Ahmedabad.	With all the equipment, including compu ters available at the media unit of KMVS at Bhuj, the reporters produce the rough edit and with some help also the Master.

Participatory development communication that reflects a transactional process is defined as 'a two-way, dynamic interaction between grassroots receiver and the information source, mediated by development communicators, which facilitates participation of the target group [*sic*] in the process of development' (Nair and White, 1987: 37). If this approach is adhered to in the message development process for community radio, it can become a training ground for rural people to participate in other development activities. It will also add a new dimension to traditional roles of a development communicator, that of catalyst, initiator, facilitator, negotiator or mediator. The transactional model based on the participatory development communication framework of Nair and White (1994) goes further to present a typology matrix of participation from receivers' perspective that depicts the degree (low, quasi or high) of participation of the 'intended receiver' vis-à-vis the 'development communicator' (see Table 5.2). This 'nature' of participation characterised by the different cells of the matrix can be used to determine the participatory mode perceptible in the different stages of the participatory message development process of community radio in each of the case studies. For the purpose of analysis, we have divided the message development process of community radio into three phases—design or planning, production, and post-production.

It may be mentioned here that in the case studies of community radio projects we have carried out, we have observed that the NGOs who had facilitated these initiatives had been following participatory development practices for several years in their interventions. Considerable amount of mobilisation and conscientisation efforts had spurred people from the community to take on the roles of development communicators for the NGOs (NGOs are referred to as information sources or intervention agencies in the model/definition) and to be involved in all the developmental activities, including community radio, in different capacities. Thus we find that the project coordinators and reporters in KMVS and AID community radio initiatives as well as the studio managers and radio women in DDS and VOICES/MYRADA community media centres are all local people belonging to the villages and *mandals/talukas* where these development projects are based.

The analysis of KMVS and AID presented in detail earlier reveals that in both the initiatives, the planning and design stage is 'top-down' (see Table 5.2) where the intended receiver has little or no say and the decision-making rests with the development communicator or rather the NGO itself. The reporters who are people selected from

Table 5.2: ***Nair and White's Typology of Participation from the Receiver's Perspective***

Intended Receiver	Development Communicator: High	Quasi	Low
High	Ideal (1)	Active (2)	Bottom-Up (3)
Quasi	Passive (4)	Transactional (5)	Elective (6)
Low	Top-Down (7)	Selective (8)	Haphazard (9)

Source: Nair and White (1987, 1994).

the community and also form part of the intended receivers are now managing the production and post-production functions. Local people are also approached to give information and create content, making the production stage 'transactional' while the post-production still has characteristics of being 'passive' as it is limited to the reporters and the trained production personnel deployed by the NGO.

The participation levels among DDS women and the involvement of community in radio are high in all the three stages of the community radio programme production process as the station is (wo)manned by the DDS women themselves. However going by the transactional matrix of participation of Nair and White (1994), the design and planning stage of the community radio message development process in DDS is 'transactional' involving a constant give and take and a synergistic dialogue among the members of the community for deciding on the programmes. The production and post-production stages have features of being 'active' as the production has been handed over to the DDS women with inputs coming from outside experts as and when desirable and needed.

In the first phase of message construction, the purpose, needs and objectives for which the message is being developed are defined. DDS has had a presence of over two decades in the villages that are also the coverage area for the radio in its present narrowcasting mode. It uses participatory tools for its developmental activities that enable women to do things themselves and carry out their own agenda. Radio technology was adopted by the DDS women with a mandate to use it as another strong tool for peoples' participation and 'to talk about the things that we are doing'. In a consultation with Mr James Bentley, Regional Communication Adviser (Asia), UNESCO, about 35 DDS *sangam* women explained to him why they must have their own radio. Sammamma, a 35-year-old non-literate Dalit organic farmer from Bidakanne village, sums up the need for radio in these words:

> We are working on so many alternative issues. The dissemination of this message is now the burden of a few women leaders who travel around, work till after midnight in *sangam* meetings, talk to their fellow women to try and convince them about the things we are talking.
>
> If we have our own radio, the issues we are talking about will have a much wider dissemination even outside the *sangam* circles and will reach a larger community of women. This radio will also enhance the credibility of our messages by lending them the 'weight' of the medium.

> The mainstream radio disseminates some dominant values. We must fight these dominant values that are anti-poor and are against village people. Therefore we must have the control of the media (http://www.ddsindia.com/www/radiostn.htm).

This phase also involves taking decisions about the content 'design' and its presentation. DDS women carry out this process through their own radio committee consisting of the women who manage the radio station, *sangam* supervisors, coordinator of *sangams* and *karyakartas* (workers) for various activities like *balwadis* (day-care centre), Public Distribution System, health, traditional crops, education, etc. Based on the feedback from the *sangams* and the progress of DDS initiatives and seasonal requirements, it is decided on which subject the programme is to be made for the month. The 'local' experts to be called for the programme are also identified. Details such as dates and the locations for the recording are worked out. Algole Narsamma explains further:

> We (production staff) make suggestions to the committee about how to do the programme, whether the message should be conveyed in the form of a song or drama or as discussion, or in story telling mode. Sometimes we decide to go for *burra kathas* (folk tales). We use more than one way of dealing with the same topic for one cassette (interview, Pastapur).

The three women from DDS villages who have been trained in radio production carry out the next two phases of message 'production' and 'post-production' which includes recording, dubbing, editing and preparing the log sheet. Algole feels that till the permission to broadcast does not come, 'for all this work, the two of us are enough. When the licence comes, there will be more work and we will give training to others.' A fourth or the distribution and feedback phase allows scope for participation of the facilitator and also of the *sangam* women directly in their respective villages. The cassettes are sent to all the villages where DDS *sangams* are working. The cassettes are played and the DDS staff seek reactions of the people. This is also a method of identifying potential participants for future programmes. A new list of 'local' experts on various issues is also built up. Satheesh says,

> Today we have a kind of an inventory, if you ask who should be called for, let's say tree-related programmes; there is a whole list of who can be invited. It's almost like, a kind of an audition you do in AIR, but here it is purely

> for localised expertise, localised articulation, localised vision and localised perception. That is how the community gets involved in this thing (interview).

At *Namma Dhwani*, the subjects and the formats are worked out by the management committee constituted by representatives from each of the ten MYRADA-facilitated women *sanghas* in the Budhikote village, about two to four volunteers, the studio managers and community radio programme coordinators of VOICES and MYRADA. They meet 'without fail' on the fifth and 25th of every month and discuss about 'what kinds of programmes the local people need; what are their needs; what more can be done; how to run the station better; what kind of cooperation is needed; what training is required—they discuss about all such things,' says Amaresh, who is one of the studio managers for the audio studio. According to Seema Nair, the VOICES programme coordinator for the community radio project, the 10 *sanghas* are 'our inroads to the community'. She explains how the functioning of the station is the 'ultimate' responsibility of the members of the management committee:

> It is the women of the *sanghas* whose responsibilities include first cultivating goodwill with the community and talking about *Namma Dhwani*. Second is to initiate programming from among the people that they know—it is mandatory for the *sangha* members to give two programmes in a month. Third is to persuade volunteers to get associated in the different stages of the programming process. The women are also the representatives of the community for the visitors who are visiting out station. Fourth is to get other people involved, to pick people identify talents and promote them. And the fifth responsibility of the management committee is to be actively involved in managing the station (interview, Budhikote).

Forty-two-year-old *anganwadi* teacher, Geeta K.R., who is also in the management committee, discloses that she has made programmes and carried out recordings and that she was looking forward to the recording that her *sangha* members had scheduled for the next day. They were going to record songs sung by old grandmothers so that 'those songs can stay alive for the future generations'. She further explains that the minutes of the meeting of the management committee are shared with the women when 'in the night our *sanghas* meet—what we do in the *Namma Dhwani* meeting, we go and narrate in the *sangha*. Two of us come for the meeting. We go back and inform the others as to what happened and plan further course of action' (FGD).

The post-production work is carried out by the three young fairly well-educated studio managers belonging to poor families of villages in Budhikote sector. They were trained by VOICES to run the radio station at *Namma Dhwani*. The volunteers also assist in programme production after undergoing preliminary training. Volunteers help in documentation, as reporters, technical hands and also motivate other people to get involved. According to 25-year-old volunteer Ramakrishna, a volunteer from the neighbouring village of Kotur, who is fond of reading newspapers and has a technical diploma:

> Voluntary means we aren't doing it for money. We are doing it as a social service. We do programmes about what's happening around to inform the poor. We go to all villages and collect information. We tell them to give programmes. We edit those programmes here and they play them in those villages through cassette player. They listen to them with interest. One group had come here for training. We played the programme that they themselves had done. Tears rolled down their cheeks. Then, if we play cassettes as to how one group has developed, the other groups will also be interested to follow them (FGD).

The participation of children is a unique feature of *Namma Dhwani*. A children's club has been started where every Saturday after the school closes at 11.00 a.m., children go to *Namma Dhwani* studio and record programmes. 'We make them do plays. They also write poetry and narrate stories. We broadcast (cablecast) the programmes they make. This encourages even the parents who don't send their children to send them,' says Mangala Gowri, who manages the studio. The children volunteers were very enthusiastic and especially enjoyed 'operating the radio and also computers'.

The participation levels in the community radio initiative in the Budhikote village, especially among the women of the *sanghas* and their families, are high in all three stages of the message development process. They are also keen participants in the evaluation process as the *Namma Dhwani* centre is part of an action research project funded by UNESCO where a systematic monitoring of the changes, problems addressed and benefits are being carried out simultaneously by the organisations to assess the effects of the ICT interventions in poverty alleviation. Going by Nair and White's transactional matrix presented here, the VOICES/MYRADA project can be considered to be at a stage of 'active' participatory interaction that puts the community at a slightly more dominant position in guiding decisions and implementing them. The development communicator takes on the role of a facilitator, making inputs as and when support is necessitated.

Before going into how the participatory developmental work in the four cases taken up here has been augmented by their community radio initiatives, it must be pointed out that there may arise inherent contradictions in the practice of participatory communication. It may be difficult to maintain 'a dynamic balance between ideology and strategy, between power and countervailing power, between conformist and spontaneous non-conformist participation' (Moore, 1986: 586–623). But one has to appreciate that there is more good than bad in the approach and participatory communication seems to be the most promising approach for building self-confidence of the people, decreasing dependency, for re-establishing indigenous knowledge into modern-day solutions to development and overcoming alienation of the powerless. However, it has been recognised that there are certain limits to participation and a cautious and sensitive approach to participatory communication is thus indispensable. An international seminar of practitioners and researchers working in the area of participatory communication for development affirmed three caveats at the conclusion of their meeting:

(*a*) participatory communication processes may not be suitable for solving all problems in all contexts. The mother whose child is dying of diarrhoea does not want to 'participate'. Participatory processes usually involve long-term goals but short-term solutions are also needed;

(*b*) the interventionist who attempts to 'sell' solutions to 'target population' is accused of being manipulative as s/he is may bring along an alien set of cultural premises. A participatory social communicator who enters a village hoping people will come to perceive their oppression the way s/he sees it is equally manipulative;

(*c*) it should not be assumed that the villagers have nothing better to do with their time. For every hour spent 'participating' there is an opportunity cost: the villager may be foregoing more productive activity if the participatory process does not lead to long or short-term benefits (summarised from White, 1994; Yoon, 1996).

Addressing Social Problems: the Tangible Benefits

This section endeavours to infer to what extent the participatory and democratic principles of community radio have been successful in generating a community-based communication environment, with opportunities for articulating localised and people-centred development needs. Some of the sub-concepts that are functionally related to the act of participation and should ideally form an integral part of any development communication initiative claiming to be participatory in nature have been listed here.

> *Self-Reliance*: developing self-reliant individuals who are confident enough to speak up their points of view, unite together to define communities' needs and have a strong voice in setting priorities and action agendas.
> *Power and control*: refers to the generative idea of power whereby people have the potential to generate their own source of power to accomplish objectives they set for themselves and the community.
> *Knowledge sharing*: makes a case for a partnership between experts and people at the grassroots (Gramsci's 'indigenous intellectuals') for knowledge generation that is contextual and applicable.
> *Liberation*: Signifies the ability of the people to determine the course of their own lives if given access to appropriate knowledge and opportunity (White, 1994).

Genuine participation in development, as interpreted and operationalised in the earlier sections of the chapter, along with conscientisation and the sub-concepts outlined here are long-term goals of any participatory communication activity. However, short-term tangible outcomes of a participatory development initiative help in reinforcing the faith in its potential for working towards self-reliant progress, social inclusion, sharing of meanings, resolution of conflicts, knowledge generation and ownership of responsibilities at the community level. Table 5.3 gives details of the issues and subjects on which programmes have been produced in the four community radio projects and the analysis that follows discusses the perception of the respondents about the benefits and some tangible outcomes of these programmes.

Many of the people we met during focus group discussions in Jharkhand, with the exception of the elderly and some women, identified the major issues on which the programme is made, viz., alcoholism, dowry problem, superstition, bribery, literacy and child marriage (see Table 5.3). Though unverifiable, several people claimed that consumption of alcohol in the villages has come down after the programme started. Loki Mahato of village Mahe asserted that *Chala Ho* is gradually having an influence on several critical problems of the area, including the drinking problem, which has been a major burden on rural life economically and socially. 'The programme had a lot of impact here. Many people here who used to drink three to five bottles of liquor now run away even from its smell' (FGD).

Suresh Kumar of AID spoke of a dramatic intervention made by the organisation in which several people were invited to record a song against alcoholism. The song involved people swearing on their mothers that they would give up drinking liquor. He said the organisation tried to take advantage of this public pledge and urged those people to stand by it.

The pathetic condition of government-run primary schools and of delinquent teachers was discussed repeatedly in various focus group discussions. Rajmani Yadav, another community reporter, narrated this episode where the threat of doing a radio programme helped solve a problem in the school. This incident is also illustrative of the perceived power of the medium.

> One of our schoolmasters used to siphon off the grain meant for the children's mid-day meals. When many people in the village complained about this, we made a surprise visit to the school. We raised this issue with him and told him that there are other complaints as well regarding lack of books and facilities for students to sit. We told him that we have recorded all these things and will broadcast it on radio. He pleaded with us not to do it. We put him on alert and agreed not to go on air for now (FGD).

According to some participants in the focus group discussions, *Chala Ho* has also addressed the issue of superstitious interventions against illnesses and brought about some changes in health practices. Ajay Kumar, a 21-year-old post-graduate in history at Cheri village, pointed this out clearly: ' In the old days people used to bank on faith healers to invoke spirits, even for such diseases as malaria, and never got the patient any medical treatment. Now after listening to radio dramas on the subject, more people are beginning to take patients to the hospital instead' (FGD).

According to Preeti Soni, the project coordinator for the KMVS community radio initiative, the first radio programme *Kunjal Paanje Kutch Ji* (KPKJ) was an effort to meet women's demand for training

Table 5.3: *Issues on which Programmes Produced*

Chala Ho Gaon Mein	*KMVS Community Radio*	*Namma Dhwani*	*DDS Community Radio*
Literacy	Women's leadership and governance	Electricity and water problems	Seed sowing
Education	Girl's right to education	Health issues	Land ploughing
Superstition	Violence against women	Crop patterns	Seed preservation
Child marriage	Harassment of brides for dowry	Panchayat activities	Food security
Health	Uunnatural deaths and suicides of women	Panchayat elections	Biodiversity
Alcoholism	Pressure on women to produce boys	Indigenous medicine	Old crops
Environment	Female foeticide	Current affairs	PDS
Dowry	Maternal mortality	Agriculture	Watersheds
Gram Swaraj	Liquor	Insurance	Lands tenancy
Child labour	Corruption	Cookery	Crop insurance
Bonded labour	Communal harmony	Widow pension	People's verdict
Corruption	AIDS	Folk songs	Vision 2020
Migration	Disregard for natural environment	Government schemes	Gender justice
Women empowerment	Lack of water resources	Children's programmes	Women empowerment
Gambling	Cyclical drought	Youth debates	Adult literacy
Public distribution	History and legends of Kutch	SHGs' development	Night school, *Balwadis*
Rural banking	Construction technology	Insurance	Summer camps
Veterinary issues		Computer education	Education—formal/ Non-formal
Day care		Sericulture	Health/hygiene
Development schemes		Employment opportunities	Women's diseases, Children diseases
Unemployment		Micro-credit	Animal diseases
Gender equity		Education	Local knowledge
Population		Environment	Folk songs
Elections		Organic farming	Festivals

to participate in political processes, specifically in the village panchayat activities. This is represented through the character of Rani, the woman *sarpanch* located in the fabled village *Ujjas* where the *saras* crane (*kunjal*), she is also the *sutradhaar* (storyteller), comes to live once a year. The theme song reflects on the central focus of the serial:

> Salutations, Salutations to *Sarpanch* Rani
> Many salutations to *Ujjas* village
> She wrote applications, raised objections
> She went time and again
> To the TDO's (*Taluka* Development Officer) office
> Her shoes are worn out
> With all the running around
> She exposed the Engineer's misdoings
> She put up a struggle
> That's when the government buckled!
> That is how she wrangled the permission
> To deepen the old village pond
> As part of the government drought relief works!
> Salutations to *Sarpanch* Rani
>
> (translated from Kutchi in Virmani, 2000).

Preeti explains how the programme has revealed cases in several villages where women's role in panchayats have been undermined by their male counterparts owing to their repressive control on the governing procedures. The women *sarpanchs* are reduced to mere rubber stamps by the vested interests of *sarpanch patis* (husbands of women *sarpanch*) who promote their spouses to this post only to hold sway in the panchayat. The politics of pressure building, caste structure and family restrictions that curb the development work of panchayats and specifically women *sarpanchs* have also been brought out in the programmes.

The content development of KMVS radio programmes is based on the fundamental issues of concern in the area, especially those that people are reluctant to talk about. In the focus groups we conducted, almost all of those who claimed to be regular listeners had a good recall of the issues discussed in KPKJ (also referred to as *Kunjal*) and KLJB, like women's marriage-related problems, panchayat, water, literacy, alcoholism, midday meal and problem of mid-wifery. Some women empathised with the character of 'Dhanki', a victim of domestic violence and were happy that she protested against the atrocities of her husband. They mentioned that *Lokvani* brings information about the history, achievements, incidents, cultural practices and development initiatives from different rural settlements in the district. A Muslim *Jat* woman in her forties, Bhasra Bai of Mohaldi village declared that she actually fought with her husband who switched to another station when she was listening to the programme:

> When *Kunjal* comes, I don't let anyone disturb me. It talks about our lives, about the problems that women are facing and information about government schemes like 'Indira Awaas' that we can make use of. When there was discussion about construction of a village well by women themselves, we talked to our *sarpanch* about it (FGD).

Several men identified KPKJ and KLJB (Kutch Log Ji Bani) as the only programmes that talk of the problems in the villages of Kutch. 'There is no other programme on radio in which the villages of Kutch figure.' They recalled programmes about model villages where *guthka* (tobacco) has been banned and about the community that shuns alcohol and displayed faith in the potential of the radio in bringing about *sudhar* (improvement) in their situation and in dissemination of pertinent information—'*sudhar hota hai, jankari milti hai*' ('the programmes bring about change for the better and give us useful information!') Almost all men and women wanted the Kutchi language programmes, produced by '*mahila mandals* or their village reporters', not to be discontinued as they felt that if their village has not benefited from the programmes so far, they do learn from the experiences of other villages and are hopeful that *hamari bari bhi aa jayegi* (their turn will also come one day). However they were not very sure that 'the government will take action even if they listen to our voices'.

Pardafash, the investigative journalism segment of KLJB was praised for its efforts to expose corrupt practices of the officials. The men in Dhoravar as well as in Mandvi said that it is indeed important and useful to get information about the wrong doings of government officials, or if children are not getting mid-day meal or about corruption in forest department or malpractices in the Primary Health Centres. They were convinced that *pardafash* benefits people who do not have power and resources and are exploited by the rich. They felt that the government officials were scared of radio as it brings things out in the open. The advantage of radio is that that once something is on radio, 'all know it' and the people who are doing wrong feel insulted. Some listeners expressed a wish to hear more follow-up programmes that would give particulars of the action that was finally taken in the cases.

Namma Dhwani programmes in Budhikote, Karnataka include songs sung by schoolchildren, talks and discussions by young girls on the evils of dowry and eve-teasing, women explaining to others how to open a bank account and farmers debating the vagaries of the weather and fluctuating crop prices (see Table 5.3). According to Seema Nair, who helps the villagers run the station at Budhikote, 'Community radio in India is not about playing alternative rock music, it is a source of strength for poor people for addressing their most basic development needs.' Several instances of socio-economic, cultural and political problems have come to light in the brainstorming sessions that *Namma Dhwani* holds for deciding on the subjects of the programmes. These include lack of market information, poor transparency in government offices, poor health facilities, water, electricity, superstitions, animal sacrifice, crop failures and even lack of local entertainment.

The *Jagruti Sampanmoola* (Awareness Resource) that has been created as a constituent of *Namma Dhwani* provides timely information to the farmers regarding various departments that should be approached 'if there is no rain and there is drought, for example'. Balu, the programme coordinator from MYRADA explains, 'Farmers come to us and want to know about the facilities given by the government. So we collect information from the welfare department of the government and broadcast that. The farmers are also free to contact the *Namma Dhwani* resource centre for more information about any particular scheme or facilities.'

He said that people from the horticulture department and agriculture department are invited to the studio and farmers can interact with them directly and these programmes are also broadcast. Giving the example of how a radio programme helped them deal with corrupt government employees, Hamesh, a volunteer from Linkaldurga village which falls in the Budhikote sector said,

> This sericulture department—they have swallowed all the pesticides and other facilities that are meant for farmers. Through *Namma Dhwani* we are informing people of the facilities the sericulture department offers. On being informed, our people went and enquired about the pesticides and the department people who had been taking advantage of people's ignorance had no choice but to give them (FGD).

Sujata, a young woman from Lakshmi *sangha*, was vocal about the prevalence of superstitions in the village and spoke about how 'people go to the God for everything. They never went to the doctor. After *Namma Dhwani* programmes, people have started going to the doctor. They still go to the God. They won't stop going there. But, now they are also going to the doctor.'

Another member of the same *sangha*, Sarasamma narrated the case of measles.

> Most of the time what happened was, as soon as they realise their kid is having measles they go to the temple and roll around the god, they think its gods curse. You know three children died in that village and four others were suffering. So, we went and made a programme and told them what is to be done if a child gets measles. We covered live what a doctor was telling the parents about measles. Our reporter was there capturing how the doctor's intervention saved the life of a child. It shook many people (FGD).

The incident of how *Namma Dhwani* helped women solve the water problem in the Budhikote village has made it to the pages of *The Washington Post*. The news item aptly highlights the power of media that is in the hands of the people.

> Crushed under the weight of three years of drought, the villagers lost their patience when the public water pipes dried up last June. For eight days, there was no water for cooking, cleaning or washing. There were murmurs of protest everywhere. Women came out of their homes with empty pots demanding that the old pipes be fixed and new wells dug. Men stood at street corners and debated angrily. The village chief made promises, but nothing happened. Then, a young man ran over to the village radio station and picked up a recorder. 'Women complained and shouted into the mike and vented their anger at the village chief's indifference. There was chaos everywhere. But I recorded everything,' said Nagaraj Govindappa, 22, a jobless villager. He played the tape that evening on the small community radio station called *Namma Dhwani*, or Our Voices. The embarrassed village chief ordered the pipes repaired. Within days, water was gushing again (*The Washington Post*, 17 September 2003, p. A17).

According to 'General', Algole and Sukkamma, the three radio women, sharing local knowledge and two-way flow of applicable ideas are the main objectives of the DDS radio. DDS women have a long-term view of their future and an unambiguous idea of family, children and how they should get better. The development paradigm that these women subscribe to combines economic and ecological improvement, and an incremental movement towards the well-being of the people. Women have a lot of commitment and, therefore, over the years they have been able to put in place alternative processes for their development on a firm ground while maintaining a close relationship with nature. The women find radio to be a tool for direct expression of people's problems and for horizontal learning that adds to the larger community knowledge. DDS radio women have canned more than 400 hours of programming on various issues (see Table 5.2). The women in the focus groups felt that they had benefited from the radio programmes especially those related to traditional crops, seeds preservation and health.

In Kalimela, 25 km away from the DDS office in Pastapur, the farthest village among the ones we visited, the group of Dalit women, between the age of 25 and 55 years, all of whom were non-literate, participated actively in the discussions. Everyone was eager to make a point about the benefits of the 'cassettes' of DDS radio programmes. Chandramma's immediate response was 'We feel happy that they (cassettes) speak about our crops, the crops which we eat. There are old crops' songs also on tape recorder.' Kantamma added, 'We are cultivating those crops, old crops are good for health, good for stamina.' Tukkamma came out with a list of forgotten crops, '*Jowar, Ragi, Korra, Sajjal, Samalu, Togar, Minumulu, Pesarrlu, Jonnalu, and Pachajonnalu.* We should eat *Korra* and *Ragi.* Our health keeps well.' Sukkamma informed us that, 'We used to eat that only, but they became outdated. Now we are storing the seeds also.' Basantpur Syamala, the *balwadi* teacher, who is a matriculate explained, 'We used to cultivate *Samalu* and *Sajjal*. Later we forgot. Rice! Rice! We said and ran after it. After listening to the tape, it reminds us again that we should cultivate and eat traditional crops and improve our health.' The women told us that they had even suggested to the *Patel* (landlord) and *Sarpanch* (head of local governing body), who would not eat these marginalised grains, that these crops are beneficial for health and that 'we'll grow old crops in your fields for daily wages.' Kalimela Sunderamma asserts:

> It is now deep-rooted in our brains that cow dung, organic waste are to be used for crops as manure. Crops produced from traditional manure will give good strength. Otherwise we were selling this natural manure to others. Pesticide sprayed crop is not good. We were using pesticides for crops, but for traditional crops pesticides are not needed and the output is good (FGD).

The personal experiences of women from different villages on a particular subject serve to guide those without specialised knowledge. According to Erra Annasuya of Raipally village:

> For example, if they come up with a theme like how do we ensure that our crops don't get attacked by the pests. And, a number of women come up with their personal experiences, and all these experiences are grouped. And when they are played back in the villages, those who haven't done well will get a lot of strength, confidence that they can also do it (FGD).

The radio is also looked upon as an archive of indigenous knowledge. This timely dissemination of information at hand 'guides and educates us about what is good for us and to know what we did not know. This information would be available even for our future generations.' Tahirabi of Pastapur village gives an example: 'Earlier people used to sow only the seeds kept with a clever woman who knew the method of keeping seeds. Now with a radio programme on seed preservation, all are learning the methods of keeping seeds' (FGD).

Byagar Sangamma, 50, a childless widow from Pyalaram also makes a point.

> Before the coming of radio cassettes, we used to depend on wise men who would guide us say, if animals fell sick. Like that so many diseases will come, that may even attack men or women. During *sangam* meetings, we cannot discuss such issues fully. When we listen to cassette about overcoming common diseases or problems of animals or precautions to be taken if a snake bites, the information is very useful (FGD).

DDS women are extremely disappointed that the government is denying them a licence to broadcast and giving it to people in urban areas. 'They should keep two points in mind, this radio is in village and that is in city. For how many this is useful and how many that is useful? To whom this is useful and to whom that is useful? Think like that!'

Conclusion

The participatory projects considered earlier are all endeavouring to put radio stations run by local communities at the heart of development. They have devised ways and means of disseminating community-produced radio programmes not only for facilitating participatory development but also for the preservation and spread of traditional practices and culture. One realises that community radio is not meant to be a 'quick fix' for social problems—it is only a 'means' to enhance genuine participation in development and promotes participatory democracy as an 'end' in itself. Community radio has the capacity to consolidate participatory communication into a thread that weaves through the development process and endows it with avenues to strengthen and give voice to all stakeholders, particularly the poor.

6 REVITALISING CIVIL SOCIETY

Forging Counterpublics with Community Radio

> As for the radio's object, I don't think it can consist simply in prettifying public life... The radio would be the finest possible communication apparatus in public life, a vast network of pipes... That is to say, it would be if it knew how to receive as well as to transmit, how to let the listener speak as well as hear, how to bring him into a relationship instead of isolating him.
>
> Whatever the radio sets out to do it must strive to combat that lack of consequences which makes such asses of almost all our public institutions... But it is not at all our job to renovate ideological institutions on the basis of the existing social order by means of innovations. Instead our innovations must force them to surrender that basis. So: For innovations, against renovation!
>
> —Bertolt Brecht, 1932

The Brechtian mandate to use radio for social change seems never more pertinent than the present times when the mounting influence of media globalisation has eroded diversity and quality of information in the public sphere, rendering civil society increasingly ineffective. The concentration of media and modes of communication in the hands of a few oligarchic multinational corporations is infringing freedom of expression, diversity of information and media plurality. As firms grow larger, they become reluctant to take risks on innovative or progressive information or cultural forms that could potentially challenge the status quo or strive toward even limited structural change. However, the global media juggernaut has been facing stiff resistance all over the world from citizen groups, community organisations and media activists. In their effort to forge a more responsible and responsive civil society, these groups have been pushing for a democratic, community-based media that foster cultural diversity in addition to freeing people from the passivity imposed upon them by the mainstream media.

The earlier chapter endeavoured to analyse how community radio is being mobilised (mainly by civil society organisations) for participatory development. This chapter goes a step further to focus on community radio as a means to effectively enhance 'a process of public and private dialogue through which people define who they are, what they want and how they can get it' (The Rockefeller Foundation, 1999: 15). It addresses the critical question of citizen empowerment by examining the potential of community radio to subvert differential access to technologies and structural inequalities in knowledge or cultural production. The first section of the chapter argues that as a consequence of the media globalisation and the centralisation of ownership of the electronic media and communication sector (which ranges from telecommunication networks and the Internet, through to radio, television and film), gigantic media corporations have gained a firm foothold in the cultural and information marketplace of every region of the world. Various civil society organisations are pursuing the cause for public access to information and communication technologies (ICTs) for empowerment at the grassroots and emphasising on the intricate link between communication and culture. They are advocating that free and pluralistic media alone can guarantee every community the opportunity to express its concerns without exclusion or discrimination.

The second part reviews the potential of community radio to revive plurality of viewpoints and strengthen the submerged local forms of social and cultural expression. It also explores how community radio, with the specific characteristic of citizens' access and participation, influences perceptions of self-identity among marginalised communities excluded from the mainstream media. The third section of the chapter investigates how community radio helps to strengthen communicative and analytical skills of the people and their participation in democratic governance. If technology is demystified for the marginalised and capacities of communities enhanced to take control of radio, would it lead to new forms of political action and empowerment in contemporary, mass-mediated societies? The final segment describes the ability of community media to create a new relationship between media and citizen's empowerment in accordance with the contemporary ideas of participatory democracy. Is there a possibility that access to radio could transform the dominant public sphere by establishing decentralised public spaces for dialogue and collaborative action controlled by the marginalised sections in India?

Media Globalisation

> Since the Industrial Revolution, society and culture have been subservient to technology. One of the compelling tasks today is to reverse the process and make technology serve culture and society (Bagdikian, 1992).

'Globalisation' has been used in scholarly literature as a catch-all phrase to include an array of processes such as: time–space compression (enabled by expanded transportation and communication infrastructure); technological, commercial, and cultural homogenisation; and a general 'intensification of the consciousness' of the world as a whole (Robertson, 1992; Pieterse, 1994; Appadurai, 1997). Wilson and Dissanayake (1996) underline the dialectics of globalisation when they direct our attention to a new terrain of cultural production and national representation that is simultaneously becoming more globalised (around the dynamics of capital) and more localised (into contestatory enclaves of difference, coalition and resistance).

The post-industrial society, heralded by scholars like Bell (1974), was supposed to put an end to centralisation and standardisation and bring about diversified production processes and democratic decision-making. However, the worldwide trend toward economic liberalisation since the 80s and the advent of satellite communications, technological convergence and subsequent globalisation of media belied these expectations. Control over ICTs became more centralised and the power structure between the information-haves and information-have-nots has been reinforced. In the face of the increased volume of information on specialised subjects, where more and more is known about less and less, where access and skills required to exploit complex technologies are unevenly distributed in the society, information becomes a source of power only under specific conditions of equity (Lyon, 1988; Wresch, 1996). As long as ICTs cater only to the interests of the most powerful sectors of society, i.e., those who control and manage information, the information revolution remains only a myth (Traber, 1986).

The onslaught of capitalist globalisation has led to concentration of ownership of the cultural industries in the hands of ever fewer corporate communications conglomerates at every level—production, distribution, regulatory environment, access to globalise markets and the political processes. This is evident in the fact that even as we have an expanded menu of media outlets, the uniformity of the content renders meaningless the increase in the number of information sources. Deregulation and privatisation are most visible in the broadcasting sector, which in many countries had been maintained by the state as a non-profit, public service. The transition from national public ownership to global private ownership is almost total. As the role of the state declined, transnational media corporations began to invade domestic markets by entering into collaborative ventures with national media firms to produce, provide, and/or disseminate news and entertainment. Advances in satellite broadcasting and advances in digitisation have helped these gigantic media corporations gain a firm foothold over the terms of public debate and discourse (Pavarala and Kumar, 2002).

We all know that distance is dead. What used to be far is near, what is local is global. An important outcome is that nations are facing the dilemma of having to balance the advantages of global satellite technologies against conflicting assertion of regional identities within the country. Collins, Garnham and Locksley (1988), in their analysis of developments in Europe, contend that transnational satellite media are part of the same process of globalisation as integration of financial markets. They threaten not just national sovereignty and identity, but the concept of citizenship that goes with it (Page and Crawley, 2001). We are spectators to what Lipschutz (1992) calls 'a leaking away of sovereignty from the state, both upwards to supranational institutions and downwards to sub-national ones' (cited in Page and Crawley, 2001: 27).

While Anderson (1992) also talks of the possible implications of transnational media technologies for nationalism, Williams (1983) visualises a world pulled between 'false and frenetic nationalisms' and 'reckless uncontrollable transnationalisms'. His fear is that the development of technology would ultimately cater only to state and transnational commercial and political interests. An expression of this widely shared anxiety could be seen in the countervailing public demand for greater decentralisation of political power and distribution of the benefits and control of media technologies. The state is no longer seen as the sole transmitter of culture and negotiator of development. Appadurai (1997) has argued that satellite television has helped to create 'diasporic public spheres, a phenomenon that confounds theories that depend on the continued salience of the nation-state as the key arbiter of important social changes.'

Elaborating further on the social consequences of the globalisation of media and communication sector, Siochrú (2004) argues that this sector is a leading 'enabler of globalisation' as ICTs facilitate overall globalisation, and media industries spread world-circling cultural influences to promote consumerist and individualistic lifestyles. Another characteristic of the globalisation of the media and communication sector is that it acts as 'a powerful agent in the transformation of social, cultural and political structures'. The 'side effects' of the gradual commercialisation of media and communications on the formation of individual and community identity, cultural and language diversity, the capacity to participate in the political process, the integrity of the public sphere, the availability of information and knowledge in the public domain and the use of media for development, educational and human rights purposes (Siochrú, 2004), highlight the major risks that are involved in the current process of media globalisation. Siochrú (2004) emphasises that these critical social functions that media must play in a society that respects democracy are seriously hampered by the 'global commodification of media outputs' that 'subsume media and communication "products" under general market rules.' He clearly identifies the need for an alternative route that would lead media and communication to focus on fulfilling social needs and reinforcing human rights.

As media globalisation diminishes freedom of information, erodes the diversity and quality of information in the public sphere, civil society becomes increasingly ineffective. This has raised questions about the free flow of information to and from citizens, which is an essential prerequisite if the realm of civil society must include 'organized and substantial capacity for people to enter into public discourse about the nature and course of their lives together' (Calhoun, 1994). Civil society or civil institutions refer to the totality of voluntary civic and social organisations or institutions which form the basis of a functioning society as opposed to the force backed structures of a state (regardless of that state's political system). While there are myriad definitions of civil society, the working definition by the Centre for Civil Society, London School of Economics, is illustrative:

> Civil society refers to the arena of uncoerced *collective action* around shared *interests,* purposes and *values*. In theory, its institutional forms are distinct from those of the *state*, *family* and *market*, though in practice, the boundaries between state, civil society, family and market are often complex, blurred and negotiated. Civil society commonly embraces a diversity of spaces, actors and institutional forms, varying in their degree of formality, autonomy and power. Civil societies are often populated by organisations such as registered charities, development non-governmental organisations, community groups, women's organisations, faith-based organisations, professional associations, *trades unions*, self-help groups, *social movements*, business associations, coalitions and advocacy groups (http://en.wikipedia.org/wiki/Civil_society).

In discussing the role of the media here, the concept of 'civil society' used is one whose institutional core is constituted by voluntary unions outside the realm of the state and the economy. The term remains a valuable one, despite the fact that it has sometimes been taken to exclude categories of gender and ethnicity, which are central to contemporary ideas of participatory democracy. Siochrú (2004) discusses three trends in the organisation of civil society around the issue of reinvigorating the democratic core of media and communication structures.

(*a*) The emergence of international advocacy concerned with pushing for enhanced democracy and the right to communicate.
(*b*) The inclusion of the right to communicate in statements and goals of (non-media) NGOs and civil society events.
(*c*) The growth of community, 'alternative' or 'people's media' in several countries across the world, motivated by the need to provide an alterative to the mainstream media and to democratise media structures and access.

The Communication Rights in the Information Society (CRIS) campaign launched in November 2001 by the Platform for Communication Rights, an umbrella group of international non-governmental organisations and local networks active in media and communication came out with a document setting out some of the reasons for the significance of community media for the civil society (AMARC,

2003). The document describes community media as providing 'a vital alternative to the profit-oriented agenda of corporate media'. They are driven by social objectives and empower people and do not treat them as passive consumers. Instead of replacing local knowledge, they nurture it and are committed to sustainable approaches to development. Ownership and control of community media is rooted in the communities and they provide the means for cultural expression, community discussion, and debate. Community media provide a voice to the civil society and prevent 'the world's poorest communities from becoming a cultural dumping ground for mass market products'. Community media are integrated with practices of community life and a greater awareness of the development potential of community broadcasting, and particularly community radio is needed among governments, intergovernmental agencies and the private sector.

Civil society organisations the world over are advocating that communication should serve to create social inclusion and respect for individual or collective points of view, regardless of the source. Information and communication technologies must be instruments for a holistic, democratic and sustainable human development, and citizen's communication networks and media must be strengthened. The first ever UN Summit on Information and Communication issues, the World Summit on the Information Society (WSIS), held in December 2003 provided an opportunity for media activists to assert that civil society participation as fundamental to the WSIS.[1] The Civil Society Declaration (2003) devoted to shaping people-centred, inclusive and participatory use of ICTs sought to broaden the WSIS agenda to deal fully with issues of information and media in addition to playing a catalytic role in civil society engagement with media and communications.

Building Identity: Nurturing Local Language and Culture

Because of the recent developments where civil society organisations are seeking to deploy 'alternative media' as agents of societal and media democratisation, there has been keen scholarly interest in the nature and practices associated with alternative media. Though various scholars have delineated the characteristics that differentiate the fundamentally citizen-controlled alternative from the typically state or corporate-controlled mainstream media, there is much heterogeneity within the single category of alternative media. In a comprehensive overview of definitions that reflect on the multiplicity of alternative media, Atton (2002) declares that in order to deploy 'alternative' as an analytical term, we would need to be more specific than saying 'non-mainstream'. Alternative media are characterised not only by their critiques of mainstream media, but also by the alternative socio-cultural values and frameworks which underlie their organisation and production process. In contrast to mainstream media's liberal democratic ideal of the 'informed' citizenry, alternative media promote the participatory democratic ideal of the 'mobilised' citizenry.

McQuail (1994: 132) also supports a 'democratic-participant' model of communication that does not limit the use of alternative media for political 'resistance' and seeks to position them 'for interaction and communication in small-scale settings of community, interest group and subculture' that generate 'horizontal patterns of interaction' where 'participation and interaction are key concepts'. Thus, alternative media conceive of themselves as 'facilitators of social communication' rather than mere 'sources of information' (Tomaselli and Louw, 1990: 213). Atton (2001b: 15) clarifies that from a sociological point of view, there is a discrepancy between what the two terms, 'alternative' and 'oppositional' signify. He refers to the distinction Williams made between alternative and oppositional practices as interpreted by McGuigan:

> Alternative culture seeks a place to coexist within the existing hegemony, whereas oppositional culture aims to replace it. For instance, there is a world of difference between a minority 'back-to-nature' cult and the ecology movement's global reach (1992: 25).

The alternative media thus go beyond simply providing a platform for radical or alternative points of view and lay emphasis on the organisation of media to enable wider social participation in their creation, production and dissemination than is possible in the mass media. Williams (1980: 54) highlighted three aspects of communication as foci for this re-alignment: 'skills, capitalisation and controls'. Hamilton (2001) evokes Williams to contend that alternative media must be deprofessionalised, decapitalised and deinstitutionalised to distinguish them from the mass media. Thus alternative media must be available to ordinary people without excessive cost, with negligible professional training, and their structure must offset other media institutions. According to Rodriguez (2001: 160), 'what is most important about [alternative] media is not what citizens do with them but how participation in these media experiments affects citizens and their communities.' She uses Laclau and Mouffe's (1985) notion of radical democracy to build a case that alternative media have the ability to alter individual and group self-perception, challenge oppressing social relations, and thereby enhance participants' access to power. By opposing mass media's 'hierarchy of access', (Atton, 2001b: 5) and being 'self-managed' (Downing, 2001), 'non-hierarchical' (Atton, 2002), or 'collectivist-democratic' (Hochheimer, 1993), alternative media aim to include people normally excluded from mainstream media. This means alternative media encourage 'such access, where working people, sexual minorities, trades unions, protest groups—people of low status in terms of their relationship to elite groups of owners, managers and senior professionals—could make their own news, whether by appearing in it as significant actors or by creating news that was relevant to their situation' (Atton, 2001b: 5).

Atton (2001b) considers the range of voices that are able to speak directly through alternative media as a Foucauldian 'insurrection of subjugated knowledges' (Foucault, 1980: 81). He looks at alternative media as enabling the representation of 'the Other' and where Spivak's (1988) 'native informants' are able to speak with their own 'irreducibly heterogeneous' voices. He regards alternative media as 'heteroglossic (multiple-voiced) Text' (Buckingham and Sefton-Green, cited in Gauntlett, 1996: 91, and drawing on the dialogism of Mikhail Bahktin) that gives full voice to all those 'Others'. Atton looks for heterogeneity in the principles of organisation, production and social relations within these alternative media. Community radio initiatives in India analysed here provide for democratic communication where access to media in local language and cultural forms seeks to achieve active reception and living responses.

It was a conscious effort on the part of KMVS radio programmes to employ local *Kutchi* language as a means to represent and strengthen Kutchi identity. According to Nimmi Chauhan, Core Member, Drishti Media Collective, the Kutchi language today has no written form and the spaces for cultural expression of the language are few and shrinking further. Kutch has a distinct stature in Gujarat and there is a local AIR station in Bhuj. But the station airs only one Kutchi programme although there is an audible demand for more. KMVS decided that for rural communication to make a difference in the everyday lives of people and for radio to become a medium for self-articulation of development priorities in villages, the language must be right. Most of the focus groups identified strongly with the language of the programmes and many stated that it gave them a feeling that the programme was their own.

For Mani, a 22-year-old, non-literate, single woman from the Bhil tribe and an enthusiastic radio listener in the distant Chapar village, 'the difference between this and AIR programmes is that one is in Kutchi, other, in Hindi. One takes interviews of people of our villages, other, talks to people we do not know about.' Another young woman, Gangabai, a Dalit, of the Valka village in Nakhatrana block, who listens to the radio programme regularly in the sessions organised by 'Lakhi bhai' who has been presented with a radio set by KMVS for this purpose observes, 'This programme comes in Kutchi language, so we like it. We prefer listening to Kutchi language programmes on radio. Kutchi is our language. I find the Kutchi language very sweet. It is more enjoyable to listen to a programme that is in our own language. Familiarity with reporters also attracts us to the programmes' (Focus Group Discussion—FGD).

When asked what makes them listen to the community radio programmes regularly, many people in the Palamau district of Jharkhand felt that it is the local content of the programme and the language in which it is broadcast that attracts them. Prakash Narayan, one of the community radio reporters, asserted that *Chala Ho* was very different (*sab se bhinn*) from other radio programmes because the people's language used promotes active listenership (*apni bhasha apni ore kheenchti hai*). Except for the news, which is in Hindi, the rest of the programme uses a mixture of Bhojpuri and Magadhi, the *lingua franca* of the region. Moturam, a 60-year-old *adivasi* from Rajhara village, compared mainstream radio to *Chala Ho Gaon Mein*: 'There is a big difference between programmes broadcast from Patna and Delhi and *Chala Ho Gaon Mein*. Those programmes are in "pure" (*khari*) Hindi, while *Chala Ho* uses the language of the village, understood even by every child in the village' (FGD).

The language of broadcast in *Chala Ho* also clearly evokes a sense of pride in local culture and identity. Surender Kumar, an 18-year-old resident of village Harsangra who studied till the ninth standard, emphasised the relevance of the language that sets apart the programme. 'The Akashvani programmes are all in Hindi. Their language and ours are spoken differently. *Chala Ho* is in our local (*dehati*), broken (*tooti-phooti*) language, so we understand it well. Our people are able to participate in the programme because it is in our language' (FGD).

Rajender Oraon, a tribal youth from Purushottampur, said that the formal language of mainstream media is not understood easily by the non-literate, whereas *Chala Ho Gaon Mein* is easily accessible to everyone.

Keshav Ram, a 25-year-old literate man from village Mahe in Panki block, pointed out the importance of local production. 'One major difference between *Chala Ho* and other programmes on radio is that one can never tell whether the other programmes are getting made in the city or the village. *Chala Ho* is our own, local programme. They go from village to village recording news of the village' (FGD).

A young social worker, Rabinder Kumar from village Cheri thinks that the familiarity of the participants in the programme serves as a source of encouragement to others. 'When people you know perform on radio, we also feel encouraged to participate in the programmes. We develop an interest because we relate to them better' (FGD).

Most of the women in the focus groups in the DDS villages in the Medak district of Andhra Pradesh identified with the language of the programmes, and said that they could understand what was being said in the cassettes. Sukkamma points out, 'Ours is villager's language. On the other radio, they will speak Andhra language, for example for she-buffalos they will say *gede*, we will say *barre*, like that.' DDS staff reveals another difference in the programme made by the local people themselves and the conventional radio. 'They will tell us to speak in five minutes about one subject. Our discussions are long and in depth and we discuss problems in a holistic manner, even the nitty-gritty of it.' Tuljamma, an older woman from Pastapur, who owns a radio set added, 'there is also language difference between these two radios. In the government radio they speak "soft" language, which is difficult for us to understand. For that reason we don't feel interested to listen to it because we speak our "rough" language. In our radio the language is similar to ours, so we find it interesting.'

DDS radio relies completely on local talent and indigenous experts for their programmes. If an identified local expert is to be called to the radio station, one of the radio women will simply engage an auto and bring her/him. Women sometimes sing songs that are as long as 20 minutes and deal with issues that they face in their routine lives. The songs are not sung individually. One woman will lead and 10 will sing after her. The songs offer motivation, direction and even solutions to fellow women. Whether it is an old man telling a story of his village or beggars singing folk songs in exchange for minor millets from people, or other forms of folk narrative, items that are recorded for the radio are the ones that are found in their villages. 'Any programme that is done by the radio; it doesn't go for outside experts. We invite people from our villages only and record programmes and they only will listen to them,' says Algole Narsamma (interview).

The residents of Budhikote village in the Kolar district of Karnataka have ample exposure to mainstream media, including the Kannada language newspapers and television. 'Every other house has a television and since they all have cable they hardly watch the national channel,' says Mangala Gowri, the studio manager of *Namma Dhwani*. They also listen to AIR but the women in the focus groups were clear that *Namma Dhwani* is 'different'. 'We ourselves do this, isn't it?' they stated. Geeta K.R., a member of the management committee elaborated, 'This is now our own. Akashvani (AIR) isn't like that. If our village people have the desire to give programmes, can they go to AIR and give? Here, they come freely and give programmes. Even we call them and ask to touch the table, recording system etc. This gives them pleasure. Hence, if it is of the community and for the community, it is better' (FGD).

The women also revealed that after *Namma Dhwani* started, AIR had recorded their programme once for broadcast and given them a date and time, 'If that is missed, we can't listen again. But, it's not like that here. If we want, we can listen four times in a day. Where to go and ask in Akashvani?' The women posed queries like, 'if we go on our own to AIR, will they let us in, so we must have its second form here?' Mangala Gowri offered an explanation:

> We could have gone with AIR but this is our own. We have sent around 20 programmes made by us to AIR, but they select and play. Here, we play a programme in whatever way it is. Another thing is that they play it only once,

> whereas we can play it again and again here. People ask us to replay. The very first day we cablecast, we received a phone call, 'you should speak a bit away from the mike—the sound is too loud'. Now, people come and ask if they can also do a programme on festivals or sing a song. That is how the people have a sense of ownership (interview).

In the discussions with volunteers, they outlined some of the noticeable distinctions between the two radio programmes and what makes them listen to the *Namma Dhwani* programmes on a regular basis. They said that while the 'other' radio gives information about big cities and there is nothing about Budhikote, *Namma Dhwani* talks about 'our problems' that are 'of interest' to them. 'Nobody knows the persons who make programmes or announcements on AIR. But, if a person from the next village speaks, people will listen with interest because they know him. Also, when people do programmes related to their problems themselves, they learn how to solve them.' The women of the Purnima *Mahila Sangha* focus group also identified *Namma Dhwani* programmes as those that represent their realities. The following exchange of comments brings out some of their views:

> Lalita: This radio station is ours because it speaks about us—in our language and in our accent. When I turn it on, I hear the voices of people I know.
>
> Pushpa: Everything in *Namma Dhwani* is ours. We have the children's club; the programmes are all done by our own people and children; about our village, and all these appeal to the people.
>
> Sulochana: People who we don't know speak there [AIR] whereas in *Namma Dhwani*, our own people talk. You see '*Akasha*' means programmes related to the universe come there. Here it is 'our voice' and our own programmes (FGD).

Building Capacities: Awakening Abilities of Self-Expression

Traber argues that mass media marginalise the role of the 'simple man and woman' and foreground the elite and the powerful whereas for alternative media, 'the aim is to change towards a more equitable social, cultural and economic whole in which the individual is not reduced to an object but is able to find fulfilment as a total human being' (Traber, 1985: 3). He divides alternative media into 'advocacy media' and 'grassroots media'. The advocacy media represents alternative social actors including, 'the poor, the oppressed, the marginalised and indeed the ordinary manual labourer, woman, youth and child as the main subjects of [their] news and features' (Traber, 1985: 2). In grassroots media, information and messages are generally produced by the same people whose concerns they represent through direct engagement and participation. The involvement of professionals is only to the extent of enabling 'ordinary people' to produce their own media. Traber's primary concerns are not just the production of information in areas where the mass media do not penetrate, but also to provide a counter to the state-run media. Traber argues when media production is placed in the hands of ordinary people with the help of minimal guidance, they can develop their own news-gathering networks and become confident reporters, writers and editors. This type of information and the manner in which it is presented will be more appropriate and more 'useful' for the communities in which it is produced and distributed.

Such community-based media facilitate access and participation and 'a conviction that the means of communication and expression should be placed in the hands of those people who clearly need to exercise greater control over their immediate environment' (Nigg and Wade, 1980: 7). This ensures a process of internal dialogue in the community, providing opportunities for developing alternative strategies. Enzensberger (1976) maintains that interactivity between audiences and creators, collective production along with a concern with everyday life and ordinary needs of people would make media politically emancipatory. Downing (2001: 45) argues that such media would then perform the dual functions as 'counter-information institutions' and 'agents of developmental power'. Drawing on Benjamin's (1934/1982) idea of 'the author as producer', it may be said that a community radio initiative 'is better the more consumers it is able to turn into producers—that is, readers or spectators [listeners] into collaborators'.

Perhaps the one area that KMVS in the Kutch region of Gujarat could boast most about is its team of 14 community radio reporters and the capacity-building efforts that have enhanced the abilities of these young rural men and women who had negligible exposure to media production before getting involved with the project. During our formal and informal interaction with them, they not only exhibited competence and palpable enthusiasm for their work but also an exhaustive knowledge of the demographic profile, political and social system, history, issues and problems concerning their designated *talukas* and villages.

There are an equal number of men and women reporters, all of whom come from rural background, their level of education ranging from Class four to B.A. They belong to villages within the areas they cover for reporting, and are accountable to their respective *sangathans* at the *taluka* level. Preeti, coordinator of the KMVS community radio initiative, explains that the criteria for selection of a reporter were a certain level of literacy, his/her motivation to work in the social sector and familiarity with Kutch and its rural areas. The men had been pursuing occupations like farming, labour, etc., whereas most of the women had never stepped out to work before joining KMVS as full-time reporters. The women reporters said that they had never interacted with men on a one-on-one basis as colleagues earlier. Most of them whether an unmarried Muslim or Patel woman or a homemaker from a conservative family, had never dreamt of working outside their homes. A woman reporter, moderately literate and abandoned by her husband, has now developed proficiency in scripting and production apart from reporting.

Another married woman Jyoti Ben, 35 years old and a mother of three, confessed that she was an old-fashioned Brahmin and had 'no awareness of the outside world' before joining the KMVS team. She now considers herself 'progressive' and listens regularly to other radio broadcasts, besides the KMVS broadcasts. In terms of training, apart from learning on-job, the reporters have gone through several workshops which not only included a process of conscientisation and confidence building, but also training in technical aspects and the art of seeking information and community participation. They are clear that theirs is a *bhagidari wala radio* (participatory radio) and they as reporters had to go to the people and not like AIR that asks people to come to their studio for recordings all the time. Ahmed, who has completed his education till matriculation and has been associated with KMVS radio project from the time of *Kunjal,* gave details of the training that he and his fellow reporters have undergone.

> We were first given an orientation about the functioning of the developmental groups, especially the philosophy and approach of KMVS and the purpose of the radio programme. We were also given some idea about concepts like

> social justice, human rights and gender issues. After this we attended a workshop to pick up basic recording skills in Ahmedabad. When we started working, we would discuss our problems, doubts, ideas and findings among ourselves and with Drishti Media people when they visited us. There have been periodic training sessions on interviewing, drama direction, investigative journalism and radio production techniques (interview).

Women reporters in their 20s, Bhavana and Geeta said that earlier they were shy and even scared to move out of their homes or to talk to men. Today, with suitable training and field experience they are more open and are not afraid to question *sarkari* (government) officials. They are aware of the functioning of government offices and of their own rights to seek information as *nagrik* (citizens). Men feel they have developed a knack of collecting relevant *mahiti* (information). Habbu, a 22-year-old Dalit reporter declared that now he is not only more aware of the issues around him but has also developed a *drishtikon* (perspective) and the courage to be critical.

For all of the reporters the ability to use equipment for recording, production and to operate computers gives a sense of achievement. Harish Parmar feels that a technology that had been inaccessible to them has now become a part of their daily job and in his words, 'is quite simple to use'. The media team now handles the post-production work in the newly set up studio in the KMVS Bhuj office. The reporters feel empowered in terms of technical know-how and are enthused about their ability to forge solidarities with their community, garner information, talk to the government officials and secure a full-time employment with satisfactory remuneration.

The community radio project started in Jharkhand with AID organising a content development workshop at Lesliganj and gathered volunteers from villages across Lesliganj and Panki blocks, who had been associated with one or the other AID projects in the past. Out of these, 16 community representatives, including four women, were identified to form the core group of the project and were given initial operational training for field recording. Each volunteer was asked to identify two more villages in addition to their native village for which he/she could act as local reporter-cum-project motivator. The volunteers were imparted further training in the techniques of audio presentation and production in two subsequent workshops. Presently, there is a team of 14 community reporters at AID who carry out recordings in the field using portable cassette recorders and help to integrate the community radio initiative with the ground level work of AID.

The reporters constantly assess the acceptability of the programmes among the members of the local communities and encourage them to come out with programme ideas and to participate in production process. As the awareness about *Chala Ho* and the rapport of the reporters with the people grew, many villagers expressed their desire to participate in the community radio initiative and utilise it for social education. Residents of several villages told our research team that there are other basic problems on which episodes of *Chala Ho Gaon Mein* should be made.

Some of the issues they cited as more basic and on which they would like to see more programmes include: roads, water, electricity, land, employment, hunger, poverty, and drought. The programme does touch upon some of these problems occasionally, but it seems like, given the political disquiet generated by Maoist groups in the state, AID is compelled to stay away from contentious issues such as land distribution. An argument between a poor Dalit resident of Goradih Khas village and an AID worker revealed how radical demands for land reform place reformist NGOs in a dilemma. In the focus group at Mahe-Dema, an interesting suggestion was made to broadcast prices for their produce in the local markets. The idea was, as one participant puts it, one could listen to the rates on the Sunday evening programme and take one's produce to the Monday market. Ramcharitrasa, a 55-year-old backward class resident of the same village, drew attention to the need for discussing the problem of middlemen. 'We would like to discuss on radio the problem of middlemen. We never even get to hear about the funds for new facilities that come to the village. The middlemen gobble up all this and the work is also not done properly' (FGD).The fact that many of the people we met during our focus group discussions even came up with an inventory of additional issues on which radio programmes should be made, shows that people have tremendous amount of faith in the medium to solve their problems. They realise that if they could come together as a collective, deliberate on their problems and then make programmes on these issues, the radio would become a stronger and more effective medium. Many felt that concrete benefits would flow from the programme if it were heard by authority figures such as the Block Development Officer, the MLA, or a Minister. They saw the programme as an important tool to reach out to the outside world.

Fourteen-year-old school student, Akanksha Rani of Nawadih village was most enthusiastic about *Chala Ho* and insisted that the programme would motivate people to work for the village.

> When people listen to the programme about the problems of the village, they are inspired to do something for the development of the village. People could then sit together and come up with a plan to tackle the problem. Gradually, our problems could be solved in this fashion (FGD).

VOICES in Karnataka decided to work with MYRADA for its community radio project, as it was looking for a partner that adopts a participatory mode of development, observed Seema Nair, project coordinator for *Namma Dhwani*. When VOICES and MYRADA discussed about community radio as a strong tool for participation in development with the *Sanghas*, people said, 'a radio station of our own, locally is a necessity' as 'our own people will be able to speak' and 'we can make our own programmes that we need here'. At the time when the studio was being constructed, the training of volunteers was taken up simultaneously and 32 men and women belonging to different villages of the Budhikote sector participated in the first training workshop. According to Amaresh, *Namma Dhwani* studio manager, 'Some who did not have interest left and others continued. Five of us locals continued. Once the studio was completed, the community people themselves chose us to run the station with the help of the management committee constituted by the nominated members of the women *Sanghas*.' He further explained that after the studio was operational, volunteers came in large numbers and took training. The members of the *Sanghas* and their children are given first preference.

Mangala Gowri, who also manages the studio along with Surya Prakash and Amaresh added, 'Earlier women used to fear to send their daughters. After we went and talked to them, they have started sending now. They themselves bring them (daughters) here, to give programmes and take them back. Now they all have courage. Since, the women run this, the middle school girls come here during lunch break, also' (interview).

Shilpa, a 16-year-old student of Class X and her friends Madhavi and Lakshmi visit *Namma Dhwani* studio regularly to participate in the making of the programmes and feel that it is a place that gives them opportunity to 'learn and to gain courage':

> It is for us to learn. We can come here without any fear. We can learn to talk, sing our songs, tell stories and also learn computers. Namma Dhwani has been started so that we get courage. When we tell other girls also to join us, they are afraid and think—what would they say? What would they do? It is fear, isn't it? When we tell them that we are taught many things here, they come (FGD).

The women in the focus groups talked of the days when they would go to the meetings of the *Sanghas* and 'simply listen to some of the members and come back'. But after *Namma Dhwani* started and they learnt how to give programmes, 'we could learn whenever we had time, or holiday', they now speak confidently in meetings also. 'We had skills. But we did not know how to let them out. *Namma Dhwani* has created a way for us to let out our skills and to speak out our minds.'

In the context of the DDS radio project, Satheesh declares, 'The people themselves do it all'; 'In terms of their capability to use their language—it's a very, very strong oral culture—they can express themselves brilliantly'. He feels that with bare minimum formal training, radio technology enables people to articulate themselves without having to look for outside mediators. At the time of writing the book, there were two women managing the DDS radio station. They have been part of the DDS family for a number of years. Algole was part of DDS as a small child studying in *balwadi*. She was selected to work in radio as she was articulate, while 'General' was chosen for her ability to think and analyse issues deeply. Both of them were given very basic training in radio production. According to Satheesh, 'I don't think, in all their career in radio, last five–six years, they have had more than ten days of training, in all spaced over the first year or two and some specialised sessions later.'

'General' recalls,

> When the foundation was laid for radio station and I was asked to work there, I thought I am not fit to work in Radio. In the beginning, I was afraid to touch the big machines since they are so delicate. Almost for one year I used to be afraid that if I touched the machine, something might happen, I may spoil it. Now I am not afraid and use them freely. I am confident of getting them repaired also if there is any damage. We did not know how to operate a tape recorder before, now I am picking up editing on computer also (interview).

Algole remembers that first she was told how to use a tape recorder and where the buttons were for recording, and the stop button and simple things like putting a cassette into a recorder, and to take it out. Then she learnt how to look at various meters, how to measure the audio that is coming in, how to avoid the wind noises, what are the kind of microphones that are in use, how to hold the microphone, how to use the microphone in large meetings, and things like that. Eventually, in the studio she was explained the use of a 16-channel mixer and faders. The women also refined their skill of asking questions, dialogue delivery and script writing through interactions with resource persons who visited them for short durations. Satheesh is very apprehensive about what is now seen as a training manual for community radio, especially the ones prepared by those who neither have an idea of community nor the kind of new expressions that the community can build for itself. He narrates his experience at a consultation workshop on 'ICTs for Women' that he had attended at IGNOU, New Delhi:

> Someone was explaining how he or she was involved in working with rural women and had given them radio training. We asked, what is the training that you give? They said that when women come to the studio, they talk a lot. We trained them, how to talk for short period. I was absolutely stunned. I think, the whole character of community radio is that, it's a very different kind of articulation, it's a different kind of oral culture, it's a different kind of expression. And if you curb that, then you have completely contained that culture. That is the reason we are worried about sending our women for the so-called radio training where they are taught how to capsule and manipulate their expressions (interview).

DDS has therefore engaged in training the women to handle the hardware and then they are completely left to start using the radio. The concept is to provide them with a tremendous amount of flexibility so that their ideas about how to use the radio are not manipulated. Otherwise they will 'only become copy cats of the larger broadcast medium instead of thinking about and discovering their media for themselves'.

Building Solidarities: Putting the Community First

Alternative media as a vehicle of participatory democracy and a resource for community development help local populations to reconnect with the civic and cultural life of their communities. In the face of a nexus between the national government and the corporates to control commercial and political power, community media are key to creating a strong, socially responsible civil society and to promote local democracy. Many scholars have noted that involvement in alternative media production can be politically empowering for participants (Atton, 2002; Downing, 2001). In contrast to mainstream media, which consistently have been found to exclude the voices of ordinary citizens, alternative media offer spaces that broaden the scope of public debate by introducing topics and participants generally excluded by mainstream media. Streitmatter (2001) argues that alternative media have the potential to serve as conduits for the political agendas and have helped ignite social movements through their advocacy of various disenfranchised social groups. Culturally and politically, such media may thus be considered as 'oppositional' in intent, as their 'information for action' has social change at their heart (Atton, 2001b: 6). This harmonises with Williams' (1983: 250) optimism that the culture of the new social movements, while being termed an 'alternative' culture, was 'at its best ... always an oppositional culture' (as cited in Atton, 2001b: 16).

During our field trips, we asked why people would want to listen to the programme even when their own village and its problems do not always figure prominently. While people were eager to have the problems of their village being represented in the programme, they offered a much broader understanding of the functions of a radio programme such as *Chala Ho Gaon Mein*. The following exchange among members of the focus group at Mahe-Dema reveals their hope that the programme can help forge some kind of solidarity among the marginalised sections.

> Keshav Ram: Even if there is no benefit to our village, other villages in the neighbourhood are gaining something from the programme. At least it is the poor somewhere who are getting benefited.
>
> Loki Mahato: When we hear on the radio that another village's problems have been solved, we will also make an effort to do something about our own situation.
>
> Tilak Singh: We hope that when someone else could develop, so will we. We feel happy that some development is taking place somewhere (FGD).

In order to assess what people are deriving from the programme, beyond the tangible benefits, we asked all the focus groups, 'How would you feel if this programme is stopped from next week? What difference does it make to your lives?' Apart from those who reacted with utter disbelief at the suggestion, responses ranged from the more philosophical to those who felt it would stop all development in the area. Shashikant Mahato, a 22-year-old visually impaired man in village Pipra, thought that the programme promoted an atmosphere of debate and discussion on important issues, such as illiteracy and child marriage. In his words, the programme has 'brought light to those who have been living in darkness' (*andhkar mein jo log rahte hain, unko prakash milta hai*).

Fifty-six-year old Jogeshwar Singh, a small farmer in village Dema, retorted angrily to our hypothetical question. 'Close down the programme, no problem. If the programme is coming today, we listen. If that were stopped, we would not even come to know what's happening outside' (FGD).

Radhakrishna Oraon, a 25-year-old teacher in AID's non-formal school from Purushottampur, predicted dire consequences if the programme were to be stopped.

> It will certainly make a lot of difference. Word does not reach from one village to the other. Society will remain just the same—poverty and unemployment. We eagerly wait for the programme every week. We like it. If you stop broadcasting this programme, our villages will become weaker. People gain some experience from listening to the programme, there is some influence (FGD).

Sixty-year-old Lokì Mahato of Mahe was confident that the programme has had a positive effect on the lives of the people. 'When all of Jharkhand listens to us, including the minister and the MLA, everyone will come to know that the people of our village are now awakened. Through radio, we started understanding each other's problems better and we started tackling them together. We got new strength' (FGD).

An educated young man, Ajay Kumar in village Cheri called *Chala Ho* 'a tonic' for the people in the region. Prakash Narayan, one of the community reporters for the programme, suggested that one of the significant gains from *Chala Ho* is the coming out of women from their homes to participate in public life. This view finds its echo in the opinion expressed by 21-year-old Sanjukta Devi, who is an active member of a self-help group in village Cheri. 'We women were earlier very inhibited. When the men used to sit outside for discussions, we used to sit inside. Today, after this programme, we feel we too have a voice and are confident to come out of the house to even take part in processions' (FGD).

The *Ujjas* radio programmes' popularity in the Kutch region is to a large extent because of its focus on locally relevant issues. The community reporters of KMVS travel in and around the villages, carrying back with them reports of local problems and developments, folk songs and folk tales from the region, and record plays on local issues with performers from the villages. When broadcast, these issues strike a chord in the listener invoking instant recognition of familiar names and places and forging solidarity among those placed in a similar socio-economic situation. 'Also, because it talks about our daily problems and issues—*Hamari baat radio par aati hai.*' The community reporters say that it is their responsibility to highlight people's problems at the village level and help give a voice to the marginalised. The programmes of KMVS use local folklore, legends, music and characters to voice silenced cultures and to stoke up a debate between tradition and modernity. The programme, they add, is also aimed at giving opportunities for suppressed artistic talent (*dabe hue kalakar*).

The space for the rural poor within public media is consistently shrinking and the private media have always been oriented towards urban, young, rich people and the elite. DDS people, therefore, gradually started looking at autonomous media that would be rooted in the ground realities of the region, so that people can identify with its content. Pushpalata, a 40-year-old single woman from Pastapur puts it succinctly:

> We want to talk about *Saama* and *Sajja* (some minor grains). We are always talking about marginalised grains, marginalised people, marginalised language and marginalised issues. This does not interest the mainstream radio. This is the reason we should have our own radio to allow us to discuss our issues (FGD).

The 36-year-old *karyakarta* (active member) of the Bidekanne *sangam*, Samamma, pointed out definite advantages of 'our radio' over the 'government' radio in terms of local appeal:

> They talk about issues happening in our country, which we do not listen to so often, where as our radio talks about our problems, our difficulties, our agriculture, our development. We make these cassettes, so we find them very interesting. We have got special affection towards this radio, because the

> people who talk in it belong to our villages, our community. We feel very happy when we hear familiar voices. We often discuss with each other about that. The people of our village feel proud about the people who talk in it (FGD).

In the focus groups where we had assembled the radio committee of DDS, the members said that their radio programmes always covered issues that touched the lives of the people directly and came out with several examples. Machnoor Raju said that there are programmes 'about festivals, about Dalits, poor people, and divorced women, about women who are away from their husbands due to quarrel and about farmers when there are no rains and no crops, or if the crop of a farmer gets damaged because of excess rainwater.'

When we made a suggestion that the government could be persuaded to open a radio station here that could help preserve their language, culture and talk about their issues, a 28-year-old Dalit woman, Metlakunta Susilamma, reacted:

> We can't accept government radio. It becomes their propaganda tool. They will go to a village and say we have given so many buffaloes in this village; we have given so much land in this village... that radio will not allow poor women to dialogue on their own problems and issues. Our radio helps us in our own analysis of our experiences and our problems (FGD).

Algole Narsamma pointed out the difference between their and mainstream radio. 'Mostly they will advertise on fertilisers, pesticides or Colgate paste or on soaps. We will do the programmes that will be useful for the poor. We will take poor people, village people, but they will go for educated people' (interview).

'General' Narsamma elaborated further:

> Those programmes are meant for only big farmers—how much fertiliser to put; how much DAP to mix; which pesticide to use—what we are doing is only for small farmers. How much organic manure you have; when to breed cattle; where to buy the seeds; And how to store them. We will explain about the crops which will give good strength like *jowar, korra*, etc. How our people are using hybrid food grains and facing health problems; how people should send their children to school—all this is useful to the public and for me also (interview).

The popularity of *Namma Dhwani* in Budhikote, Karnataka may be gauged from the fact that people in the villages surrounding Budhikote also wish to be connected through cable to access its programmes. Several volunteers, who assist in the production of programmes and in covering local events, belong to the villages of the larger Budhikote sector. They are unable to listen to the programmes and are hoping that the license to broadcast would be given soon for the sake of other villages.

Twenty-three-year-old Hamesh, a volunteer from Linkaldurga village, says, 'When we see things here [Budhikote village], we feel that what all is happening is good. But how will the people in the other villages know? We know that *Namma Dhwani* hasn't got the permission, but then what about the other villagers? There has to be some way to give them access also.' His associate Baithapa from Kotur village adds, 'We are not doing this for our own sake, but from the point of view of the people. We are doing this so that the surrounding areas and we ourselves can improve' (FGD).

Women in all focus groups in Budhikote village were keen to see all-round prosperity in their village and considered *sanghas* as a means to prosper and to 'stretch out our hands for those who are relatively more poor and underprivileged.' The women informed that there are various castes and sub-castes in the village. There are people belonging to both scheduled caste (SC) and scheduled tribe in the village. The Ambedkar (SC/Dalit) colony is separate, at a distance of 1 km. From the discussions with the management committee it was clear that Dalit women too have joined the *sanghas*. The members said that after they had joined the *sanghas*, people sit and talk with them. 'Earlier they weren't admitted inside the compound. Now they are. Though they can't enter the house they have got the chance to come till the door.' The Muslims are treated at par but the backward caste people are still singled out in several ways. 'It will change slowly,' the women said and acknowledged that *Namma Dhwani* was promoting this change by providing open access to 'all kinds of people—there is no discrimination here.'

Twenty-six-year old vegetable vendor Triveni, a member of the management committee said,

> They also have a chance of progressing and associating with members of other *sanghas*. If they prosper, there's no problem in that—they too must have the chance—if we move up and leave them there, it will not be good. We are all the children of one mother, humanity. *Namma Dhwani* provides a means for all *sanghas* to come together—otherwise, you live to yourselves and we live to ourselves (FGD).

Forging Subaltern Counterpublics

Community radio may thus be seen as providing to the marginalised an arena, outside the state apparatus, that may be used as a potent instrument for democratic deliberations and negotiations. Such an institutionalised space for discursive interaction and for political participation through the medium of talk could be looked at as an alternative post-bourgeois model of public sphere that Habermas (1962; translation: 1989) stops short of developing in *The Structural Transformation of the Public Sphere*.

While Habermas' idea of the public sphere is indispensable to the understanding of democratic political practices, certain assumptions underlying the concept are problematic. His assumptions that proliferation of other forms of public discourse and activity necessarily weakens the democratic attributes of the single all-inclusive public sphere or that it is possible for interlocutors in a public sphere to bracket status differentials and deliberate as if they are social equals are farfetched in stratified societies. Also, his bourgeois conception of the public sphere stresses its claim to be open and accessible to all but in practice women of all classes and ethnicities were excluded from official political participation on the basis of gender status, while plebeian men were formally excluded by property qualification.

Fraser (1992) critiques the singularity of Habermas' public sphere and argues that arrangements that accommodate contestations among a plurality of competing publics better promote the ideal of participatory parity than does a single, comprehensive overarching public. She claims that such a public sphere tends to operate to the advantage of dominant groups and renders subordinate social groups less able to articulate and defend their interests. She proposes the forging of what she calls *subaltern counterpublics*, spheres parallel to that of the dominant social category where 'members of subordinate social groups invent and circulate counter discourses to formulate oppositional interpretations of their identities, interests and needs' (Fraser, 1992:123). She claims that subaltern counterpublics on the one hand, function as spaces of withdrawal and regroupment; and on the other they also function as bases and training grounds for agitational activities directed towards wider publics. This dialectic enables subaltern counterpublics partially to offset, although not wholly to eradicate, the unjust participatory privileges enjoyed by members of dominant social groups.

Our analysis of community radio initiatives suggests that they offer to people opportunities to debate issues and events of common concern and to set counter-hegemonic agendas. Such forging of subaltern counterpublics through a process of shifting control of media technologies to those excluded and marginalised from the dominant public sphere helps expand the discursive space, which could eventually facilitate collective action and offer a realistic emancipatory potential.

Note

1. Representatives of governments, international and regional organisations, civil society and the private sector attended the second phase of the UN-convened World Summit on the Information Society (WSIS) held in Tunis from 16–18 November 2005. The agenda was to promote people's access to and use of information and knowledge for human development.

7 COMMUNITY RADIO FOR EMPOWERMENT

The Gender Dimension

Participatory communication for development envisages, among other things, democratised and decentralised media systems as key agents of empowerment for those who have traditionally been marginalised socially, culturally, economically and politically. Feminist activists and women's movements have argued that the conventional ideology of male superiority and the control of productive resources by men have affected women's options and opportunities for a better life. 'Gender Equality and Empowerment of Women' is one of the core *Millennium Development Goals* stated in the *Millennium Declaration* adopted by all 189 member states of the UN General Assembly in 2000. Gender is a significant dimension in community radio initiatives launched by community-based organisations that are seeking to deploy communication technologies for social change in general and empowerment of women in particular. As is evident from the profiles of the non-governmental organisation (NGO) initiatives (see Chapter 4), three of the four community radio projects under study carry out their developmental activities through women-only collectives/self-help groups (SHGs).

Women in these organisations use community radio to talk about their issues and concerns and to augment their own developmental activities. Community radio helps to build the capacities of discursive interaction of women for collective action and also their media competencies. Equipped with the confidence that their voices and lived experiences would not be disregarded, more and more women are participating in producing programmes that are locally relevant and gender sensitive. Through a comprehensive analysis of the data we have collected from focus group discussions and interviews with women engaged in community radio production and reception, this chapter attempts to reflect on women's involvement at various stages of the project, their participation in the programmes and enhancement in their capabilities to communicate and develop messages. Some of the questions to which answers were sought from field experiences include:

(*a*) Are women engaging actively in critical reception of community radio programmes?
(*b*) To what extent is women's participation discernible in the various stages of the initiative? Do women's issues and their ideas get transformed into radio programmes? What is the media competency among women?
(*c*) Have community-driven media initiatives helped in creating new mediated discourses that amplify the voices and concerns of marginalised rural women and serve as a platform for expression of alternative development strategies?
(*d*) How and to what extent are women in grassroots communication creating avenues for democratic communication and fostering social change? What role is communication playing in activating women's alternatives to support their social struggles?

The chapter begins by examining the intersections of development frameworks and feminist theorising, and how they have been influenced by debates and critiques of globalisation. The two main feminist development frameworks—Women in Development (WID) and Gender and Development (GAD)—are analysed to highlight the gender mainstreaming practices stirred by them, especially those that address issues of regional and cultural differences. The relationship, paradoxes and synergies among the discourses originating in development, feminist and communication scholarships offer insights into a new agenda for empowerment of women, which is discussed in part two of the chapter in the form of a typology of women's participation in communication for social change. This conceptual framework was derived from two powerful movements, of gender and of participation, that have generated major implications for the role of communication in transforming the rhetoric of local-level development into reality. This is then applied to analyse gender as an analytical category in the case studies of community radio initiatives at the grassroots level.

The third section looks at women in community radio initiatives as conventional receivers of programmes to determine if media has reinforced the crucial objective of generating a process of conscientisation among rural women. The next two sections discuss the degree of participation of women in programme production taking into consideration how the recent approaches to development have moved away from their preoccupation with top–down economic growth and towards social and participatory development practices that are more inclusive. The aim of these approaches seems to be enlargement of people's choices and human capabilities. The subsequent section probes the manner in which management, control and ownership of media technologies by community (SHGs) of marginalised women has provided rural women access to representation and decision-making in the practice of participatory development. The concluding section reviews the extent to which community radio has initiated or furthered the process of transformation of power relationships at the village level and helped in activating women's alternatives for fostering social change by forging gendered *subaltern counterpublics.*

GENDER AND DEVELOPMENT: THEORETICAL PERSPECTIVES

'Look at the world through women's eyes,' proclaimed a poster at the venue of the Fourth World Conference on Women held in Beijing in September 1995. In the context of development, this is an indispensable tenet today, as it calls for redefining the existing approaches to development and making them gender responsive. The *Beijing Declaration* as well as the *Platform for Action* (1995) and the *Outcome Document* (2000) adopted by the UN General Assembly Session on Gender Equality, Development and Peace for the twenty-first century, have identified several critical areas that must be addressed for achieving the advancement and empowerment of women. These include:

- unequal access to education and training;
- violence against women;
- violation of the rights of the girl child;

- inequality in access to economic resources;
- inequality between men and women in the sharing of power and decision-making at all levels; and
- inequality in women's access to and participation in all communication systems, especially in the media.

Although in the past decades, the status of women has improved in some important respects, there still exist major barriers of inequality that hinder women's participation in the decision-making processes, their access to key resources and sharing of power. Unless a feminist perspective is unambiguously integrated in the design, implementation, monitoring and evaluation of all existing and prospective development initiatives, their outcome will rarely enhance gender equality or lead to empowerment of women. A sustained effort by feminist activists and theorists, women's movements and poor women's grassroots organisations to mainstream gender in development discourses has contributed significantly to challenging oppressive structures of patriarchy, introducing alternative practices and redefining the goals of development (Abbot, 1997; Singha Roy, 2001).

Until the end of the 60s, the role of women in development projects of modernisation was limited to being recipients of welfare and development messages. They were considered reproducers, while men, who were identified as producers, were given access to information, training, technology, credit and decision-making. This exclusion along with the sex-role stereotyping and patriarchal biases led to women's increased marginalisation as the 'benefits' of development never 'trickled down' to reach them. Ester Boserup's book, *Women's Role in Economic Development* (1970) highlighted how the development planners and policymakers had failed to acknowledge the productive roles performed by women especially in agriculture and to involve women in development activities as contributors to the economy. This resulted, in the mid-70s, in women getting increased attention globally through the Women in Development (WID) project (Blumberg, 1989; Melkote and Steeves, 2001). Women in Development sought to provide greater visibility to the role of women in development and several agencies worked to secure the benefits of modernisation for them by integrating women into the mainstream of economic development through limited, stereotypical, 'traditional' work roles (Bhasin, 2000; Humble, 1998).

The WID approach was criticised by feminist theorists for subscribing to the dominant modernisation and Marxist models and failing to question structures of patriarchy that limited women's access to resources and power (Humble, 1998; Melkote and Steeves, 2001). The liberal conception of the public–private dichotomy that views the household as being isolated in the 'private' sphere and distinct from the public sphere of market economy was challenged. It was pointed out that the gender-blind categories of conventional economic development excluded household work, caretaker roles, childbearing and childrearing from the purview of productivity (Knobloch, 2002; Verma, 2004). 'An unequal division of labour within the family presents obstacles to women in their lives outside the family; and these inequalities are often supported by social traditions and expectations' (Nussbaum, 1992: 3–12). The role of the 'universal caregiver' and the 'invisible' work meant solely for household consumption restricts the full-wage work opportunities available to women outside and sustain the notion that women are dependents. This curbs women's entitlements to land, credit and control over physical resources (Knobloch, 2002; Verma, 2004).

Feminist interventions also contested the contentions of the WID advocates that women's participation in labour force and enhancement of their 'productive' potential is a necessary condition for improving their social status. The dominant development theories assumed that higher productivity and improved standards of living would resolve individual conflicts over resources (Parpart et al, 2000; Verma, 2004). These theories, preoccupied with economic growth, failed to acknowledge that the factors determining women's status might be culturally specific and related to traditional work roles. An analysis of the internal economy of the household, the sexual division of labour within it and the hierarchical relations that it generates between members of the household was deemed essential to understand the implications of domestic economy for the distribution of benefits and burdens of development (Blumberg, 1989; Verma, 2004).

Feminist activists and women's movements in the developing world also questioned the hegemonic Western feminist theories and their universal definition of modernity that was central to liberal feminism. They objected to the WID approach as it ignored the issue of cultural relativism. They called for dismissing value judgements about traditions by the West and developing sensitivity to distinctive worldviews and the complex material and multi-layered cultural realities of women in the non-Western world (Parpart et al., 2000). Depicting 'Third World' women as a homogenous group of acknowledged victims of oppressive norms was contested as it misrepresented the lived experiences of women in specific socio-cultural and local/regional contexts. Feminist scholars in the Third World pointed out that while the ethical universalism of Western feminist theories of justice had suitably condemned gender-based dominations and obsolete customs that subject women to physical and mental abuse, the ideology of possessive individualism of the women's rights approach totally overlooked the cultural membership of women in their community (Verma, 2004). This has led to adverse consequences especially for women from poor and rural households because of their dependence on village commons—forests, pastures, *gram-sabha* lands for basic necessities (Agarwal, 1997). It was proposed that without falling into the trap of idealisation of tradition and blindness to local power structures, an alternative set of theories must focus on human-centred development that recognises the centrality of women and nature, respects indigenous knowledge systems and gives people greater access to and control over their natural resources (Shiva, 1988; Verma, 2004).

The mid-80s thus saw Gender and Development (GAD) approach questioning the prevailing socio-cultural, economic and political structures that generated and underpinned a disadvantageous status for women relative to men. The focus of this empowerment agenda was not on women alone, but on relationships between women and men. The GAD framework emerged from the grassroots experiences and writings of Third World feminists and was articulated lucidly by Development Alternatives with Women for a New Era (DAWN), formally launched at the 1985 Nairobi international NGO forum (held parallel to the official World Conference on Women) (Parpart et al., 2000). The GAD theory recognised that both the ideology of male superiority (patriarchal ideology) and the control of material and productive resources by men at the global, national, community and household levels have affected women's options and opportunities for a better life (Humble, 1998; Melkote and Steeves, 2001) An urgent need to redefine socially constructed gender patterns in the three spheres—economy, home and the community—and to redress power imbalances in gender relations was articulated by women's movements.

Women experience oppression differently, according to their class, caste, colonial history, culture and position in the global economies (Moser, 1993). Third World scholars stressed the need to adopt a more democratic and pluralistic approach to women's issues and on the need to ground solutions to women's problems in the spatially and culturally specific realities and experiences of women. This focus on context and on recovering women's silenced voices and knowledge resulted in an increasing importance of identity and difference (Parpart et al., 2000). Feminist critiques of development asked for the use of women's experience as a resource for any programmes or policies that fundamentally affect their lives and stressed that knowledge based mainly on male experience represents a partial and distorted perception of reality. The GAD scholars and activists thus emphasised that while gender-sensitive policies must be specific to the country, region and locality, they must also reflect an understanding that the needs and interests of women and men who belong to the same country, caste, and/or social class may also be in conflict with each other, despite their intersecting life experiences (Kabeer, 1994).

Gender, Media and Participatory Development

During the past two decades, concepts like 'participation', 'community-based action', 'empowerment' and their varied interpretations have also been transforming the discourses, frameworks and practices of development (Chambers, 1997; Gujit and Shah, 1998; Cornwall, 2000; Parpart et al., 2000). In the context of globalisation and resurgence of grassroots movements, conventional development strategies are giving way to more participatory approaches that are recognising the involvement of those who have suffered systematic and systemic inequalities and deprivations as 'partners' in development. The two powerful movements of gender and of participation are seeking to appropriate communication avenues, and specifically media for the advancement and empowerment of women especially at the grassroots level.

There is an increasing consensus amongst communication and feminist scholars and organisations that media and new technologies of communication informed by a gender perspective have an immense potential to strategically promote agendas that advance the status of women in society and support women's empowerment. They can be harnessed as indispensable tools for reversal of women's marginalisation by generating spaces for expression of women's issues; dissemination and exchange of authentic information and images about women; enhancing women's equal participation in civil and public life; activating women's representation in development; and facilitating women's alternatives for designing solidarity campaigns and collaborative actions for their own futures.

Riaño (1994b) argues that feminist scholars and media campaigners have in the last two decades raised issues of lack of women's representation in communication channels, including news and current affairs and of sexist portrayal of women in mainstream media. They have also highlighted the disadvantageous position of women with respect to access and control of communication technologies. Feminist works in communication studies have confirmed that women's role as 'communicative subjects and producers of communication' is still being disregarded in mainstream media. She further indicates that all these demands for women's equity in representation and against negative portrayal have not been met with far-reaching changes in communication policy or the structures of media industries. The situation has worsened due to the unrestricted operations of transnational media enterprises.

But Riaño and a growing school of scholars and practitioners feel that the gender specialists attending international conferences and focusing on publications and presentations have ignored the contribution being made to democratisation of communication by women's social movements that are involved in building new communication alternatives for change at the grassroots level (Nair and White, 1987; Kidd, 1992; Riaño, 1994; Gujit and Shah, 1998).

Riaño (1994a) provides a typology of women's participation in communication based on various analytical frameworks that address the relationship among women, participation and communication (see Table 7.1). This typology identifies the principles and approaches of four basic frameworks, i.e., development communication (women as subjects of information); participatory communication (women as participants); alternative communication (women as subjects of change); and feminist communication (women as producers of meaning). Riaño clarifies that while all these types of communication have been used by women's groups to achieve their development goals,

Table 7.1: ***Typology of Women, Participation and Communication***

Type	*Perception of Women*	*Objectives*	*Societal Context*	*Participation*	*Empowerment*	*Communication Process*
Development Communication	as subjects of information originating from outside the control of the community	to encourage women to change certain key practices, elicit active support, mobilise community	national/ international development projects; development -support communication agenda, extension work, social marketing	defined as cooperation with planners, administrators and power elites, and a willingness to adopt new ways, feedback	little scope for strategies aimed at empowering people to control the programmes; through acquiring information	one way; people do not use communication equipment or formulate messages, media act as loudspeakers to reinforce project messages
Participatory Communication	as participants in development, leading to self-reliance	to enable women to take control of their own lives, develop confidence through learning, encourage socio-cultural change, influence public policies	critique of diffusionist and one-way models of development, participatory approaches to development, policy making	practiced as transaction between receivers and information source	process through which individuals acquire knowledge, and skills to take control of their lives, capacity to benefit from involvement	interface of top-down and bottom-up information flow; participatory message development
Alternative Communication	as subjects of struggle and	to support social struggles, awaken	development of alternatives to	viewed both as a dimension of and	developing individual	multidimensional, cyclical flow of

	change	women's consciousness to their subordination, advocate and defend rights, promote group reflection and popular communication	commercial media and to one-way communication system, social movements	a condition for social change, a measure of control over the process of development	and collective capacities to struggle for rights and impact change	messages, alternative communication strategies based on community access to media production and decision making
Feminist Communication	as producers of meaning	to speak about gender, race, class and other oppressions, negotiate fair representations and equal participation, build identity, produce alternative meanings	feminist politics and advocacy; formation of independent women's communication networks, grassroots communication alternatives	conceived as ownership, inclusion and accountability that acknowledges differences of race, gender, class, and sexual orientation, identity articulation	involves the transformation of women as social subjects of struggle and as active producers of meaning, breaking silence	communication as exchange, networks of meanings and development of messages as a project of naming their own experiences and identities

Source: Adapted from Riaño, 1994a.

development communication and, to some extent, participatory communication frameworks seek consent and support and are adopted by the state and development institutions. Alternative communication and feminist communication identify with social movements and respond to the logic of social projects that seek out shared reality and new culture for all aspects of life (Riaño, 1994a).

Riaño's typology takes into account distinct interpretations of 'participation' and the differences in 'perceptions of women', 'goals', 'societal contexts' and conceptions of 'empowerment' that distinguish each of the four frameworks and introduce us to the message development processes in the four types of communication. We have used this typology here as a reference framework to connect our empirical work of community radio case studies with the discourses originating in development, communication and feminist scholarship. This is done with a view to evaluate, from a gender perspective, the various communication approaches that are being adopted at different stages in the grassroots initiatives.

Community Radio and Women: The Listening Context

Before attempting to analyse the participatory, alternative and feminist communication features of community radio initiatives, this section first looks at women as receivers of community radio programmes. This development communication viewpoint seeks to bring out the different kinds of communication practices and media that women are exposed/used to that influence their listenership of community radio programmes, which are produced by people of their own community and are a representation of local expression and culture. AID and KMVS community radio programmes are aired through the local All India Radio station on fixed days and at a particular time. The habit of group listening by men, with friends or neighbours, as well as the domestic division of labour ensures that women rarely get an environment conducive for listening to radio at home. As a result, many women said that they listen to the community radio broadcast while cooking—'*roti banate hue sunte hain*', and are therefore not able to listen to the programmes attentively (*dhyan se nahi sun paate*). Many women said that even if they do listen, they forget what was said—'*yaad nahin rahata'*, some attributing it to the fact that they are uneducated. During the focus group discussions it was obvious that this has not only affected their ability to recall the content of the programme, but also rendered them incapable of stating any benefits from the programmes. Women wish to be regular radio listeners, and do listen to radio 'when men are not around', the preferences of programmes being *bhajans* and folk songs. One woman said that they would start listening only when there is some benefit (*faida*) to the village.

Fifteen-year-old Rukiya studying in KMVS school in the border village of Hajipir said that she had never listened to radio till *Kunjal* started, 'but I cannot remember anything after the programme is over'. Her friend, sitting next to her remarked, '*Humare ghar mein TV hai to radio kaun sune'*—we have TV at home, why will I listen to radio? Women do not have access to radio as they do not get time from work and men take the radio set outside the house to listen with friends. Chatni Devi, a 50-year-old agricultural labourer of Kundari village in Lesliganj block, said, 'We have FM radio at home. I try to listen to *Chala Ho* every Sunday. But I can only listen while doing housework. When my husband or his brother takes the radio outside the house, I can't listen' (FGD).

Kunti Devi of Bhalmanda and Biphni Devi of Chandaigir village in Palamau, among many other women, echoed this problem. Thirty-year-old Malti Devi, member of a recently formed self-help group in Chandaigir, explained, 'We have a radio at home, which can receive FM. But I don't get to listen much because the younger brothers of my husband keep taking the radio set outside the house to listen with their friends. I listen sometimes, but I have so much work that I can't listen with concentration' (FGD).

The women in the Jhumara village of Kutch are preoccupied with the fate of their animals because of continuous droughts in the area and are tensed up that their men have to go long-distances and even migrate to look for work. When Mohammad Yakuf, who has been given a radio by KMVS, invites them to listen to the programme, they sometimes get very irritated. Those like the 30-year-old Amina Bai, who do go to listen to the programme sometimes, comments: 'I normally don't sit to listen to radio. If I sit, only then I will listen. I don't get time, I have to look after children, go to get fodder for the cattle, it is not easy to find, and animals are dying. When I listen also, I cannot understand anything, so why should I listen' (FGD).

There are exceptions to the above cases among women who are keenly involved in *mahila mandal* or *sangathan* activities or those who have participated either in the programmes or in the panchayats. Many women interviewed for the study felt that women's groups or collectives in the village provide a more conducive environment for reception of radio. In DDS villages, the supervisors of the women *sangams* carry audiotapes of programmes produced by their women and play it on the cassette players in the monthly meeting. This listening session is followed by discussions and the feedback is carried back to the radio committee, which then takes necessary action to produce new content and improve programming. Women in the DDS village Raipally find those programmes useful that give information specific to their agricultural needs and about indigenous knowledge systems, health and hygiene, food security, gender justice and the narrative traditions of song and drama. Manayama, a Dalit woman in her early 40s explains, 'We are illiterate and poor people. We cannot follow writing material. We thought it is better to listen to these programmes and learn more about issues that affect our lives so intimately.'

Fifty-year-old Dalit, non-literate woman, Sunderamma of Kalimela village not only identifies with the programmes about crop and bio-fertilizers in 'our cassettes', but also finds the 'other radio' gives them only film songs. She looks forward to the cassette that the *sangam* supervisor brings to the meeting 'sometimes'.

> We like to listen to whatever Tukaram brings and plays. In the 'other' radio we understand some, and some we don't understand. Who will keep the work aside and sit to listen to that radio? For example, we are cleaning our utensils and the radio starts. We keep doing our cooking and the radio starts. Radio programmes will come once only, no replay facility. This one we hear whenever we want to hear. That one will come and go and we will not come to know (FGD).

Nagamma, a 28-year-old Dalit Christian belonging to one of the oldest and more organised *sangams* in Pastapur village explains,

> Manjula brings cassette exclusively for us and keeps tape recorder among the group. There will be announcement that we are going to listen to so and so programme and no one should make noise. We maintain silence, and lend our ears to it. This is easily understandable, this is our language and our words, and so we can understand it. Those [radio] are difficult words. We like this one (cassette) only.

Thirty-five-year-old, expressive and enthusiastic woman *sarpanch* of Mohaldi village of Abdasa *taluka*, Hawa Bai endorses that she has obtained useful '*jankari*' (information) from the KMVS programmes.

> We all wait for this programme, gather together and listen to it. Some women in my village started listening to radio only after this programme was started. I make my daughter's to write letters and send feedback to the programme. I am illiterate but I have come to know about panchayat and about our own history. I get *jankari* (information) from radio only (FGD).

Some active *sangha* members contended that by talking about the progress they have made through *sanghas* on *Namma Dhwani,* they would be able to motivate more women to join these self-help groups. They explained that this motivation could come, 'if we make programmes about how women have saved money and increased the number of their goats from one to ten or prospered economically by selling milk.' Usha Rani, a 33-year-old woman, who has been a member of the Shalini *sangha* for the past six years, had an interesting version of her listening experience.

> In my house my husband says, 'What is that you always want *Namma Dhwani*? All your interest is in it. Put some film or other programme.' But, I don't put anything other than *Namma Dhwani* till it finishes. I tell him, 'Look! This is for just half an hour and the programmes are all very useful for us. They tell us about doctors, diseases, schemes and what to do when. You can watch songs and films anytime later' (FGD).

At Rajhara village in Jharkhand, after we finished our focus group discussion with older tribal men, we ran into Sonamati, an articulate middle-aged woman, who was involved in *van samitis* (forest protection committees) and *mahila sangathans* (women's collectives). She was enthusiastic and articulate about the role of the radio programme in various development efforts in the region. She represented for us the potential for building participation of women in radio production where there was some amount of prior mobilisation and conscientisation of women.

Older women seemed alienated from the radio programme while younger women in Jharkhand demonstrated a high recall and were eloquent about *Chala Ho Gaon Mein* and its benefits. Kamala Devi, who joined the discussion at Kundari towards the end, demonstrated a high recall of at least two different radio dramas, one of which was about the dowry problem and the other on over-population. She was a younger woman who was married into a literate family and insisted that the programme has many benefits.

Listenership among women also seems to be tied to their participation in programme production—discussions, drama, *lok geet* (folk songs), etc. At Nawadih, the adolescent girls, who formed a focus group for our study, had participated a number of times in *Chala Ho Gaon Mein*—in discussions, drama, *lok geet*, etc. They recalled in great detail a short play they had recorded on the issue of post-natal health of the mother and the child. The active participation of these young girls in programme production owed, in large measure, to the tireless efforts of the community reporter who works with them.

Namma Dhwani is an important component of the *sangha* (self-help group) activities of women in the Budhikote village and their representatives are involved in the decision making process at every stage. The women in the management committee exchange feedback and programme ideas in the *sangha* meetings and also motivate their members to participate. Most of the women in the focus group were aware of the content and its format. Everyone who was part of the discussion claimed to be keen listeners of the programmes (that are cable cast and received through TV sets), 'If *Namma Dhwani* programme is coming we leave all our work and listen to it.' A middle-aged *anganwadi* teacher, Uma affirms, 'There is no TV at my place. My neighbour calls me when the programme is on and I leave my work and go to her house and listen.'

Seventy-year-old Ramba of Kalatalav village in Kutch is the 'Parma *dadi*' in the *Kunjal* programme. She is also an enthusiastic *sangathan* member and was actively involved in the Savings and Credit programme when she was picked to play a character in the radio serial. Now she owns a shop, and is a dedicated listener and promoter of the radio programmes in her village. She says that the women in her village are enthusiastic about the programme and listen to radio even if they have work to do. The women in the DDS village of Bidekanne manage their *sangam* activities independently. Eight women from the village have participated in the radio programme. The women who had gathered for our focus group not only promptly recollected all the 10–12 issues of the radio programmes that they had heard in the listening sessions but also gave details of the contents and participants of the programme. Some of them said they had heard some programmes two-three times to grasp them fully.

GENDER ISSUES IN PARTICIPATORY DEVELOPMENT

The processes of genuine participation with their goals of social inclusion and societal transformation essentially aim at handing over the control of natural and shared resources to the marginalised people and empowering them with skills and confidence to have a say in decision-making over their circumstances (Chambers, 1997; Gujit and Shah, 1998). The paradigmatic shift towards participatory development appears to offer prospects of giving everyone who has a stake a voice and a choice. In reality, the legacy of a highly unequal and hierarchical society, the embedded notions of gender and power and the ideology of male superiority affects women's options to intervene in discussions or participate in any decision-making process (Cornwall, 2000).

'Community' has usually been perceived and dealt with as a harmonious collective with equitable internal dynamics. Too often the prevalent hierarchies, differences and conflicts, that are crucial to positive outcomes, are overlooked. It has been observed in numerous cases that community-driven development is not gender-sensitive, and 'the language and practice of "participation" often obscures women's worlds, needs and contributions to development making equitable participatory development an elusive goal' (Gujit and Shah, 1998). For any participatory development approach to be gender responsive, it ought to provide women with the enabling resources which will allow them to take greater control of their own lives and to devise the strategies and alliances that help them to choose the kinds of gender relations they want to live within (Kabeer, 1994). It is only by integrating Gender and Development (GAD) philosophy into participatory development practices that the slippage between 'involving women' and 'addressing gender' may be redeemed, thus enabling women to gain a voice and subsequent representation and agency in development initiatives (Humble, 1998; Cornwall, 2000).

However, participatory processes aimed at producing consensus and identifying a common set of priorities for action, can work both to enable different voices to be heard and to mask dissent. Context sensitivity could easily turn into communitarian relativism leading to acceptance of too many local norms and cultural traditions that maintain women's subordination within the family and the community. Feminist theories of social justice informed by notions of pluralism warn against acceptance of local traditions and practices that violate a woman's individual agency to pursue a way of life that she affirms as good. Nussbaum (2005) defends a liberal feminist position, even as she displays sensitivity to cultural differences and religious liberty, when she stresses that there should be an ethical consensus around ideas of human dignity. She maintains that it is the prerogative of people to sustain a religious view or any cultural outlook that gives their life meaning, but respecting the freedom of religion should not grant a select number of religious leaders 'limitless license to perpetuate human misery' (Nussbaum, 2000).

She lists various 'central human capabilities' that members of any particular culture ought to possess, i.e., 'what a person is in a position to do and be' (Nussbaum, 2000). She identifies 10 of these capabilities as essential to human dignity—those that ascertain the 'threshold level of capabilities beneath which truly human functioning is not available'. The list of central human capabilities include, the ability to live a normal life span, bodily health, to be secure against violent assault, the use of senses, to imagine, think and reason to play, to live with concern for and in relation to animals, plants, and the world of nature and to make economic and political choices (Nussbaum, 2000: 78–80). Nussbaum considers this list as open-ended and subject to ongoing revision through cross-cultural dialogical reflection among people with different conceptions of the good. Nussbaum advocates this latest version of her capabilities approach as an alternative to the human rights discourse that could provide a basis for governments as well as development actors to provide people, especially the poor and disadvantaged women, with the required conditions for actualising these central human capabilities.

Women's organisations and gender workers who participated in the first-ever international conference on women and communication held in Bangkok in 1994 explain that having women 'empowered' by communication is not enough, and declared their commitment 'to communication that is enriched by women's perspectives, and whose structures are responsive to women's participation' (WACC, 2005). The participants of the conference put together the Bangkok Declaration that outlines a vision shared by gender and media activists worldwide even today.

> It is essential to promote forms of communication that not only challenge the patriarchal nature of media but strive to decentralise and democratise them;

> to create media that encourage dialogue and debate, media that advance women's and peoples' creativity, media that reaffirm women's wisdom and knowledge, and that make people into subjects rather than objects or targets of communication, media which are responsive to peoples needs (Bangkok Declaration, 1994).

Degree of Participation in Programme Production

Significant capacity-building efforts by all community radio initiatives have enhanced the abilities of the rural women, who had negligible exposure to media production prior to their involvement in these projects, to be eloquent radio reporters and dexterous studio managers. Algole Narsamma of Pastapur village in Medak district of Andhra Pradesh and Mangala Gowri of Budikote township in Kolar district of Karnataka are young, rural women, matriculate, and belong to poor daily-wage earner families. Over the years they have joined *sangams/sanghas* (self-help groups) and have been trained in radio production as part of the community radio initiatives of the grassroots NGOs, DDS and MYRADA/VOICES, respectively.

Shy and hesitant once upon a time, today they proficiently manage audio studios in their villages along with a few other women and volunteers and produce programmes in the local dialect that they feel would 'benefit their community'. Algole and Mangala carry out planning, recording, scripting, editing, narration, mixing, mastering and doing voiceovers for production of programmes in the local dialect. These women had never seen the inside of a radio studio earlier and never had the opportunity to formally voice their opinion and experiences. Today, their studio archives boast of 300 hours of cassettes on information specific to the region's agricultural needs, indigenous knowledge systems, health, food security, gender justice and the narrative traditions of song and drama recorded with the participation of women of their communities. Vijayaben, a middle-aged woman with formal education till class four, who covers the Mohaldi and Abdasa *talukas* for the KMVS community radio programme explains how she had attended conscientisation, confidence-building and technical training workshops as also one on the art of seeking *mahiti* (information) and community participation. She and her fellow reporters are aware that theirs is a *bhagidari wala* radio (participatory radio) and that they have to go to the people and not like AIR that asks people to come to their studio for recordings all the time. Most of the women reporters in KMVS confessed that earlier they were shy and even scared to move out of their homes or to talk to men. But with suitable training and field exposure they have now gained confidence and are not afraid of handling any kind of work related to radio production, whether it is interviews, feature or the technical tasks of recording, editing or doing voiceovers.

Shilwanti Biranchi, the dynamic reporter at Bhalmanda village, told us that she made her own family members participate in plays and other programmes for *Chala Ho Gaon Mein* before others could be convinced that it was not only harmless, but could also be fun. Another reporter, Prakash Narayan had his wife act in a drama in order to overcome the resistance from women to participate in the programme.

Surendra Thakur, the AID reporter for Harsangra village, among others, narrated his experiences with mobilising women's participation in radio plays.

> Recording a radio drama involves a lot of practice and rehearsals. Some plays require women to play the roles of wives. They would say "how can we become some strange man's wife" and hesitate to come forward to take on such roles. So we persuaded women members (*didi log*) of our own group to take the lead and show the other women that there is nothing wrong. Gradually some women started feeling that if this programme is being made for the good of our village, then they too should participate (FGD).

For VOICES/MYRADA, the 10 women *sanghas* of Budhikote village are their 'inroads to the community' and the functioning of the station is the 'ultimate' responsibility of the management committee consisting of representatives from among the members of each *sangha*. The primary aim of the project is 'to bring poor women who are at the periphery of information and communications networking into the centre of it, thus giving them the power to make more informed decisions, better organise themselves and take actions', according to Seema Nair, the project coordinator. As women themselves are the content providers and the producers of radio programmes, the participation levels and involvement among *Namma Dhwani* and DDS women are high in all the three phases of radio message development, viz., definition of problems, production and post-production.

The DDS women in the focus groups were aware of 'how cassettes are made' and for what purpose. They stated unambiguously that it was the *sangam* women who had asked for the radio station. It was sought as a medium for horizontal communication among women to dispense timely information that is helpful to the community and to discuss the things that women are doing at DDS. The design and production process is carried out based on the feedback from the *sangams*, and the 'local' experts as well as the production staff are women of their own community. Narrowcasting is a means of seeking reactions of the women and the regular interaction of the *sangam* supervisor with the radio committee ensures that issues and perspectives of women from all villages get represented in the programmes.

Sammamma, a non-literate woman of Bidekanne, 32 years of age with seven children, said:

> We have been to radio station at Machnoor and know how these cassettes are made. Normally we gather at that place and few people among us will sing the songs before the mike. They will play those cassettes for us. We feel very happy to hear our voice in the tape (FGD).

An articulate member of the *sangam*, Sarojamma of Pyalaram village informed us that though there was no TV in the entire village, people had 'tape player'. She has sung songs composed by DDS women themselves on subjects like old crops, seeds, organic farming at *Pachh Saale* (Green School) next to the radio station where the recordings are carried out sometimes. She describes that the women from the village are called and made to sit in order and the mike is placed in the centre, 'like you are doing now'. After that they are asked to sing songs or talk about various issues. This is recorded and played back to seek the opinion of the participants.

Many women felt that participation could be further enhanced in programme production if the amount of woman-centred programming on issues such as dowry, child marriage, literacy, reproductive health, etc., was increased and women other than reporters were given opportunities to participate in discussions. Twenty-one-year-old Sanjukta Devi, who is an active member of the self-help group in village Cheri (AID) states:

> We women were earlier very inhibited. When the men used to sit outside for discussions, we used to sit inside. Today, after this programme, we feel we too have a voice and are confident to come out of the house to even take part in processions.

In the opinion of 40-year-old Sarasamma of the Lakshmi *sangha* in Budhikote,

> the programmes on women issues, of young girls talking fearlessly about the evils of dowry and admonishing boys for teasing them at school or of women giving out recipes and teaching others how to open a bank account interest and benefit us more. When we get the factual information and are able to express our problems, we will develop.

KMVS has been engaging with the concerns of rural women by making direct interventions in villages to set up *mahila mandals* that work towards self-managed *sangathans* (rural women's groups) at *taluka* (block) level. The radio programmes of *Ujjas* radio are devised with a clear gender focus and seek to enhance the socio-economic and political status of rural women in Kutch at home and in society and also to boost their dignity of work and livelihood. The focus of the programmes is to enable women to be decision-making partners in development at the village, community and regional level. The women who are members of KMVS *mandals* and *sangathans* are aware of all stages of the production process of the community radio programme. The reporters are answerable to the *sangathans* of the respective blocks they cover. Interaction with women of the block *samiti* (managing committee of a *sangathan*) is a regular feature for finalisation of content.

Addressing Women's Issues

Media concerns related to women and the role communication technologies can play in enhancing gender equality, and equity have been debated in several international conventions of women working in the information and communications sector. In most countries, the media is overwhelmingly male-controlled and women still lack the power to determine the nature and shape of media content or to influence media policy. Documents produced at these important conventions urged media enterprises, professionals, international and national governmental and non-governmental organisations, educational and media training institutions, to dispel gender disparity and encourage greater involvement of women in the technical, decision-making, and agenda-setting activities of communication and media (Frankson, 2000). They also point towards the need for creating new opportunities to 'promote a balanced and non-stereotyped portrayal of women in the media'. The *Toronto Platform for Action* (1995) specifically advocates the following among several other measures as essential:

- to increase women's access to expression in and through the media (paragraph 1.1);
- to increase women's access to and participation in decision making and management of the media, so as to encourage media to promote women's positive contributions to society (paragraph 1.2);
- to use communication as a driving force in the promotion of women's active and equal participation in development in a context of peace and equality, while preserving freedom of expression and freedom of the press (paragraph 1.3);
- to recognise the importance of women's media networks worldwide, both those that supply news in women's activities and concerns to media outlets, and those that utilise alternative media channels to reach women and women's groups with information that assists and supports them in their personal, family and community development activities (paragraph 1.4);
- to recognise the rights of all women to have access to expression and participation in the media, in particular those from discriminated groups such as other-abled, indigenous, women of colour and women of diverse sexual orientation (paragraph 1.5);
- to recognise women as authoritative information sources, experts, and opinion makers, therefore, news sources on any issue and not confine women to the role of speaking only on 'women's issues' (paragraph 2.5);
- to include women on a parity basis in government reform committees, parliamentary, advisory, policymaking and other regulatory bodies that consider advertising and communications policy (paragraph 5.1);
- to introduce, support and extend community radio stations as a way of increasing women's participation and contribution to the media and local economic development, especially in areas of high illiteracy (paragraph 6.4); and

- to conduct research into various alternative, traditional, local, and folk forms, as well as new communications technologies used by women (paragraph 6.12).

According to Algole Narsamma, the programming content of the DDS station seeks to serve the information, education and cultural needs of the women in the region and to communicate their problems, raise their issues and find solutions through the medium of radio. It is an extension of their *sangam* activities that have benefited the women immensely. Tuljamma, who is a health supervisor and also a member of the radio committee, believes that participating in DDS activities, including making radio programmes, have made women more confident. 'Before that, we were scared about meeting and talking to people. Now we discuss matters in our *sangams*, make radio programmes and even talk to any higher officials including *Patwari*.'

Zaheerabad Anuradha, the *balwadi* supervisor adds,

> Women are now participating in Panchayat meetings. We sit along with men and we participate in decision making. Earlier, there were no women in Gram Panchayat. Nowadays women are *Sarpanchs* also and ward members. These women are no longer just dummies, they are questioning also. They visit different areas and do not leave until the work is done (FGD).

Almost all women in the focus groups were convinced that their involvement in collective developmental activities and their relative improvement in the financial status have led to an observable, and in a few cases, major changes in attitudes of their husbands towards them. Kishnapur Chilkamma, who is also a board member of DDS, recalls how there was a time when men would not allow their wives to go out for *sangam* meetings in the night. They would beat them up if women would wish to go for a radio station meeting and order them to sit at home. Now they are gradually recognising the potential of women and giving respect. 'Today men even come forward to facilitate our work.'

Some radio programmes have also made a difference in this respect. The women in Raipally and also the video women have similar versions about a radio programme that highlighted the importance of saving.

> Previously our husbands were irresponsible, now they work more for the wellbeing of the family. At work, the wage for women is Rs 10 and for men

> it is Rs 20. Out of that Rs 20 they used to give only Rs 10 to us and rest they would keep for tea, *bidi* (hand-rolled cigarette) and toddy. Now they give it to us for saving in our bank account that we have learnt to operate (FGD).

The experience of Nagamma of Pastapur, in her late 20s and already a mother of five, is very different with her husband who is an alcoholic and she feels that some men are incorrigible.

> After all other efforts had failed, I brought a DDS cassette home, which had songs about the ill effects of drinking, but my husband switched off the tape recorder saying this is 'nonsense'. *Sunane wale sunte hain, nahin sunane wale nahin sunte; galian dene wale dete hain, rahne wale rehte hain.* [Some men listen and change, but others don't even listen. I continue to stay with him even though he drinks and uses abusive language] (FGD).

Women in several focus groups pointed out the problems they faced because of men who were habitual drunkards. A shelter for destitute women, who are beaten by their husbands or tortured by in-laws has been built by DDS. The radio women recorded a programme that talks about these problems women face and about the attitude of the parents who tell them that after marriage, their life is with their husbands. The women are left with no choice but to stay back and suffer or commit suicide. The programme explains to women about this shelter and also the legal committee that helps to get free legal aid.

'General' and Algole narrated an incident where they had used the microphone to record information that later served as evidence before the law for young girls in two different cases.

> One girl in Idlapalli was raped and murdered. DDS people went to the police station. I went there with a microphone in my small coin pouch, as they'll not allow me to record. I just stood holding my pouch and recorded completely the facts the policeman was revealing. When we asked them later to file a formal FIR, he denied that there was any such case. We brought the evidence and played, and filed a case to get justice for the parents of the girl. Similarly, we used our recording to get a girl from Madiri village married to her lover who had ditched her. Our recorded evidence made the police warn him not to misbehave with the girl after marriage. Now they are leading a happy life with children (interview).

The community radio projects have also contributed in creating awareness about social problems that perpetuate women's subordination to men. The tradition of *tilak/dahej* (dowry) is quite deeply rooted in the culture of the Jharkhand region and it is unrealistic to expect that the AID radio programme would make a dent in that so soon. However, it is apparent that the programme has managed to put the issue firmly on the agenda and that people are at least discussing the problem. Thirty-year-old Kamoda Devi, the only literate woman in the focus group in Bhalmanda village (AID), hoped that the programme would make a difference. 'If I take dowry for my son now, I will realize the problem later when my son has a daughter and he has to give dowry. So it is important to stop this practice. If this can be done through the programme, it will be good for society' (FGD).

Adolescent girls at the Nawadih village (AID) also condemned the practice as a blot on society and hoped that the radio programme can address the issue. Surendra Thakur, one of the community reporters, offered an example of a specific outcome of *Chala Ho Gaon Mein* in the area of gender equity:

> Before this radio programme started, people used to send only their sons to school and make their daughters work at home. However, after this programme started talking about treating sons and daughters equally, many parents came forward and, with our help, enrolled their daughters in school (FGD).

The women in the focus groups in Budhikote felt that the maximum benefit that *Namma Dhwani* can provide to the village is through its programmes for women. They stated with fervour that a family could not prosper without the support of a woman. In the focus group with the management committee of *Namma Dhwani*, the women came up collectively expressing their views:

> A woman has more responsibilities and problems. Men simply go out and work, but we have to struggle with husband, children, our health, cooking, home, various chores and our relatives from morning to night. A woman maintains everything at home and sometimes even goes out to work. She is the main switch. Everybody else is a bulb. The bulbs burn only if the main switch works. That's why they call us 'Mother'. If she rests due to ill-health for a day, the house is all topsy-turvy (FGD).

The women listed out a number of issues that they felt *Namma Dhwani* addresses and that have proved beneficial for them. Twenty-one-year-old Byatappa, from the management committee remarked,

> Whether it is the question of eating well for the sake of our health or the facts that help women progress economically, such programmes are useful. There

> are programmes about legal help that women need in case of dowry harassment. Earlier women used to fear going to the police station for any help because there were wrong notions that they lock you up in the room or exploit you. Now women are more aware of their rights (FGD).

The *sangha* members also pointed out that they never used to come out and participate in programmes earlier. But, now, after listening to members from their own *sangha* on *Namma Dhwani*, they are coming out voluntarily to give programmes like '*Mane Maddu*' (Home Remedies) and to exchange issues discussed in various *sanghas*. Bhavani, a volunteer, spoke about how self-conscious she was about talking in public and now 'I love participating in live radio programmes,' she smiles. To prepare for the task, she reads newspapers, participates in self-help group meetings and uses the computer to access information. The women are now also asking for news about panchayat and its activities. Some women mentioned the change in men's attitude who had earlier said no to the *sanghas*. 'But now, they say—it is time for the *sangha*. I will do the remaining cooking, you go.'

Sujata of Navjyoti *sangha* clarified that 'All this happened slowly, step by step. The change did not happen all of a sudden. The other day my husband asked me to go with Amaresh on his scooter because it was late. "They have come for you. How long do you make them wait," he said.'

KMVS awareness of issues at grassroots level gets reflected in the programme *Kunjal Paanje Kutch Ji* (Saras Crane of Our Kutch), its first community radio programme, which sought to augment the ongoing efforts in thrust areas of KMVS. The demand for a programme to cater to the information needs of the women of Kutch came from *Ujjas* (rural women's newsletter) women, those involved in the various activities of the organisation and women *Sarpanchs* of the village panchayats. The central focus of the serial conceived in docu-drama format is participation of women in political processes, specifically panchayats at the village level. By exploring the entry of women from the private to the public domain, KPKJ was able to generate a debate on gender issues on the one hand, and *swaraj* (democratic self-governance) on the other. Gradually, other issues got interwoven into the central theme addressing gender inequities in the development process and engendering a sustainable socio-economic transformation in the region.

These issues that also get tackled in the various segments of *Kutch Lok Ji Bani* include: girl's right to education, female foeticide, harassment of brides for dowry, dowry deaths, violence against women, unnatural deaths and suicides of women, pressure on women to produce boys, and maternal mortality. Identifying KMVS community radio broadcasts as the only programmes that talk of their concerns, most women respondents who are involved in the activities of KMVS or are regular listeners of these programmes had a good recall of the issues that dealt with the problems of women. Some women empathised with the character of 'Dhanki'—a victim of domestic violence and were happy that she protested against the atrocities of her husband.

Forging Solidarities

In this section, we seek to contextualise the use of democratised communication spaces, especially community radio, by women for identity articulation and as counter-hegemony to the patriarchal structures of the media as well as the negative forces of media globalisation. A significant contribution is being made to the gender and communication movement by the growing numbers of coalitions at the grassroots level that are constructing democratic 'we' spaces for women to develop their own narratives, 'voice their concerns, name who they are, share and build projects of change' (Riaño, 1994a: xi). Women, through interpersonal communication networks and as barefoot journalists, independent film makers, alternative press owners, community radio reporters, process video producers, radical song writers, people's theatre activists, communication facilitators and participatory researchers are organising themselves across differences or around the commonalities of gender, class, caste and culture as subjects of struggle and transformation (Riaño, 1994b).

The programmes of community radio have enabled women to radically change accepted 'media languages' by providing them with a space and a process for expressing ideas and issues linked to their unique experiences. Women are central to development, and women's media production competencies help them to develop their capacities as socio-political actors and spearhead popular movements. For women radio reporters, the first tough task is to adequately address the concerns of their own village/community and have a *pahchan*—identity, that imparts other women with faith in them and the potential of the medium to bring about *sudhar*—improvement, and prompts them to participate in media activities.

P.V. Satheesh, Director DDS says, 'For us, a community radio is total control of the communities over the radio. And that includes everything, it includes the language, it includes the format, it includes the expression and entire sequence of what will come there.' He recalls the answer that the women gave when they rejected the offer of a slot on AIR to air their programmes. They said:

> Look, that is a kind of a continuous chain of broadcast and within that they will give us a particular position. And we don't know what comes before that and what comes after that. Like for example, we are all talking about organic agriculture and may be there is a pesticide advertisement before that and then our organic agriculture comes, after that somebody from an agricultural university may give a talk about hybrid seeds. So, we don't want our programmes to be positioned in a radio channel where that positioning may be very awkward for us.

He quotes Chilukapalli Anasuyamma from Pastapur, a 30-year old non-literate Dalit single woman, who, when she was asked to suggest what they could do with their own radio, said:

> In our *sangams* (village associations of dalit women), we are carrying on a number of tasks that used to be done by men. Our men are doing a number of tasks, which were only being preserved for women. This way we have been able to erase the boundaries between man's work and woman's work.' 'The mainstream radio is still steeped in the traditional gender roles. If we depend on it, we have to go back in time. All that we have done in our *sangams* will come to a nought. If we have our own radio it can help us continue this progress we have made on gender issues (interview).

The women in the focus groups of DDS confirm that earlier there was no communication on developmental issues among women within a village or from different villages. Now because of the *sangams* there is interaction and new relationships are beings forged. They are now discussing their problems with each other. Kalimela Tukkamma affirms that the attitude has changed now and we feel that 'If we talk about an issue, it will be solved. Because of the *sangam* activity and discussions on radio, we can talk now. Otherwise we used to sit silent. Government officials will come and we let them talk. Now we question them.'

Sammamma of Bidekanne maintains,

> Earlier on we did not have the courage to even discuss politics. If any political leader comes, we would listen to the one who gave money. Nobody thought in a united manner. The scheduled caste women were anyway limited to their masters' mansions. They would exercise their vote and be seen again during the next elections only.

Humnapur Laxmamma, a senior media activist with DDS's participatory video team elaborates further:

> Previously we used to bother only about our own problems. We were not keen on the problems of others. Now we are doing collective work. We share each others' sorrows and happiness. We want to help women in other villages and expect the same for them. Before radio, we used to do lot of good things which were not noticed by society. But now everyone knows all our activities. We cannot write all these things in a book, we are recording it in the cassette. It is easy for the people to understand. Moreover, after me, my next generation can also hear this cassette and know about the works, which we have done (FGD).

Namma Dhwani and its programmes seek to provide support to the endeavours of women self-help groups of Budhikote in addressing their own poverty situations by positively steering the abilities of women to voice their concerns, access productive information and by increasing their bargaining power to affect changes that address their lives directly.

A young and active member of Purnima *Mahila sangha*, Sulochana was definite that it is only avenues like *Namma Dhwani* that can help the lot of women.

> The women folk are still inside homes. If we want to come out, our men and mothers-in-law don't allow us. So, we definitely want *Namma Dhwani* so that we can go out and talk there. Even to this day women are oppressed. We don't have the freedom we want. Then there are problems of dowry. We should make programmes on these issues that will help us, women (FGD).

The women in the management committee were positive about the outcome of *Namma Dhwani* in forging solidarities among women.

> We are the police in our village now. The police don't come to question us about our meetings or *Namma Dhwani* programmes. Seeing us women together, they fear. They have understood that if they trouble even one of us, the entire *sangha* would protest. They know very well that we have unity. They don't poke into our affairs.

The programmes of the KMVS *Ujjas* radio are devised with a clear gender focus and seek to enhance the socio-economic and political status of rural women in Kutch at home and in society and also to boost their dignity of work and livelihood. The focus of the programmes is to enable women to be decision-making partners in development at the village, community and regional level. At village Cheri, 19-year-old Chintamani said confidently that specific episodes of *Chala Ho* on the dowry problem are already beginning to make a difference in the thinking of women about the need for collective action.

> Prior to the radio programme, we girls were never even allowed to go outside the home, leave alone participating in meetings. After this programme started, we got together and formed a young women's group. Now we all sing together, attend meetings, and discuss issues. A lot of change has come in our attitudes (FGD).

Although the women radio reporters of Bhuj and the community radio representatives of Palamau negotiated with the contemporary state policy for airing their programmes, their voices harmonised with those in Budhikote and Pastapur for demanding a radio of their own. All of them believe that in order to deploy radio as a tool of empowerment, participation of people is not enough. The ownership, control and management of the radio station must be in the hands of the community for it to function as an autonomous media space open to the need for self-expression by the socially and culturally marginalised sections of society, especially women. The media unit of KMVS that wholly handles its community radio production aims at being a training ground for the community radio reporters to equip them to start media activity for *sangathans* in their respective villages. The DDS Community Media Trust has eight radio and video women as trustees and its preamble reads, 'In fulfilment of the wishes of thousands of women from DDS *sangams* who wish to have their unrecognised voices heard and recognised by the world outside.'

Conclusion

It was satisfying to observe that the gender dimension in the community radio projects in India is not limited to identifying the gender of the participants or simply including women-related issues in communicative interaction. The women also influence the nature of message production. Although the socially ascribed roles for women in the communities inhibit their frequency of listening to radio and their full participation in the community radio programmes, their capabilities to develop messages cannot be underestimated. Women listen to radio, especially those who are part of the social networks at the local and community levels. The women whose skills and confidence have been enhanced through media production, now act as agents to mobilise other women to participate. This participatory process further helps women in raising their collective consciousness and understanding of their own social reality and problems (see Table 7.1).

Women produce programmes related to issues that affect them intimately and also come out with alternative solutions. They also seem to discuss some concerns related to the ways in which they may be marginalised because of not only their gender but also their class and caste. They are gradually seeking to transform existing gender relations by changing the distribution of resources and responsibilities to make it more equitable. The extent to which the changes have taken place may be difficult to assess, but community radio programmes have surely achieved some success in helping consolidate women's views and perspectives on gender subordination and social transformation. In cases where the ownership and management of community radio is in the hands of women, the process of re-socialisation of women and men is visible. Changes in traditional attitudes, behaviours and roles that perpetuate gender stereotypes and inequalities are more perceptible. As women create, control and consume the information presented by the community radio, they are seeking, despite the odds, to correct these imbalances.

For those who have traditionally been unacknowledged and silenced, socially and culturally, the opportunity to have one's voice heard can be an imposing experience of self-worth. In Bell Hooks's words:

> Moving from silence into speech is for the oppressed, the colonized, the exploited, and those who stand and struggle side by side a gesture of defiance that heals, that makes life and new growth possible. It is that act of speech of 'talking back', that is no mere gesture of empty words, that is the expression of our movement from object to subject—the liberated voice (1989: 9).

8 CONCLUSION

Community Radio in India—Opportunities and Challenges

Several community-based media initiatives in different parts of the world are making an attempt to promote participatory local development, the right to communicate, multiculturalism and gender justice. Media and communication scholars internationally are engaging in research that seeks to analyse such communication processes and their ground realities. Our book may be regarded as an useful contribution to the existing body of knowledge about global developments in the area of communication for social change. It also hopes to enrich the contemporary social science discourses about alternative media in non-Western societies. Community radio is one of the genres of community-oriented democratic media that civil society organisations are struggling to develop for facilitating more people-centred development and as a means for empowerment at the grassroots.

Community radio campaigners in India have struggled through the good part of a decade for the creation of a new tier of not-for-profit radio stations, owned and run by local people, typically in rural areas, which would enable marginalised communities to use the medium to create opportunities for social change, cohesion and inclusion as well as for creative and cultural expression. This fight for freeing of the radio spectrum has become a key to challenge the global march of capitalist media industries and the unidirectional flow of information and communication from the northern metropolitan countries to the rest of the world. This movement is also concerned with providing an alternative to the dominant media and a means of expression to a wide spectrum of social actors who have been socially, culturally, geographically, economically and politically excluded from power. That the Government of India in late 2006 finally saw good sense in opening up the airwaves to community-based organisations is a good augury for the entire South Asian region.[1]

Communication critic Armand Mattelart, in his keynote address 'What is Community Radio?' delivered at the Third Convention of the World Association of Community Radio Broadcasters (AMARC) held in 1988 in Nicaragua, referred to the differences in definitions and contexts of community radio, but said that the common orientation was the 'construction of a collective identity to build a more just society' (cited in Kidd, 1998). He urged the delegates to reflect on the practices of community radio within the changing historical contexts of social change and orient them towards the long-term project of democratising communication. Referring to Brecht, Mattelart reiterated his proposal to convert radio from a distribution system to a communication system which would allow the listener to speak as well as hear. Mattelart also affirmed that the legacy of community radio was in three historical movements. The first was the struggles for national liberation in which revolutionary leaders had made radio and other communication technologies 'instruments of struggle' for popular power and, later, consolidation of state power. The second historical period was the political and cultural resistance to the US practices of development and its 'monolithic conception of communication'. Finally, the third period in the late 70s and early 80s was the challenge to the monopoly control of communication by both state and commercial broadcasters (Kidd, 1998).

The obstacle to expanding access to communication technologies for marginalised groups lies in a lack of political will and in policies that fail to recognise the importance of communication in political, economic and social development. The indispensability of community participation at all stages in a genuine development initiative and the rights of all peoples and segments of society to communicate through mass media by word, voice and image has been widely recognised since the late 70s. Radio is the most economical electronic medium to broadcast and receive messages and leaps the barriers of isolation and illiteracy. A community-owned and run radio station can work as a forum to facilitate participatory, public dialogue which is essential for determining development inputs that meet local needs. Community radio can serve as a mechanism to pressurise local authorities to adopt practices of good governance and transparency.

Policy for Community Radio in India

Media policies and broadcasting systems the world over are undergoing changes in response to the demand to accommodate the voices of the marginalised and to create spaces for the agendas of disadvantaged communities. However, broadcasting in India, for nearly 80 years since its inception, has been dominated by the hierarchical and paternalistic 'public' and the profit-oriented 'commercial' models. Little has been done by the government to promote decentralised, autonomous, horizontal and reciprocal broadcasting practices that can respond effectively to the socio-economic and development needs of the country, deal with local issues in the local languages and encourage cultural plurality. The practices of radio in India, until recently, reinforced existing economic and geopolitical hierarchies by limiting full access to users outside of the state, military and corporate interests. Privatisation of broadcasting in India has merely escalated the corporate monopolisation of the spaces being made available for public use. The possibility of a change towards democratic communication from the grassroots point of view is only emerging now after years of political apathy and bureaucratic pussyfooting.

By revisiting the evolution of broadcasting in India from the vantage point of access to and control of media technologies by marginalised sections of the society, we inferred that although advancing democratic functioning of radio has been a vital concern in the continuing debates for a comprehensive media policy in India, little has been done to open up broadcasting for the non-profit social sector. This has unleashed a demand for collective re-appropriation of the airwaves for social development by those seeking a more equitable distribution of the radio spectrum. A few community-based organisations have acquired the technical capabilities to run radio stations of their own, but have been waiting for several years for government sanction to go on air. Others have taken up opportunities within the state space to come up with innovative local programming.

The Indian Government derives its current monopoly over radio and television broadcasting from the Indian Telegraph Act, 1885 which gives exclusive privileges of the establishment, maintenance and working of wireless apparatus to the Central Government. The possession of radio receivers and wireless equipment without a license is an offence under the Indian Wireless Telegraphy Act, which was brought into force by the British Government in 1933 to deal with alleged evasion of license fee and to monitor possession of wireless gear. The expansion of broadcasting in India has been guided largely by economic, strategic, engineering and administrative aspects. The rapid growth and spread of broadcasting reflects the top–down 'reach' of the medium and is sought to be justified often in terms of coverage area and population, listenership, programming and the number of languages in which programmes are broadcast. Although the use of radio for development was the cornerstone of public service broadcasting policy in India, no sustained attempt has been made to use radio innovatively to create a participatory model of development in which information flows not only downwards, from governments to the people, but also upwards from people to the government.

Some issues that must be addressed in order to resolve the persistent inadequacies and imbalances in radio broadcasting policy in India include: counterbalancing state's monopoly over broadcasting by opening up the sector for private and community involvement, regulation of private ownership, convergence directives for integration of broadcast and telecommunications infrastructure, digitisation, and support for community radio stations to improve access. The focus of discussion here is the need for reform in the form and structure of broadcasting aimed at increasing people's access to communication technologies and media content. This vital concern can have significant impact in improving governance and transparency as well as in challenging the mainstream understanding of social issues. This has been emphasised consistently in the reports of various committees periodically appointed by the Government of India to examine media-related issues.

The historic judgement of the Supreme Court delivered in February 1995 ruled that 'airwaves constitute public property and must be utilised for advancing public good'. The judgement further decreed that broadcasting media as a whole should promote freedom of expression and speech and, therefore, should be able to enjoy freedom from government monopoly and control subject to regulation by a public body. The judgement noted that private broadcasting must be regulated by a public authority in the interests of the public and to prevent the invasion of their rights. As the country still awaits a comprehensive media policy and a broadcast law to enable democratisation of media, efforts are on for carving out an alternative media sector in India, which would neither be state-run nor market-driven. The groups advocating community radio as part of the movement for an alternative public realm can only hope that the Union Cabinet's approval of the community radio policy in November 2006 would unleash the potential of radio for achieving participatory development goals and to represent the priorities of the most vulnerable sections of society.

This book makes a comparative analysis of the policy frameworks for community radio in five liberal-democratic countries of the world with the purpose of developing a set of recommendations for a policy on community radio in India. This analysis was done in the context of the political realities of broadcasting in India, our field experiences in studying community radio initiatives in India, and the discussions in various forums regarding appropriate policy to open up broadcasting for the civil society sector. The recommendations put together by us for a policy that would enable the emergence of a community radio sector in India are given in Box 8.1.

Box 8.1: ***Recommendations for a Policy on Community Radio***

1. Definition

Definition of Community: Community may be defined as a non-sectarian group of individuals who are territorially-bound and share a common socio-economic position/interest (Pastapur Agenda).

Definition of Community Radio: Community radio as having three key aspects: non-profit making, community ownership and management, and community participation. Community radio is distinguished by its limited local reach, low-power transmission, and programming content that reflects the educational, developmental and cultural needs of the specific community it serves (Pastapur Agenda).

Who can apply for a community radio license: NGOs and voluntary organisations with proven track record of community development work in the area of the license.

2. Licensing Process/Procedures

Applicants should submit a proposal to the ministry of information and broadcasting or to an independent broadcast regulator to be set up.

Assessments of the application could be made on the basis of:

- a clear definition of the community to be served;
- the level of current and expected participation by that community in the station;
- the type of programming service envisaged; and
- how they propose to resource their station.

There should be no cost involved in lodging an application for community broadcasting license. There should be no spectrum fee or bank guarantee. In the event of more than one claimant for a single frequency at a given place, the licensee will be selected by a committee constituted by the ministry on the basis of standing, commitment, objectives and resources of the applicant organisation.

3. Allocation of Frequency and Technical Parameters

The ministry could prepare a frequency allotment plan for different areas that ensures economic and efficient use of the radio frequency spectrum for broadcasting purposes, and also prioritise geographical areas least served by existing services. This would help identify suitable/available frequency to allocate licences for community sector. The nature of licences can be determined by available frequency and perceived public need.

The station should operate on FM frequency. The maximum limit for transmitter power could be 100 watts (with an approximate radius of 30 km). The permitted power could be decided on the basis of the area of work of the licensee and/or the geographic dispersal of listeners.

Where there is limited spectrum availability or limited resources and capacities of an individual applicant, frequency sharing by more than one applicant may be permitted.

4. Sustainability; Funding Sources

Community radio stations are, by definition, not-for-profit entities. Any funding or revenue generation should be for sustainability of the venture and not for profitability. Community stations should be funded from a diversity of sources. This is not only the most realistic option, but is essential if stations are to ensure that programming is determined primarily by the community served.

On-air commercial activity, including broadcast advertisements and sponsorship announcements, could be subject to the following conditions:

- No more than 50 per cent of income is secured from commercial activity;
- A maximum of five minutes advertising/sponsorship per hour could apply. (Ireland)

Guidelines for nature of advertising, broadcasting sponsorship announcements and other promotional material on community radio could be prepared and include such directions as:

(*a*) community stations may only broadcast advertisements, which relate to:

- work opportunities that exist in the specified area;
- events that are to occur in the specified area;

- businesses that are carried on in the specified area;
- services that are delivered in the specified area (Ireland).

(*b*) a sponsorship policy which:

- ensures that the content and style of individual programmes are not influenced by the sponsors of programmes;
- ensures that overall programming of community broadcasting stations is not influenced by sponsors (Australia).

Community Radio Development Fund

The Government must create a Community Radio Development Fund to support worthwhile initiatives with seed money to supplement the organisation's own resources, and for capacity building, technology upgrading, and research/evaluation. A model for such funding has been suggested in 2003 by the recent FM Radio Committee headed by Amit Mitra.

5. Management and Ownership

Stations should be owned by not-for-profit organisations.

Their structures should provide for membership, management and operation of the station by the community served. The station is accountable to the community and the community are in control of, and therefore responsible for, the station.

The importance of community participation in a voluntary capacity for community stations must be recognised. The extent to which members of the community served are willing to give of their own time, in a voluntary capacity, to support their station is a key indicator of the success of that station (Ireland).

Providing suitable training on a formal and informal level is essential.

Incorporate policies that promote equity and social justice, with particular reference to those marginalised on the basis of their class, caste, religion, physical disability and gender.

6. Programme Content

The programming should be based on community access and reflect the special interests and needs of the listeners a station is licensed to serve. Each station should set out the station's programme philosophy and detail its plans to facilitate and promote community participation. Specific programming, to be decided through participatory processes, must focus on local information, events and the occasional notifications, local culture and identity, and in the local language/dialect.

For most purposes, the programming code mentioned in the ministry's guidelines for community radio could apply.

7. Regulation and Monitoring

Need for a single, independent broadcasting regulator. The regulator and the stations to work together on the basis of cooperation and consultation, rather than conflict.

The standard licence term for stations in the community sector is generally five years.

When a community broadcaster comes up for renewal of license, the relationship between the station and the audience could be assessed by public hearings and/or external, independent evaluations. If by any of these methods, it can be shown that the station's past functioning violated the community's interests or that the station did not fulfil the purposes for which the license was obtained, the license may not be renewed.

All licensees must maintain a six-month log of broadcasts, as mandated in the existing provisions.

There has been intensive lobbying by community radio activists in India after the Government of India announced the 'Guidelines for Community Radio' in 2003, but limited its access to established educational institutions. The lobbying efforts were based on a consensus document prepared by community radio campaigners following the suggestions, recommendations and experiences of several academics, activists, researchers, NGOs and grassroots workers in this field. After many rounds of consultations with the lobbying groups, the Ministry of Information and Broadcasting officials came up with a draft policy on community radio in June 2004 that incorporated provisions to allow both non- governmental organisations as well as civil society groups to get licences to start radio stations. This was finally submitted to the Union Cabinet for approval around July 2005. In the cabinet meeting held in October 2005, the government referred the policy to a Group of Ministers for further discussions, prolonging the unrelenting wait for a workable community radio policy in India. In a campaign that started around the same time, more than 50,000 people from around the country, including activists, academics, non-governmental organisations and rural communities have joined hands to demand that the expanded community radio policy be announced without delay. In November 2006, the Cabinet finally gave its seal of approval to the community radio policy.[2]

Community Radio: Lessons from the Grassroots

Community radio is indeed a unique tool that employs media technologies for development and empowerment of marginalised, rural communities. This community-driven initiative takes on a special significance in economically deprived areas, marked by illiteracy and the relatively indifferent attitude of the state as well as the mainstream media towards the problems of the region. In the community radio initiatives analysed in this study, within a short time, the programmes have generated a great deal of enthusiasm among the people. They feel that the programmes are geographically and culturally more intimate to their lives, and gradually a sense of attachment to the programme is beginning to build up. Suppressed local artistic talents have come to the fore, women caught up within feudal social structures are beginning, albeit slowly, to find a voice of their own, and there is a sense of optimism that the radio programme would help solve many of the intractable problems of the people. Community radio initiatives, therefore, deserve to be encouraged for facilitating participatory communication and development.

In examining the patterns of reception of the various community radio initiatives under study, it was observed that radio serves as a lifeline in regions such as these, which are under-served by other media. Though radio listening is popular among the villagers, there exist problems of unequal access. The existing hierarchies in the household, socio-economic position, division of labour and fulfilment of basic needs come into play. These affect the listening patterns unfavourably and inhibit discussions that community radio programmes are mandated to trigger. Women, older men, poor, illiterate and the less articulate often tend to be excluded from active listening.

For building meaningful democratic spaces within villages, it is crucial to create a listening environment in which everyone from the community gets access to community radio programmes and enters into deliberations on the issues raised. Organising regular group listening sessions to elicit feedback would give people an opportunity to collectively analyse their problems, decide on the changes that affect their lives, and become active in implementing these changes. Such an interactive process prompts people to express their viewpoints, share their knowledge and also moves them to participate in programmes. This has been successfully achieved in initiatives where a culture of popular, local participation in development efforts has been integrated over the years. In projects where the NGOs are not working exclusively with women, we felt that a conscious attempt should be made to provide a more relaxed and comfortable listening environment for women, perhaps through collectives at the village level. Audio tapes could be played at their regular meetings. This would facilitate more attentive listening and promote discussion among women.

Participation is the key to increasing listenership and involvement in community radio. If any village has participated in production of a programme for community radio, its residents listen, pay attention and identify with it more closely. Those engaged actively in the participatory developmental activities within their community are fairly regular listeners of the community radio programmes that are rooted in local issues and culture and even feel disappointed if they miss any broadcast. Copies of the episodes must be made in audio cassettes for narrowcasting and must be available freely for repeat listening in places such as schools, panchayats, and other village-level collectives, especially of women. Audio tapes could also be used as audio documents to enhance interaction between block-level officials and villagers, who otherwise feel that government officials rarely visit them or pay attention to their problems.

Community radio's strategy to convert the traditional 'receivers' into producers of programmes is visible in all initiatives but the extent of participation is not total. The community radio programmes are produced in all initiatives by people from the local community who have been trained as reporters and studio managers. The awareness among their 'audiences' about the processes of community radio programme production seems to vary according to the degree to which these reporters are active in their assigned villages. People in several villages said that they had been interviewed for the community radio programmes and others had visited the studio to participate in a discussion, play or rendering of songs. Very few of those who participated in the focus group discussions, however had been involved in the designing or planning of programmes and also displayed little awareness of the post-production process. A few of those motivated appear to be utilising the opportunities of access to the use of media provided by community radio, while a large majority is still on the receiving end of programmes that are made 'by their own people' on themes that touch their lives closely. There is still a fair amount of awe about the medium and we did not get the impression that the projects had gained much in terms of demystifying the technology for the listeners in general and women in particular.

Community participation should, therefore, be enhanced in identification and definition of issues, programme planning and production. Conscious efforts should be made by all the community reporters to involve as many villages as possible in programme production as it has been observed that those villages, which have contributed to programme content, also tend to be more committed audiences. Participatory approaches to needs assessment, including research techniques such as Participatory Rural Appraisal (PRA) and Rapid Rural Appraisal (RRA), should be taken up periodically so that the NGO's own programmatic agenda does not supersede in decisions related to the issues on which the programmes are produced. The number of people involved in the production and post-production process should also be gradually increased, if the quality inputs for local programming during the field recording have to be enhanced. The issue here is of building the capacities of more and more people to produce radio programmes so that they can participate directly. This would provide them with opportunities for democratic deliberations and collective action.

In order to build a sense of identification and ownership among members of the community, visits to the radio studio may be arranged periodically. It was observed that the content of the programmes appropriately reflects the local identity and culture of the region. People identified with the issues on which the programmes were made and the recall was encouraging. The radio was also described as an archive of indigenous knowledge. However, the projects in our study have a long way to go in addressing social issues and producing tangible results in terms of sustainable goals of social change. There is no doubt that small beginnings have been made in various spheres.

Although there are some issues related to greater participation, community radio projects can serve as examples of how alternative media spaces act as powerful sites for nurturing local language and culture and building identity. The radio programmes produced in the local dialect go a long way in enhancing the potential of community radio to serve as a medium for self-articulation of development priorities in the rural setting. All focus groups identified strongly with the language of the programmes and many stated that it gave them a feeling that the programme was their own. The local content and their 'own' language of broadcast promote active listenership and distinguish community radio from its mainstream counterpart by clearly evoking a sense of pride in local culture and identity. The community radio programmes feature local talent and indigenous experts. The feeling among the community is that while the mainstream radio gives information about big cities or plays music, this radio is about 'our problems'.

In the four case studies of the community radio initiatives taken up for analysis, three work entirely through women's collectives and self-help groups. The women who are part of these participatory developmental efforts by the local NGOs have endured multiple marginalisations including those based on gender, caste, class, literacy and ethnicity. They have participated as active agents of change in the development processes set off by the NGOs for several years and are now seeking to use radio for building new communication alternatives for furthering change at the grassroots level. Depending on the stage of their involvement in the development endeavours, community radio provides women with opportunities for participating in the communication process as subjects of information; as participants; as subjects of change and as producers of meaning as explained in Riaño's typology (see Table 7.1). All these types of communication are used by women's groups at one or the other stage of the community radio project to achieve their development goals.

Women who wish to be initiated into the development projects engage actively in critical reception of community radio programmes. Others participate in the various stages of programme production of community radio and ensure that women's issues get adequate representation. When women develop media competencies, they utilise community radio to garner support for their social struggles, awaken women's consciousness to their subordination, advocate and defend rights, promote group reflection and popular communication. The community radio initiatives have helped in amplifying the voice of rural women and served as a platform for expression of alternative development strategies. However, there still exist social hierarchies along the lines of caste, class and other oppressions that inhibit women to negotiate fair representations and equal participation socially and politically to produce alternative meanings. Community radio has the potential to support these efforts of women in grassroots communication to create viable avenues for democratic communication that could foster long-standing social change.

The team of community radio reporters and studio managers in all community radio initiatives are their main strength and their biggest achievement. Young rural men and women with negligible exposure to media production and average literacy now manage radio production deftly. The reporters are driven by the zeal to serve their community and are also ideologically inclined towards the local issues and the ideals of community participation. They can take on local *sarkari* (government) officials when necessary. The community radio reporters view themselves as representatives of the community. They look upon the community programmes as an opportunity for people 'to learn and to gain courage'. With minimum formal training, radio technology enables people to articulate themselves without having to depend on outside mediators and thus provides a forum for consolidating their developmental and social agendas.

The democratic significance of community radio resides in the opportunities it provides to people to focus on locally relevant issues and events of common concern. Such a medium provides the means for cultural expression, community discussion and debate. It also fosters stronger community ties based on culture, language, human values and shared meanings. It may, however, be pointed out here that in the case of the two projects where the programme produced is aired on the AIR station, the structure appears to be superseding the process. The rigid structure of the fixed format, the painstaking rehearsals, the over-emphasis on quality and the relative lack of freedom for reporters should not result in robbing community radio of its flexibility or simplicity and render it completely professional.

Community Radio, Civil Society and Counterpublics

What is community radio? This question has been dealt with in its diversity and specificity from various descriptive positions in the book as also from the point of view of policy. The role that community radio plays in participatory development and in empowering the marginalised sections of society, especially women, has also been analytically examined in the context of relevant theoretical frameworks in the thematic chapters. To fathom deeper into the significant characteristics that identify community radio and for an understanding of 'community radio' as a conceptual category in itself, it may not suffice to work within a single theoretical framework. We are therefore making use of a combination of conceptual and theoretical underpinnings from disciplines such as community development, media studies, sociology and political science for a more elaborate analysis.

For this purpose, we are taking into account the three distinguishing aspects of community radio as emphasised in its definition, i.e., community participation, non-profit making and community ownership and management. The first aspect of community radio listed here can be explained in terms of its mandate to involve and serve a 'community'. The second feature sets community radio apart as an 'alternative' to mainstream media, while the third characteristic links community radio to 'civil society'. Our research suggests that these three processes of community radio facilitate the shifting of control of media technologies to those excluded and marginalised from the dominant public sphere. This helps to expand the discursive space through the formation of 'counterpublics' which could eventually facilitate collective action and offer a realistic emancipatory potential.

Conceptualising 'Community'

Community radio as the voice of the under-represented and a tool for social change first seeks to engage itself with the community. In any working definition of community radio, the concept of 'community' explicitly highlighted is that of the 'geographical community', while the 'community of interest' that may even extend 'across conurbations, nations and continents' (Lewis, 1993: 13) is also accounted for in some cases. Within the discipline of sociology, 'community' has been among 'the most fundamental and far-reaching of sociology's unit ideas' (Nisbet, 1967 as cited in Jodhka, 2001) and the dichotomy between 'society' and 'community' has been an influential framework for analysing social change. According to Tönnies (1955), 'community' is defined by the presence of close and concrete human ties and by a collective identity. Living inside a community (*gemeinschaft*), fosters a high degree of social cohesion that Morris and Morten (1998: 12–13) have exemplified as the 'notion of a big family'. Society (*gesellschaft*) or association is a collectivity of atomised individuals who come together guided by interests (Carpentier et al., 2002; Upadhya, 2001).

This dichotomy has been the basis of mainstream sociology and Western theories of evolutionary change and modernisation. The term 'community' in Indian sociology is also viewed as 'the relic of the pre-modern tradition and large, universalistic and impersonal political identity as the hallmark of modernity' (Chatterjee, 1998: 278). Upadhya (2001) argues that the term 'community' is associated with the modes of social organisation in pre-colonial Indian society such as caste (*jati*), village or religious sect and communities are regarded as natural groupings that endure over time by passing down shared traditions, customs, languages and social norms that get manifested as their specific 'culture'. The social organisation represented by community is generally understood as opposed to the individualism of the 'modern' society of the Western world. On the other hand, the growth of modernity is considered inimical to 'community' which is considered a repository of culture, language, human values and tradition in the non-Western world.

Most sociologists are now aware that the culturally defined and organically integrated communities may not necessarily be internally harmonious and homogeneous entities and are often marked by internal conflict, oppression and patriarchy. But their modes of 'civic association' have been placed above the individualism and materialism of the West by the 'communitarian' thinkers like Gandhi and Ashis Nandy. Reflecting on the notion of 'Community in the East', Chatterjee (1998: 278) observes:

> Guided by this modernizing propensity much of the recent history of non-Western societies has been written as a progressivist narrative of the evolution from small, local, and primordial community attachments to large, secular solidarities such as the nation....
>
> There is, however, a twist to the way in which this nationalist project of modernity was formulated as one different from Western modernity. While non-Western nationalists agreed that many of the traditional institutions and practices in their societies needed to be thoroughly changed for them to become modern, they also insisted that there were several elements in their tradition that were distinctly national, different from the Western, but nevertheless entirely consistent with the modern. Borrowing the categories of orientalists or colonial thought, they frequently posed this difference as one between Western materialism, individualism and disregard for traditional values and Eastern spiritualism, community solidarity and respect for tradition.

In posing the questions of individualism in the West and communitarian values in the East, the nationalist thinkers insisted that the latter represented a more appropriate version of modernity for non-Western states. A number of scholars have also sought to replace the 'primordialist' conception of community with a 'constructive' understanding of community, which is a result of the modern bureaucratic state, introduced in India by the colonial rule and the modern governing practices (Appadurai, 1997; Kaviraj, 1992; Ludden, 1992). Chatterjee's description of community also does not invoke primordial ties; rather it has been constructed 'to struggle for survival through networks of mutual support and collective action by the residents of a settlement'. Thus Chatterjee's communities are active sites of political and social action, the most significant feature of which is 'the way in which the imaginative power of traditional structure of community, including its fuzziness and capacity to invent relations of kinship has been wedded to the modern emancipatory rhetoric of autonomy and equal rights' (Chatterjee, 1998: 282).

The role of community radio to serve a community may thus be interpreted as facilitating access to and participation by members of the community who would then use it in the manner that Berrigan (1979: 8 cited in Carpentier et al., 2002) eloquently summarises:

> [Community media] are media to which members of the community have access, for information, education, entertainment, when they want access. They are media in which the community participates, as planners, producers, performers. They are the means of expression of the community, rather than for the community.

Community radio gives an opportunity to 'ordinary people', i.e., people who are not part of a societal elite (including politicians, experts and media professionals) and societal groups that are misrepresented, disadvantaged, stigmatised, or even repressed to have their voices heard. This process helps them to strengthen their internal identity and enable social change by manifesting this identity to the outside world (Carpentier et al., 2002).

An 'Alternative' to Mainstream Media

Girard (1992: 2) provides an answer to the question: 'So, why a passion for radio?'

> The answer to that question can be found in a third type of radio—an alternative to commercial and state radio. Often referred to as community radio, its most distinguishing characteristic is its commitment to community participation at all levels. While listeners of commercial radio are able to participate in the programming in limited ways via open line telephone shows

or by requesting a favourite song, for example—community radio listeners are the producers, managers, directors and even owners of the stations.

Alternative media grew as part of the counter-culture movement in the late 60s and 70s as unofficial opposition to mainstream corporate and state media. Kidd (1998), focusing on the word 'alternative', points out that alternative media advocate and work for social change. 'Alternative media are committed to altering society, to social, political and economic change.' The vision of alternative media is different from the corporate media, which view people as consumers to be delivered to advertisers. Kidd further explains that if the first part of alternative is *alter*, the last part of the word is *native*: 'Alternative media grow, like native plants, in the communities they serve, allowing spaces to generate historical memories and analyses, nurture visions for their futures, and weed out the representations of the dominant media.' This may be achieved through a wide combination of genres, from news, storytelling, conversation and debate to music in local languages.

Carpentier et al. (2002: 48) point out that mainstream media are:

- large-scaled and geared towards large, homogeneous (segments of) audiences;
- state-owned organisations or commercial companies;
- vertically structured organisations staffed by professionals; and
- carriers of dominant discourses and representations.

Alternative media take on converse positions on these matters and are:

- small-scaled and oriented towards specific communities, possibly disadvantaged groups, respecting their diversity;
- independent from state and market;
- horizontally structured, allowing for the facilitation of audience access and participation within the frame of democratisation and multiplicity; and
- carriers of non-dominant (possibly counter-hegemonic) discourses and representations, stressing the importance of self-representation.

Community radio as alternative media is a stimulus to pluralism, participation and equity and helps people wrest a grounded sense of cultural identity by engaging in ideas and expressions that catalyse social action. In *Pedagogy of the Oppressed*, Freire (1970) wrote about the US media's colonisation of the social and cultural life world of the oppressed. As a way of countering this dominance, it was necessary to recover historical memory, recollecting indigenous experiences that had been lost or denied during colonialism, and those in the process of being lost or denied during periods of military repression (Mattelart, 1983; Riaño, 1994). The method of education among the poor that Freire developed was based on the concept of *conscientisation*.[3] As part of a dialogical process, small groups of poor people from the same sector would analyse their own oppression and other social problems at work, in the family, and at school, and in their own cultural and linguistic forms, creatively counter the imported explanations and message. An individual learns to cultivate his or her own growth through situations from daily life that provide useful learning experiences. The individual reflects upon and analyses the world in which s/he lives as part of an effort to reform that world and to make it conform to his or her needs (Freire, 1970). Community radio can draw on Freire's legacy especially from his work on the recovery of historical memory and decolonising the mind from 'media manipulation'.

Community Radio and Civil Society

Community ownership and control locates community radio in the realm of civil society. These media can thus be considered the 'third voice' (Servaes, 1999: 260) between state media and private commercial media. There is a renewed interest in the concept of civil society and its political counterpart, the public sphere, as countries around the world are being undercut by the realities of contemporary globalisation. The dialectic of convergence and divergence is mounting pressure on governments to pave way for democratisation by nurturing institutions of civil society (Gaonkar, 2002). Taylor (1995: 66) defines civil society as 'a web of autonomous associations, independent of the state, which bound citizens together in matters of common concern, and by their mere existence or action could have an effect on public policy.' For Gramsci (1975), civil society comprises

> all the 'so-called-private' organizations such as churches, trade unions, political parties and the cultural associations which are distinct from the process

> of production and from the public apparatuses of the state. All organizations that make up civil society are the result of a complex network of social practices and social relations, including the struggle between the two fundamental classes, capital and labour (cited in Simon, 1982: 69).

For a further understanding of community radio as (part of) civil society, Carpentier et al. (2002) make use of Thompson's (1995: 122) model that describes the public and private domains in contemporary Western societies. The organisations related to the state are seen as constituting the public domain and privately owned economic organisations geared towards profit and personal as well as family relations are located in the private domain. Civil society is then defined as a group of intermediate organisations, separate from the privately owned economic organisations operating in the market economy, personal and family relations and from the state and quasi-state organisations. Even in societies where the public domain is repressive, different forms of what Lewis (1993: 127) named 'pockets of resistance' emerge to represent civil society.

Social and political theory in the second half of the twentieth century has been characterised by a loss of faith in the institution of the state, leading to a revival of interest in civil society (Mahajan, 1999). The democratic struggles of the people are accordingly placed in civil society, making it a domain of popular participation. Civil society thus becomes the 'leitmotif of movements struggling to free themselves from unresponsive and often tyrannical post-colonial elites' (Chandoke, 1998:30). For Kothari, the path of development that the state in India has adopted is deeply flawed: the focus on 'market efficiency', 'profitability', 'development' and 'national security' has made the Indian state unresponsive, if not hostile, to the basic rights of the common man. Civil society appears as the 'take-off point for humane governance' (Kothari, 1988: 2–3) and includes within its ambit contemporary social movements such as human rights movements, ecology movements, women's movements and the peace movement. Civil society also incorporates a 'network of voluntary, self-governing institutions in all walks of life'. Kothari associates civil society with all those forums in which people participate directly and manage their own affairs. What brings these diverse institutions together is the fact that they stand outside the state, offering an alternative to the state-sponsored forms of development.

Béteille, influenced to some extent by de Tocqueville, does not hold the same view as Kothari, who stated that civil society could take over the state's role. He specifies that civil society represents 'open and secular' institutions that mediate between the individual and the state (Béteille, 1996, 1999). He saw the civil society as a by-product of the modern constitutional state that embodies and endorses the modern idea of citizenship. He contends that the well-being of this modern state was dependant on diverse forms of mediating institutions that linked different individuals to each other on the one hand and on the other, negotiated between the citizens and the state. For Béteille, the state and the civil society are complementary and not alternatives to each other. He argues that the state performs certain indispensable functions and if those are submersed and undermined, civil society would wither in the bud (Mahajan, 1999).

The nature of civil society may vary extensively across nations and continents, but community radio as a crucial component of this segment is an important locus for the expansion of democracy. It provides communities the opportunity for extensive participation in public debate and for self-representation with an objective of bringing about social change. Downey and Fenton (2003) look at these alternative media as agents of counter-publicity in society that seek to break through into the dominant domain in their own right (rather than as decreed by corporately-controlled mass communications), providing the opportunity for ideological claims to be displaced, ruptured or contested.

Forging Counterpublics

In this context, it is worth recalling briefly the much-debated work of the German philosopher and social theorist Jürgen Habermas (1962), titled *The Structural Transformation of the Public Sphere*. In the first part of his historical narrative, Habermas traces the emergence of a bourgeois public sphere under liberal capitalism in the eighteenth century. Against the background of the demise of feudalism in Western Europe, he sketches the rise of a public sphere that consisted of spirited discussions and debates among certain sections of the educated, propertied class operating through such media as intellectual journals, pamphlets and newspapers, as well as in such settings as salons, coffee houses and clubs.

In the latter part of his work, Habermas discusses the decline of the bourgeois public sphere in the context of advanced industrial capitalism and the social welfare state of mass democracy. The refeudalisation of society (later termed, 'the colonisation of the life-world') displaces, to a large extent, the role of the public. The spread of mass media, with commercial logic transforming all public communication into public relations, advertising and entertainment, erodes the critical functions of the public. A fragmented public is reduced to mute spectators whose approbation is to be periodically mobilised.

Various versions of this story are in wide academic circulation and commentators and researchers have raised serious questions about this Habermasian narrative of the rise and fall of the public sphere. For instance, does a small group of economically and politically privileged men communicating with each other within the confines of a budding press and the spaces of salons, coffee houses, and exclusive societies amount to a genuine public sphere or is it, as Peter Dahlgren (1995) asked, 'merely an exercise in bourgeois self-delusion?'

By focusing attention on the bourgeois public sphere, Habermas neglected the significance of other forms of public discourse and activity that existed during the same period, but were outside the realm of bourgeois sociability. The work of E.P. Thompson and other historians has emphasised the relevance of a range of popular social and political movements many of which had a conflictual relationship with the bourgeois public sphere. Grounded as it was in a notion of small-scale print media and rational, conversational interaction among a small sector of smaller populations, we need to re-evaluate the relevance of Habermas' public sphere in the contemporary world dominated by large-scale societies and mass media. Further, in the face of efforts in the late twentieth century to forge a vibrant civil society through new social movements and voluntary action, the portrayal of the demise of the public sphere seems a little too pessimistic.

In an influential text, Negt and Kluge (1972) raised the possibilities for an alternative proletarian public realm for the working class and for dissident members of the intelligentsia allied with that class. Located in a Marxist framework, Negt and Kluge asserted that the development of an autonomous 'counter' public sphere would enable dissonant experience and knowledge of the working classes to be freely articulated, exchanged, debated and developed. Gradually, this new alternative public sphere could be expanded to a point at which it might replace the processes and structures of the bourgeois public sphere. Fraser's (1992) widely cited notion of *subaltern counterpublics* also indicates that alternative media represent parallel discursive spaces where participants can debate public issues of particular concern to them.

Freedom of expression and equitable access of communication media are gravely threatened in the twenty-first century, not by excessive use of state power as in an earlier period, but rather from the unhindered growth of media organisations into large-scale conglomerates. An unregulated market may develop in a way that effectively reduces diversity and pluralism, and limits the capacity of most individuals to make their views heard. So the question is: how can we stimulate a kind of publicness, which is neither part of the state nor wholly dependent on the autonomous processes of the market? This could be achieved by implementing what Thompson (1995) has called 'the principle of regulated pluralism'. This requires, in Thompson's words, 'establishment of an institutional framework which would both accommodate and secure the existence of a plurality of independent media organizations', free from the exercise of state power, but also unhindered by market forces.

Community radio allows citizens to be active in one of the many (micro-)spheres relevant to daily life and to exert their rights to communicate. These forms of micro-participation are important because they allow people to learn and adopt democratic and/or civic attitudes, thus strengthening various forms of macro-participation (Carpentier et al., 2002). Held (1987: 280) uses an apposite phrase to exemplify this, 'we learn to participate by participating'.

Notes

1. Although there have been functioning community radio stations in Nepal and Sri Lanka, they have either been operating under a general policy of privatisation or under the existing state structure of broadcasting.
2. Many of the provisions recommended here and also included in civil society submissions to the government have been incorporated in the policy announced in November 2006. For detailed guidelines issued by the Ministry, see http://mib.nic.in/CRS/CRBGUIDELINES041206.pdf.
3. In a group, participants codify and confront their social problems so that they, 'not as recipients but as knowing subjects, achieve a deepening awareness of both the socio-cultural reality that shapes their lives and of their capacity to transform that reality' (Freire, 1985: 93).

APPENDIX-I

Supreme Court Judgment on Airwaves, 1995

Operative part of the Supreme Court judgement delivered by Justice P.B. Sawant and Justice S. Mohan on 9.2.1995 in the case between the Union of India & Cricket Association of Bengal.

We, therefore, hold as follows:

(i) The airwaves or frequencies are a public property. Their use has to be controlled and regulated by a public authority in the interests of the public and to prevent the invasion of their rights. Since, the electronic media involves the use of the airwaves, this factor creates an in-built restriction on its use as in the case of any other public property.

(ii) The right to impart and receive information is a species of the right to freedom of speech and expression guaranteed by Article 19 (1) (a) of the Constitution. A citizen has a fundamental right to use the best means of imparting and receiving information and as such to have an access to telecasting for the purpose. However, this right to have an access to telecasting has limitations on account of the use of the public property, viz., the airwaves, involved in the exercise of the right and can be controlled and regulated by the public authority. This limitation imposed by the nature of the public property involved in the use of the electronic media is in addition to the restriction imposed on the right to freedom of speech and expression under Article 19 (2) of the Constitution.

(iii) The Central Government shall take immediate steps to establish an independent autonomous public authority representatives of all sections and interests in the society to control and regulate the use of the airwaves.

(iv) Since, the matches have been telecast pursuant to the impugned order of the High Court, it is not necessary to decide the correctness of the said order.

(v) The High Court will now apportion between the CAB and the DD the revenue generated by the advertisements on T.V. during the telecasting of both the series of the cricket matches viz. the Hero Cup, and the International Cricket Matches played in India from October to December, 1994, after hearing the parties on the subject.

The civil appeals are disposed of accordingly.

In view of the disposal of the civil appeals, the writ petition filed by the Cricket Association of Bengal also stands disposed of accordingly.

Operative part of the Supreme Court Judgement delivered by Justice B.P. Jeevan Reddy on 9.2.1995 in the case between the U.O.I. & Cricket Association of Bengal.

Summary

(As given in the Judgement)

In this summary too, the expression 'broadcast media' means the electronic media now represented and operated by AIR and Doordarshan and not any other services.

1. (a) Game of Cricket, like any other sports event, provides entertainment. Providing entertainment is implied in freedom of speech and expression guaranteed by Article 19 (1) (a) of the Constitution subject to this rider that where speech and conduct are joined in a single course of action, the free speech values must be balanced against competing societal interests. The petitioners (CAB and BCCI) therefore have a right to organise cricket matches in India, whether with or without the participation of foreign teams. But what they are now seeking is a license to telecast their matches through an agency of their choice- a foreign agency in both the cases–and through telecasting equipment brought in by such foreign agency from out

side the country. In the case of Hero Cup Matches, organised by BCCI, they did not ask for this facility for the reason that their foreign agent has arranged direct uplinking with the Russian satellite Gorizon . In both cases, they wanted the permission to import the telecasting equipment along with the personnel to operate it by moving it to places all over the country wherever the matches were to be played. They claimed this license, or permission, as it may be called, as a matter of right said to be flowing from Article 19 (1) (a) of the Constitution. They say that the authorities are bound to grant such license/permission, without any conditions, all that they are entitled to do, it is submitted, is to collect technical fees wherever their services are availed, like the services of VSNL in the case of Hero Cup Matches. This pleas is in principle no different freedom to right to establish and operate private telecasting stations. In principle, there is no difference between a permanent TV station and a temporary one; similarly there is no distinction in principle between a stationery TV facility and a mobile one; so also is there no distinction in principle between a regular TV facility and a TV facility for a given event or series of events. If the right claimed by the petitioners (CAB and BCCI) is held to be constitutionally sanctioned one, then each and every citizen of this country must also be entitled to claim similar right in respect of his event or events, as the case may be. I am of the opinion that no such right flows from Article 19 (1) (a).

(b) Airwaves constitute public property and must be utilised for advancing public good. No individual has a right to utilise them at his choice and pleasure and for purposes of his choice including profit. The right of free speech guaranteed by Article 19 (1) (a) does not include the right to use airwaves, which are public property. The airwaves can be used by a citizen for the purpose of broadcasting only when allowed to do so by a statute and in accordance with such statute. Airwaves, being public property, it is the duty of the State to see that airwaves are so utilised as to advance the free speech right of the citizens which is served by ensuring plurality and diversity of views, opinions and ideas. This is imperative in every democracy where freedom of speech is assured. The free speech right guaranteed to every citizen of this country does not encompass the right to use these airwaves at his choosing. Conceding, such a right would be detrimental to the free speech rights of the body of citizens in as much as only the privileged few powerful economic, commercial and political interests- would come to dominate the media. By manipulating the news, views and information, by indulging in misinformation and disinformation, to suit their commercial or other interests, they would be harming–and not serving–the principle of plurality and diversity of views, news, ideas and opinions. This has been the experience of Italy, where a limited right, i.e. at the local level but not at the national level was recognised. It is also not possible to imply or infer a right from the guarantee of free speech which only a few can enjoy.

(c) Broadcasting media is inherently different from Press or other means of communication/information. The analogy of Press is misleading and inappropriate. This is also the view expressed by several Constitutional Codes including that of the United States of America.

(d) I must clarify what I say, it is that the right claimed by the petitioners (CAB and BCCI) - which in effect is no different in principle from a right to establish and operate a private TV station - does not flow from Article 19 (1) (a); that such a right is not implicit in it. The question whether such right should be given to the citizens of this country is a matter of policy for the Parliament. Having regard to the revolution in information technology and the developments all around, Parliament may, or may not, decide to confer such right. If it wishes to confer such a right, it can only be by way of an Act made by Parliament. The Act made should be consistent with the right of free speech of the citizens and must have to contain strict programme and other controls, as has been provided, for example in the Broadcasting Act, 1991 in the United Kingdom. This is the implicit command of Article 19 (1) (a) and is essential to preserve and promote plurality and diversity of views, news, opinions and idea.

(e) There is an inseparable inter-connection between freedom of speech and the stability of the society, i. e. stability of a nation-State. They contribute to each other. Ours is a nascent republic. We are yet to achieve the goal of a stable society. This country cannot also afford to read into Article 19 (1) (a) an unrestricted right to licensing (right of broadcasting) as claimed by the petitioners therein.

(f) In the case before us, both the petitioners have sold their right to telecast the matches to a foreign agency. They have parted with the right. The right to telecast the matches, including the right to import, install and operate the requisite equipment, is thus really sought by the foreign agencies and not by the petitioners. Hence, the question of violation of their right under Article 19 (1) (a) resulting from refusal of license/permission to such foreign agencies does not arise.

2. The Government monopoly of broadcasting media in this country is the result of historical and other factors. This is true of every other country, to start with. That India was not a free country till 1947 and its citizens did not have constitutionally guaranteed fundamental freedom till 1950 coupled with the fact that our Constitution is just about forty five years into operation explains the Government monopoly. As pointed out in the body of the judgement, broadcasting media was a monopoly of the Government, to start with in every country except the United States where a conscious decision was taken at the very beginning not to have State monopoly over the medium. Until recently, the broadcasting media has been in the hands of public/statutory corporations in most of the West European countries. Private broadcasting is comparatively a recent phenomenon. The experience in Italy of allowing private broadcasting at local level (while prohibiting it at national level) has left much to be desired. It has given rise to powerful media empires which development is certainly not conducive to free speech right of the citizens.

3. (a) It has been held by this Court–and rightly–that broadcasting media is affected by the free speech right of the citizens guaranteed by Article 19 (1) (a). This is also the view expressed by all the Constitutional Courts whose opinions have been referred to in the body of the judgement. Once this is so, monopoly of this medium (broadcasting media), whether by Government or by an individual, body or organisation is unacceptable. Clause (2) of Article 19 does not permit a monopoly in the matter of freedom of speech and expression as is permitted by Clause (6) of Article 19 vis-à-vis the right guaranteed by Article 19 (1) (a).

(b) The right of free speech and expression includes the right to receive and impart information. For ensuring the free speech right of the citizens of this country, it is necessary that the citizens have the benefit of plurality of views and a range of opinions on all public issues. A successful democracy posits an "aware" citizenry. Diversity of opinions, views, ideas and ideologies is essential to enable the citizens to arrive at informed judgement on all issues touching them. This cannot be provided by a medium controlled by a monopoly–whether the monopoly is of the State or any other individual, group or organisation. As a matter of fact, private broadcasting stations may perhaps be more prejudicial to free speech right of the citizens than the government controlled media, as explained in the body of the judgement. The broadcasting media should be under the control of the public as distinct from Government. This is the command implicit in Article 19 (1) (a). It should be operated by a public statutory corporation or corporations, as the case may be, whose constitution and composition must be such as to ensure its/their impartiality in political, economic and social matters and on all other public issues. It/they must be required by law to present news, views and opinions in a balanced way ensuring pluralism and diversity of opinions and views. It/they must provide equal access to all the citizens and groups to avail of the medium.

4. The Indian Telegraph Act, 1885 is totally inadequate to govern an important medium like the radio and television, i.e., broadcasting media. The Act was intended for an altogether different purpose when it was enacted. This is the result of the law in this country not keeping pace with the technological advances in the field of information and communications. While all the leading democratic countries have enacted laws specifically governing the broadcasting media, the law in this country has stood still, rooted in the Telegraph Act of 1885. Except Section 4 (1) and the definition of telegraph, no other provision of the Act is shown to have any relevance to broadcasting media. It is, therefore, imperative that the Parliament makes a law placing the broadcasting media in the hands of a public/statutory corporate or the corporations, as the case may be. This is necessary to safeguard the interests of public and the interests of law as also to avoid uncertainty, confusion and consequent litigation
5. The CAB did not ever apply for a license under the first proviso to Section 4 of the Telegraph Act nor did its agents-ever

make such an application. The permissions, clearances or exemption obtained by it from the several departments (mentioned in judgement) are no substitute for a licence under Section 4 (1) proviso. In the absence of such a license, the CAB had no right in law to have its matches telecast by an agency of its choice. The legality or validity of the orders passed by Shri N. Vithal, Secretary to the Government of India, Telecommunications Department, need not be gone into since it has become academic. In the facts and circumstances of the case, the charge of malafides or of arbitrary and authoritarian conduct attributed to Doordarshan and Ministry of Information and Broadcasting is not acceptable. No opinion need be expressed on the allegations made in the Interlocutory Application filed by BCCI in these matters. Its intervention was confined to legal questions only.

6. Now the question arises, what is the position till the Central Government or the Parliament take steps as contemplated in para (4) of the summary, i.e., if any sporting event or other event is to be telecast from the Indian soil? The obvious answer flowing from the judgement (and Paras (1) and (4) of this summary) is that the organiser of such event has to approach the nodal Ministry as specified in the decision of the Meeting of the Committee of Secretaries held on November 12, 1993. I have no reason to doubt that such a request would be considered by the nodal Ministry and the AIR and Doordarshan on its merits, keeping in view the public interest. In case of any difference of opinion or dispute regarding the monetary terms on which such telecast is to be made, matter can always be referred to an Arbitrator or a panel of Arbitrators. In case, the nodal Ministry or the AIR or Doordarshan find such broadcast/telecast not feasible, then they may consider the grant of permission to the organisers to engage an agency of their own for the purpose. Of course, it would be equally open to the nodal Ministry (Government of India) to permit such foreign agency in addition to AIR/Doordarshan, if they are of the opinion that such a course is called for in the circumstances.

For the above reasons, the appeals, writ petition and applications are disposed of in the above terms. No costs.

Source: http://mib.nic.in/informationb/POLICY/frames.htm

APPENDIX-II

Bangalore Declaration on Radio, 1996

September 1996:

The present decade is significant for the country's development in a number of ways. Decentralization of governance, professed emphasis on social service, impact of the communications revolution and increased general awareness of human rights has opened up opportunities and challenges on an unprecedented scale. Information is a key element in socio-economic development. The capacity to communicate and have access to media greatly influences information use and its impact, and if these far reaching changes in the econômic, technological and social spheres can be harnessed to generate new and vital information with a media that is democratized, it could empower the impoverished and disadvantaged millions, and the process of development can be given a fresh impetus and a more purposive orientation.

From September 11–14, 1996, during a four day Consultation on Community Radio and Media Policy, more than sixty people representing All India Radio, universities, non government organizations involved in development activities, journalists, and members of the broadcasting establishment, met in Bangalore to discuss the problems and prospects of evolving a sectoral broadcasting. The discussions focused on the means and modalities of establishing, at the earliest, a democratic, dynamic and people-oriented system of public service broadcasting in the country. A variety of factors peculiar to the Indian situation today which tend to suggest that a liberal policy in respect of radio broadcasting with emphasis on community participation and local control, will be appropriate to the current development strategy were discussed, along with the prospects of formulating a broadcast policy in respect to radio which ensures the optimum utilisation of airwaves in public interest, facilitating community management of information exchange and participatory modes of decision making. The institutionalisation and expansion of the concept of community broadcasting was proposed, with the involvement of people at all levels across the length and breadth of this vast country. Democracy and good governance make such a change imperative, and it is an essential pre-requisite for better enjoyment of human rights. The Consultation resulted in a consensus, called the Bangalore Declaration on Radio, which outlines the basic elements of a desirable media policy on radio broadcasting.

Given the set of current policies aimed at decentralization, liberalization and people's participation in various areas, it is hoped that the Bangalore Declaration on Radio will receive the timely and earnest attention of relevant authorities, and that the concept of community radio will soon become a reality. Meanwhile, it is important that universities, public bodies, women's organizations, dalit associations–to name a few–prepare themselves for the task of establishment and participatory management of community radio stations with an agenda appropriate to, and determined by their communities: this is the near term challenge and unique opportunity. Community radio will bring fresh validity and meaning to the concept of decentralized governance envisaged by73rd and 74th Amendments of the Constitution, and catalyze the process of people's empowerment through information and education. It is with this hope and reasonable expectation that the Bangalore Declaration is being presented to the public for a wider discussion, support and follow up action.

National Broadcasting Policy: Towards Public Service Broadcasting through Community Radio

Preamble

Whereas the right to receive and impart information is recognised as a guaranteed basic right under the Constitution; and whereas the Supreme Court of India has declared airwaves as public property to be utilised for promoting public good and ventilating plurality and diversity of views, opinions and ideas, and that towards this end, the broadcasting media should be under the control of the public as distinct from the government; whereas it is necessary to promote local broadcasting through community based radio stations for the successful implementation of decentralised governance envisaged under the 73rd and 74th Constitutional Amendments; and whereas successive committees appointed by the government to examine the issue have recommended the adoption of a comprehensive national broadcasting policy with participation of the private sector, NGOs, local self government institutions and other community groups providing a framework for media development in the context of technological progress and national needs.

It is now proposed to present the elements of a National Broadcasting Policy on the basis of which Parliament could enact legislation for regulating the airwaves as a public property, whose utilisation in the context of electronic media–TV and Radio–is intended to promote public good.

Since the Bangalore Consultation was specifically focused on radio broadcasting, the statement of policy contained herein is limited only to the radio broadcasting sector, and in particular, it's community broadcasting application. It is our hope that this statement would be included appropriately in the National Media Policy which would cover all media–Television, Radio, Cinema and Print.

Statement

The Legislative Imperative

1. Airwaves are public property and must be used for public good. Public good isn't served optimally when there is a monopoly by the government over this public resource or when liberalization of broadcasting is confined to commercial use of airwaves. Access to the airwaves by everyone who acts in the public interest is the *sine qua non* of pubic good in this context. This is also part of the right to information, a guaranteed constitutional right.

Need for Community Radio

2. Centralised one-way broadcasting at various levels of aggregation has limited scope to serve the goals of development, especially in the context of pluralism and diversity which is

a singular characteristic of Indian society. As such, the regulatory framework should promote a decentralised system of radio broadcasting.

3. Community broadcasting, is a concept relevant to social cohesion, development for conviviality and national integration. Community radio is public service broadcasting in its most decentralised and democratic form. A community radio station serves a defined geographical area of a village or a group of villages, and is owned and managed by organisations serving a given community.
4. A community radio station would, besides providing education and entertainment, connect people with people through participatory or circular communication, connect people with organisations and communities, and finally connect people with government and public service agencies. These needs are not met under the current framework.
5. In a number of ways, community or public interest broadcasting can be termed Equal Opportunity Broadcasting, which is essential not only for effective democratisation of a public resource viz. the airwaves, but also in the context of our plural society with a multiplicity of languages, cultures and ethnic groups.

Policy Formulation

6. Radio combines the benefits of low cost and wide reach and access. When used in a community setting with limited area coverage, for example as in FM radio broadcasting, it offers many exciting possibilities for fulfilling the developmental goals and aspirations of the people, and wider choices in accessing information from diveıse sources within and outside the community. It's potential for creating social change has been demonstrated in many parts of the world. For these reasons, control of community broadcasting should be vested with the community rather than with the government or private commercial enterprises.
7. The present centralised structure of broadcasting isn't conducive to people-centered, participatory methods of communications. The potential of the medium to promote community

development is largely unrealised. The involvement of other public bodies, NGOs, professional associations, etc. in the utilisation and management of airwaves is essential for realising this potential to promote the welfare of millions in communities, and therefore the public good. The need for structural change in airwaves in order to accommodate local initiatives is a logical result of this imperative.

8. As recommended by the Paswan Committee (1996), while there can be a single national policy which addresses macro-level issues common to all media, medium-specific policies are required for each medium, taking into account the coverage, reach, cost-structure, technology, administration and, finally, the social application of the medium.
9. Radio broadcasting, like other media, has developed around power centres and power structures in society, resulting in disparity of access and use among different sections of society. Changes in media policy which seek to mitigate if not eliminate these disparities require political will and a people-centered, bottom-up approach already contemplated in the 74th Constitutional Amendment. Community radio is an illustration of this evolutionary process; therefore, it needs to be acknowledged and promoted.
10. At the operational level, a regulatory structure which is independent of the government and existing broadcasting organisations, public and private, should be set up in order to facilitate and support all licensed broadcasters in the country and their shared use of the airwaves under a fair and reasonable regime, consonant with national interest and priorities. The structure must address a variety of issues such as licensing criteria for various categories of broadcasting, technical and service standards, technical support and training, social and administrative auditing, funding sources and support, etc.
11. Frequency spectrum resources–particularly in the band allocated for FM radio broadcasting viz. 86-108 MHz must be made available on a shared basis with existing services for community broadcasting applications. Efforts will be made to evolve a national plan for the allocation of frequencies in this band so that the establishment of a large number of community radio stations across the country, based on a high degree of frequency re-use, is facilitated.

Note:

Far-reaching structural and managerial changes in the regulation and administration of the electronic media by the government have been recommended by the various committees appointed to examine the issue. These have been partly reflected in the Prasar Bharati Act (1990). This Act might require changes if the statement of policy contained in the Bangalore Declaration is to be adopted in legislation. At the Bangalore Consultation on Community Radio and Media Policy, a possible structure for autonomous public service radio broadcasting was discussed, taking into account the appropriate features of such a structure and also the ground realities of the country. The outcomes of these discussions, titled 'Structure of Public Service Radio Broadcasting in India: Some Essential Features.' is appended to this document as Annexure I. Admittedly, some of the features listed therein–particularly those related to the proposed structure provides a basis for discussion, once the important policy decisions on public control of airwaves and the concept of community broadcasting are taken. A list of signatories to the Bangalore Declaration is at Annexure II.

Annexure I

Essential Features of a Public Service Radio Broadcasting Structure

Regulatory Authority and Licensing Criteria

1. To regulate and oversee broadcasting activities in the country under a liberalized framework, a National Broadcast Trust (NBT) as outlined by the Verghese Committee (1978) should be established. The NBT will be an autonomous body made up of eminent professionals and other individuals, and would be free from government control.
2. The current framework adopted by national broadcasting agencies is of three-tier broadcasting, viz. national, regional and local. It is proposed here to enable the setting up of a separate and independent tier–at village/community level. The nature of community broadcasting warrants that it should be owned

and managed by the community itself. For all other purposes, community broadcasting will be entitled to the same rights and obligations as broadcasting agencies at the other levels.

3. The term 'community' for this purpose shall mean a non-rigid group of people living in a bounded geographical area which is determined by the reach of the radio broadcasting station, and who share a commonality of concerns, interests and aspirations.
4. No monopoly or exclusive control by any interest group within the community will be permitted. The community, in all its diversity, should exercise democratic control over community broadcasting and establish appropriate systems of accountability, within and outside the community, as may be necessary. Equal opportunity to all groups in the community in respect of access to communication will be the distinct feature of a community radio station.
5. Given the complexities of the local communities in India, the regulatory authority may grant licenses to other bodies serving the public interest in a phased manner. In the first phase, universities with extension activities (for example, agricultural universities, medical institutions, adult and legal literacy organisations), registered cooperatives and autonomous public bodies fulfilling minimum criteria for eligibility should be granted licenses to set up community radio stations to serve the public interest.

Programming

6. While granting licenses for community radio stations, the NBT will direct All India Radio to provide the required development and technical support to be licensees, including training of technicians and programmers. The licensee shall bear the costs of programming as well as operating and maintenance costs of the community radio station.
7. A local advisory committee, representing varied public interests within the community, shall be appointed, preferably by a local judge, for a fixed tenure. The committee shall guide the programme content of transmissions from the community radio station. The committee shall guide all other collective decisions relating to the operations of the community radio station,

as well as guide all other collective decisions relating to the operations of the community radio station, such as hours of transmission, scheduling and so on.

8. The interactive format for programming shall be encouraged to make the programmes truly participatory. A baseline-programming element will relate to environment, health, women's empowerment, education, legal matters and other such public interest issues.
9. Building linkages between private broadcasters, on the one hand, and local self-government institutions, educational and professional bodies, and special interest groups on the other hand, will be essential. It is important that these groups are provided access to the medium in order to serve the public interest in all its dimensions. Such participation would, of course, be innovative. Community radio stations should also work in concert with government agencies in reaching out to and promoting the economic and social welfare of the marginalised and disadvantaged groups within the community.
10. The NBT may lay down guidelines on programme content promotive of public interest and may monitor community radio stations. It may exercise sanctions to discipline erring stations, again the public interest as elucidated in the policy statement.
11. Community radio stations may be obliged to broadcast during an agreed period, national messages provided by AIR, for which the radio networking receiver facilities may be extended by the latter.

Role of All India Radio

12. All India Radio, with it's extensive infrastructure, trained personnel and vast experience, shall play a crucial but supportive role in the development of community radio broadcasting, under the guidance of the NBT. It's new role in this sphere shall be carried out to help carry out it's new role effectively.
13. All India Radio shall provide assistance to licensed community broadcasters in the design of their radio stations in respect of intended coverage, technical configuration of transmitter and studio, and standardisation of the service at low investment

levels; it shall also provide technical training for operation of the facilities. AIR could also evolve a Handbook/Manual on community broadcasting, based on technical/systems studies, which can be a source book for the NBT in decision making on technical matters and for potential broadcasters.

Checks and Balances

14. To ensure social and public accountability, it is desirable that each community radio station evolves its own code of conduct and strictly abide by it in its programming, transmissions and management. A local Ombudsman consisting of three persons who are widely respected for their experience and integrity shall be attached to each radio station. The Ombudsman will entertain complaints from individuals and institutions and can decide on the culpability or otherwise of the radio station concerned. Once indicted by the Ombudsman, the radio station will have to make amends and strictly abide by the directions. More than three such violations may entail withdrawal of the license, or other privileges of the station or its officers.
15. The station can also be brought under the Consumer Protection Act as a provider of services in a limited number of cases.
16. If the regulatory authority directs a radio station to close down or if the station can't for other reasons, including emergencies, AIR shall have the authority to keep the assets in trust till the problem is resolved and the station resumes broadcasting. If AIR is to finally and irrevocably take over the station along with the assets, the owner shall receive due compensation in respect of the assets taken over by AIR.

Funding and Management

17. All community radio stations will work on the principle of no-profit, no-loss. Initial capital expenditure shall be met largely by a grant through the National Broadcast Trust, contributions from member institutions, donations from the public, fees from listeners for the broadcast of local messages and advertisements, sponsorship charges, radio club subscriptions, etc.

18. The appropriate legal form for a community radio station could be either a Society registered under the Societies Registration Act, or a Trust under the Trusts Act. The regulatory authority could also examine other options for management of community radio stations and a final organisational format can be arrived at.

Interim Measures by the Government

19. In order to promote community broadcasting and the development of necessary skills in programming and other areas in the interim period when the legislative framework of the community radio and follow up action are pending, the Government could provide for the following:

    (a) Airtime in AIR Local Radio Stations for programmes developed by different community and special interest groups to provide regular community interaction with audiences within the coverage areas.
    (b) Airtime in Private Radio Stations licensed by the Government for institutions and public bodies within the community to provide regular community programming to audiences within the coverage areas.
    (c) Mandatory setting up of Community Broadcasting Stations by licensed broadcasters–government and private–as a fraction of the total number of local radio stations licensed by the NBT e.g. for every five Local radio Stations licenses granted, the licensee is obliged to set up one community radio station.

Source: http://www.communityradionetwork.org/leftlinks/advocacy/bang_decl

APPENDIX-III

The Pastapur Initiative on Community Radio Broadcasting, 2000

Pastapur, Medak Dist., A.P., July 19, 2000

A group consisting of media practitioners and researchers, educators and trainers, non-governmental organisations involved in development activities, journalists, representatives from All India Radio, and faculty and students of mass communication and law have met from July 17-20 at Hyderabad and Pastapur, A.P. to discuss and evolve a policy for community radio in India. The four-day consultation was organised under the auspices of UNESCO jointly by VOICES, Bangalore, the Sarojini Naidu School of Performing Arts, Fine Arts, and Communication, University of Hyderabad, and the Deccan Development Society, Pastapur (A.P.).

The participants reviewed the status of community radio and the potential of communities to serve as effective tools for development at the local level. The group listened to the voices of the community that are pleading for access to media in order to represent their own realities more effectively. During the consultations, the group was also given demonstrations of low-cost, affordable technologies for radio transmission by organisations and individuals familiar with them.

After carefully deliberating the overall media scenario in the country and in other democratic countries, the role of public service broadcasting, the state-initiated moves toward decentralisation and privatisation, and the role of non-governmental organisations in grassroots development programmes:

The group notes that:

Radio broadcasting in India functioned until recently under a state-monopoly public service broadcasting system. This, however, has undergone a change since the opening of the airwaves last year when the government auctioned FM radio frequencies for commercial operation.

The group shares the concerns of various communication experts and policy-makers about:

The increasing commodification of broadcasting by private operators who treat listeners as passive receivers and consumers of media content.

The group resolves that:

A truly people's radio would perceive listeners not only as receivers and consumers, but also as active citizens and creative producers of media content.

- Recalling Article 19 of the Universal Declaration of Human Rights which sets forth the freedom of opinion and expression and the right to receive and impart information and ideas;
- The People's Communication Charter which endorses that communication and information services should be guided by respect for fundamental human rights, and in the spirit of public interest;
- The judgement of the Supreme Court of India (1995) that the airwaves are public property and must be used for public good;
- The Bangalore Declaration on Radio (1996) which underlined the need for a democratic dynamic and people-oriented system of public service broadcasting in the country;
- The Government of India's stated policy objectives for local radio, as outlined in All India Radio guidelines and the report of the Prasar Bharati Review Committee; and
- The Milan Declaration on Communication and Human Rights (1998) which has asserted that communications media have a responsibility to help sustain the diversity of the world's cultures and languages and that they should be supported through legislative, administrative, and financial measures.

The group strongly urges the Government of India:

- To take the current government policy of freeing broadcasting from state monopoly to its logical conclusion by expanding the available media space and permitting communities and organisations representing them to run their own radio stations.

For the purpose of community radio as it is proposed here, the group defines:

- Community as a non-sectarian group of individuals who are territorially-bound and share a common socio-economic position/interest.
- Community radio as having three key aspects: non-profit making, community ownership and management, and community participation.
- Community radio is distinguished by its limited local reach, low-power transmission, and programming content that reflects the educational, developmental and cultural needs of the specific community it serves.

Taking into consideration, the experiences, policy precedents, and judicial interpretations from other democratic countries, the group recommends:

- The creation of a three-tier system of broadcasting in the country: a state-owned public service network (existing framework), commercial private broadcasting, and non-profit, people-owned and managed community radio stations.

The group pleads with the Government of India:

- To dedicate frequencies, specifically, for the creation, maintenance and expansion of community broadcasting in the country.

The group is of the opinion that this measure would help:

- Transform broadcasting in India into a system based on principles of universal access, diversity, equitable resource allocation, democratisation of airwaves, and empowerment of historically disadvantaged sections of society.

Considering the socio-economic and communication disparities in the country, the group recommends that:

- Priority should be given in issuing of community broadcasting licenses to rural areas and other regions and communities that are least developed in terms of various socio-economic indicators. This is based on the fact that the least developed regions and communities of the country are also least served by media.

The group recognises and appreciates:

- The long and sincere efforts of various non-governmental organisations such as the Deccan Development Society, Pastapur (A.P.), VOICES, Bangalore, the Kutch Mahila Vikas Sangathan and SEWA, Gujarat in using audio-visual technologies for the empowerment of local communities.

The group which has visited the site of the Deccan Development Society's Community Radio Station located in Machnoor village, Medak District (A.P.), near its headquarters in Pastapur, and interacted with the poor, rural women, places on record its deep appreciation of:

- The eagerness of the women of the area to have a 'radio of their own' and their state of readiness to manage a community radio station.

The group, therefore, urges the Government of India:

- To take immediate steps to license various community radio initiatives around the country and usher in an era of vibrant, community broadcasting sector in India. Finally, the following signatories strongly urge the Government of India:
- To formulate progressive and innovative policy that fosters and encourages community radio so that the developmental objectives set forth in the Constitution could be fully realised.

Source: Available with the authors and the Deccan Development Society, Hyderabad. Also available at http://community radioindia.info/index.php/topic,14.0.html, last accessed on 24 August 2007.

APPENDIX-IV

Executive Summary of Recommendations for a Policy on Community Radio Broadcasting in India

(Put together by media activists and academicians at a Workshop on 'Designing an Enabling Framework for Community Radio in India' organised by the Ministry of Information and Broadcasting in May 2004)

1. Eligibility

It was recommended that eligibility of applicants for community radio and allotment of licenses can be modeled on tried-and-proven practices of other countries, e.g., ABA, the Radio Authority of UK etc. A case was made for addressing the eligibility issue in the licensing procedure rather than in the policy framework. A basic requirement for receiving a license is that the licensee must demonstrate a proven track record of work in the community it claims to represent. Due weightage should be given to the standing, commitment, objectives and resources of the applicant organization, and an important criterion for the allotment of a CR license should be the quality and comprehensiveness of the proposal submitted by the applicant.

Eligibility criteria should not be overtly exclusive, and rather than attempting to define eligibility, it may be more logical to define who is not eligible for a CR license. For instance, religious and political entities should not be permitted to hold CR licenses. The licensee should preferably be a registered entity, though this should not be a precondition. They may be required to register themselves within a suitable time-frame. The possibility of holding 'public hearings' prior to sanctioning licenses, as in countries like South Africa, could also be looked into.

The issue of offering licenses to intermediaries like NGOs was addressed. It was pointed out that it would be difficult for an amorphous entity like a community to apply for a radio station in India, and intermediaries—like NGOs—necessarily had to be involved. However, Community Radio was not necessarily NGO Radio, and hence the need to widen the range of eligible entities.

An indicative list of groups that could apply for a Community Radio license would be: *Gram-Sabhas* and recognised community cooperatives, local self-help groups, NGOs and voluntary organisations, local schools and educational institutions.

Three aspects of eligibility would be (a) the validity of the claim that the applicant represents a local community (b) the length of time during which the entity has been actively working in the region and (c) the applicant's proven track record of community development work in the area of the license.

The question of issuing CR licenses to Panchayats and other local bodies was also discussed, but it was felt that this would be counterproductive. One of the functions of Community Radio is to assess and report on the achievements and failures of the local administration, and a community radio station owned by a Panchayat would not be able to perform this function in an impartial manner.

2. Representative Body

It is recommended that an Association of community broadcasters, like CBAA (Community Broadcasters Association of Australia) or NCRF (South Africa) should be set up in India to support community radio initiatives in various ways. While the composition of the body was not discussed, it was stressed that the representative body would act as a conduit for seed funding and assistance, mutual cooperation, content sharing, capacity building, liaising with central departments etc. It would act as an interface between the government and community radio applicants/licensees, since small communities with limited resources may not be able to deal routinely with central government departments.

The proposed national body representing CR would also be a forum to address issues of self-regulation. It would ensure codes of conduct/practices, facilitate public hearings in the community and act as mediator between the regulator and the community station. It would also form the first court of appeal by communities if they have a complaint against their local CR station.

3. License Fee & Spectrum Usage Fee

It is obvious that small and marginalised communities, especially in the rural sector, cannot afford the kind of license fees levied on commercial stations. Since community stations are not-for-profit, and are run for developmental rather than commercial purposes, a high license fee would be anomalous. Spectrum Usage Fee would be another significant non-programming recurring expense for CR stations. For instance, it was stated that Anna FM pays an annual SUF of Rs.19,500, an amount which would be a severe drain on the resources of any self-supporting community station.

It was therefore recommended that license fee and spectrum usage fee for community radio should to be kept at affordable levels.

4. Regulations and Monitoring

Some form of non-intrusive supervision by an autonomous regulator would be preferable to overt regulation.

International experience suggests that there are several ways to prevent the misuse of community radio stations. The community radio experience in Australia indicates that monitoring is done on a voluntary basis by the public, and that the government does not have to be a monitoring agency. Since broadcasting is a public activity, people tend to complain if they find anything wrong. It could be made compulsory for every CR station to advertise–on air–that if the public has any objections to its programming, they should make an immediate complaint.

CR stations could also be required to preserve recorded tapes of their programmes for, say, three months. The deployment of its revenues by the CR station should also be monitored, and its books audited once a year. It was recommended that public hearings should be organised, where the licensee has to state the mission of his CR station. Programme monitoring would then be taken up by the community.

5. Licensing Process

A simplified licensing process needs to be set in place for community radio. It was noted that the present process of seeking clearances from at least 6 ministries and departments was cumbersome and time consuming. Remote and rural communities, in particular, would not have the resources or time necessary to liaise on a continuous basis with central ministries and departments. In the interest of expediting the process, it was recommended that there should a *single window clearance system,* and that the procedure should be time bound.

It is understood that a clear time-frame has been proposed for frequency allocation and SACFA clearance, but time limits also need to be set for obtaining other clearances–including security clearance. This could be achieved by initiating dialogue with the concerned Ministries and Departments.

6. Commercials/Sponsorships

It was recommended that, to ensure sustainability, limited on-air commercial activity—including advertisements and sponsorship announcements—should be permitted on Community Radio. This should be subject to the condition that community stations may only broadcast advertisements/sponsorship messages which relate to businesses, services, work opportunities and events that are relevant and limited to the specified area. Community stations should also ensure that the sponsors of programmes do not influence either the content or style of individual programmes, nor the overall programming of the community station.

Limited advertising on community radio channels is permitted in many countries. Australia allows five minutes of commercials in every hour of programming, while in South Africa, the limit is four minutes per hour. As a means of financial sustainability, the government should permit a mix of government and non-government sponsorship and limited advertising on CR, with emphasis on local services and products. Checks and balances would have to be built into policy to ensure that community radio stations are not over-commercialised.

The Commercial Code of All India Radio would apply to the community broadcaster.

7. Funding

Community radio should be allowed to access funds from all legal sources. However, safeguards should be built in to ensure that funding agencies do not influence programming. It was agreed that restrictions on funding could be a serious constraint, especially for poorer communities that cannot afford the initial high cost of setting up a CR station. Funds can be legitimately accessed through many channels, and such seed funds would be vital to establish and sustain a community station, for the creation of infrastructure, capacity building, research & development of innovative programming etc.

Community Stations should be permitted, either directly or through their representative body, to solicit grants, donations, and other monetary contributions from Government, the private sector, institutions, groups and individuals, and also from foreign donors after taking necessary clearances.

8. Technical Parameters

Technical parameters such as transmitter power and area of coverage for Community Radio stations have to be different from those in place for campus radio. Coverage area for community radio stations must be consistent with the geographical area in which the community being served is located, and consequently, a range of transmitter power may be required depending on the coverage area and terrain. The permitted transmitter power and tower height should be decided on the basis of the area of work of the licensee and/or the geographic dispersal of listeners.

Data-casting is an important developmental tool, and would be invaluable for information-deprived communities. Data-casting, therefore, should be permitted on community radio.

Community radio applicants should be able to apply for frequency allocation and SACFA clearance simultaneously, and the procedures for technical clearances should be simplified and time-bound.

While the frequencies of 90.4, 90.8 and 91.2 MHz have been set aside for community radio, 91 MHz has been given to commercial FM operators in certain cities, where it would potentially interfere with community radio frequencies. This frequency should either be blocked, or alternative frequencies should be made available for CR.

The release of additional frequencies for CR should also be explored. Where there is limited spectrum availability or limited resources and capacities of an individual applicant, frequency sharing by more than one applicant may be permitted.

9. Codes of Conduct

It was recommended that a Code of Practice should be evolved for community radio which enshrines agreed standards among community broadcasters. The Code would guide all areas of CR activity, including station management and programming. The Code of Practice would be a document of self-regulation that would not only facilitate good programming practices and editorial independence, it would also act as a shield from interference by vested interests.

10. Accountability Parameters

It was recommended that accountability parameters should be built into the management structure of CR, its implementing structure, and content creation. At all these levels, participation by the community, the station management and the advisory body has to be ensured. To ensure accountability, and to facilitate good programming practices and editorial independence, it was also recommended that the representative body should implement codes of conduct, and facilitate regular public hearings in the community.

To address and pre-empt regulatory and security concerns, it was proposed to have a trial period or short term license for CR applicants. The trial period would also allow for examination of related issues such as who represents the community, the degree of community participation achieved, the sustainability of the station etc.

Source: Available the with authors and Community Radio Frum, India. Also available at http://communityradioindia.info/index.php/topic,15.0. html, last accessed on 24 August 2007.

APPENDIX-V

Policy Guidelines for setting up Community Radio Stations in India, Ministry of Information & Broadcasting, Government of India, December 2006

Foreword

In December 2002, the Government of India approved a policy for the grant of licenses for setting up of Community Radio Stations to well established educational institutions including IITs/IIMs.

The matter has been reconsidered and the Government has now decided to broad base the policy by bringing 'Non-profit' organisations like civil society and voluntary organisations etc under its ambit in order to allow greater participation by the civil society on issues relating to development & social change. The detailed policy guidelines in this regard is given below:

1. Basic Principles

An organisation desirous of operating a Community Radio Station (CRS) must be able to satisfy and adhere to the following principles:

(a) It should be explicitly constituted as a 'non-profit' organisation and should have a proven record of at least three years of service to the local community.

(b) The CRS to be operated by it should be designed to serve a specific well-defined local community.

(c) It should have an ownership and management structure that is reflective of the community that the CRS seeks to serve.

(d) Programmes for broadcast should be relevant to the educational, developmental, social and cultural needs of the community.

(e) It must be a Legal Entity i.e. it should be registered (under the registration of Societies Act or any other such act relevant to the purpose).

2. Eligibility Criteria

(i) The following types of organisations shall be eligible to apply for Community Radio licenses:

  (a) Community based organisations, which satisfy the basic principles listed at para 1 above. These would include civil society and voluntary organisations, State Agriculture Universities (SAUs), ICAR institutions, Krishi Vigyan Kendras, Registered Societies and Autonomous Bodies and Public Trusts registered under Societies Act or any other such act relevant for the purpose. Registration at the time of application should at least be three years old.

  (b) Educational institutions.

(ii) The following shall not be eligible to run a CRS:

  (a) Individuals;

  (b) Political Parties and their affiliate organisations; [including students, women's, trade unions and such other wings affiliated to these parties.]

  (c) Organisations operating with a motive to earn profit;

  (d) Organisations expressly banned by the Union and State Governments.

3. Selection Process & Processing of the Applications

(a) Applications shall be invited by the Ministry of I&B once every year through a national advertisement for establishment of Community Radio Stations. However, eligible organisations and educational institutions can apply during the intervening period between the two advertisements also. The applicants shall be required to apply in the prescribed application form along with a processing fee of Rs.2500/- and the applications shall be processed in the following manner:

(i) Universities, Deemed Universities and Government run educational institutions will have a single window clearance by putting up cases before an inter-ministerial committee chaired by Secretary (I&B) for approval. No separate clearance from MHA & MHRD shall be necessary. Once the WPC Wing of the Ministry of Communication & IT earmarks a frequency at the place requested by the institution, a Letter of Intent (LOI) shall be issued.

(ii) In case of all other applicants, including private educational institutions, LOI shall be issued subject to receiving clearance from Ministries of Home Affairs, Defence & HRD (in case of private educational institutions) and frequency allocation by WPC wing of Ministry of Communication & IT.

(b) A time schedule for obtaining clearances as below shall be prescribed:

(i) Within one month of receipt of the application in the prescribed form, the Ministry of I&B shall process the application and either communicate to the applicant deficiencies, if any, or will send the copies of the application to the other Ministries for clearance as prescribed in para 3(a)(i) and 3(a)(ii) above, as the case may be.

(ii) The Ministries concerned shall communicate their clearance within three months of receipt of the application. However, in the event of the failure of the concerned ministry to grant the clearance within the stipulated period of three months, the case shall be referred to the Committee constituted under the Chairmanship of Secretary (I&B) for a decision for issue of LOI.

(iii) In the event of more than one applicant for a single frequency at a given place, the successful applicant will be selected for issue of LOI from amongst the applicants by the Committee constituted under the Chairmanship of Secretary (I&B) on the basis of their standing in the community, the commitment shown, the objectives enunciated and resources likely to be mobilised by the applicant organisation as well as its credentials and number of years of community service rendered by the organisation.

(iv) Within one month of the issue of the Letter of Intent (LOI) the eligible applicant will be required to apply, in the prescribed format and with the requisite fee, to the WPC Wing of the Ministry of Communication & IT, Sanchar Bhawan, New Delhi for frequency allocation & SACFA clearance.

(v) A time frame of six months from the date of application is prescribed for issue of SACFA clearance. In the event of non-receipt of such clearance from the Ministry of Communication & IT within the stipulated period of six months, the case will be referred to the Committee constituted under the Chairmanship of Secretary (I&B) for a decision.

(vi) On receipt of SACFA clearance (a copy of which shall be submitted by the applicant), the LOI holder shall furnish a bank guarantee in the prescribed format for a sum of Rs.25, 000/-. Thereupon, the LOI holder will be invited to sign a Grant of Permission Agreement (GOPA) by Ministry of I&B, which will enable him to seek Wireless Operating License (WOL) from the WPC Wing of the Ministry of Communication & IT. The Community Radio Station can be made operational only after the receipt of WOL from the Ministry of Communication & IT.

(vii) Within three months of receipt of all clearances i.e., signing of GOPA, the Permission Holder shall set up the Community Radio Station and shall intimate the date of commissioning of the Community Radio Station to the Ministry of I&B.

(viii) Failure to comply with time schedule prescribed above shall make the LOI/GOPA holder liable for cancellation of its LOI/GOPA and forfeiture of the Bank Guarantee.

4. Grant of Permission Agreement Conditions

(i) The Grant of Permission Agreement period shall be for five years.

(ii) The Grant of Permission Agreement and the Permission letter will be non-transferable.

(iii) No permission fee shall be levied on the Permission Holder. However, the Permission Holder will be required to pay the spectrum usage fee to WPC wing of Ministry of Communication & IT.

(iv) In case the Permission Holder does not commence his broadcasting operations within three months of the receipt of all clearances or shuts down broadcasting activity for more than 3 months after commencement of operation, its Permission is liable to be cancelled and the frequency allotted to the next eligible applicant.

(v) An applicant/organisation shall not be granted more than one Permission for CRS operation at one or more places.

(vi) The LOI Holder shall furnish a bank guarantee for a sum of Rs.25,000/- (Rupees twenty five thousand) only to ensure timely performance of the Permission Agreement.

(vii) If the Permission Holder fails to commission service within the stipulated period, he shall forfeit the amount of bank guarantee to the Government and the Government would be free to cancel the Permission issued to him

5. Content Regulation & Monitoring

(i) The programmes should be of immediate relevance to the community. The emphasis should be on developmental, agricultural, health, educational, environmental, social welfare, community development and cultural programmes. The programming should reflect the special interests and needs of the local community.

(ii) At least 50% of content shall be generated with the participation of the local community, for which the station has been set up.

(iii) Programmes should preferably be in the local language and dialect(s).

(iv) The Permission Holder shall have to adhere to the provisions of the Programme and Advertising Code as prescribed for All India Radio.

(v) The Permission Holder shall preserve all programmes broadcast by the CRS for three months from the date of broadcast.

(vi) The Permission Holder shall not broadcast any programmes, which relate to news and current affairs and are otherwise political in nature.

(vii) The Permission Holder shall ensure that nothing is included in the programmes broadcast which:

(a) Offends against good taste or decency;

(b) Contains criticism of friendly countries;

(c) Contains attack on religions or communities or visuals or words contemptuous of religious groups or which either promote or result in promoting communal discontent or disharmony;

(d) Contains anything obscene, defamatory, deliberate, false and suggestive innuendoes and half truths;

(e) Is likely to encourage or incite violence or contains anything against maintenance of law and order or which promote-anti-national attitudes;

(f) Contains anything amounting to contempt of court or anything affecting the integrity of the Nation;

(g) Contains aspersions against the dignity of the President/ Vice President and the Judiciary;

(h) Criticises, maligns or slanders any individual in person or certain groups, segments of social, public and moral life of the country;

(i) Encourages superstition or blind belief;

(j) Denigrates women;

(k) Denigrates children.

(l) May present/depict/suggest as desirable the use of drugs including alcohol, narcotics and tobacco or may stereotype, incite, vilify or perpetuate hatred against or attempt to demean any person or group on the basis of ethnicity, nationality, race, gender, sexual preference, religion, age or physical or mental disability.

(viii) The Permission Holder shall ensure that due care is taken with respect to religious programmes with a view to avoid:

(a) Exploitation of religious susceptibilities; and

(b) Committing offence to the religious views and beliefs of those belonging to a particular religion or religious denomination.

6. Imposition of Penalty/Revocation of Permission Agreement

(i) In case there is any violation of conditions cited in 5(i) to 5(viii), Government may suo motto or on basis of complaints take cognisance and place the matter before the Inter-ministerial Committees on Programme and Advertising Codes for recommending appropriate penalties. On the recommendation of the Committee a decision to impose penalties shall be taken. However, before the imposition of a penalty the Permission Holder shall be given an opportunity to represent its case.

(ii) The penalty shall comprise of:

(a) Temporary suspension of Permission for operating the CRS for a period up to one month in the case of the first violation.

(b) Temporary suspension of Permission for operating the CRS for a period up to three months in the case of the second violation depending on the gravity of violation.

(c) Revocation of the Permission for any subsequent violation. Besides, the Permission Holder and its principal members shall be liable for all actions under IPC, CrPC and other laws.

(iii) In case of revocation of Permission, the Permission Holder will not be eligible to apply directly or indirectly for a fresh permission in future for a period of five years.

'Provided the penalty imposed as per above provision shall be without prejudice to any penal action under applicable laws including the Indian Telegraph Act 1885 and Indian Wireless Telegraphy Act 1933, as modified from time to time.'

(iv) In the event of suspension of permission as mentioned in para 6 (ii) (a) & (b), the permission holder will continue to discharge its obligations under the Grant of Permission Agreement during the suspension period also.

7. Transmitter Power and Range

(i) CRS shall be expected to cover a range of 5–10 km. For this, a transmitter having maximum Effective Radiated Power (ERP) of 100 Watts would be adequate. However, in case of a proven need where the applicant organisation is able to establish that it needs to serve a larger area or the terrain so warrants, higher transmitter wattage with maximum ERP up to 250 Watts can be considered on a case-to-case basis, subject to availability of frequency and such other clearances as necessary from the Ministry of Communication & IT. Requests for higher transmitter power above 100 Watts and upto 250 Watts shall also be subject to approval by the Committee constituted under the Chairmanship of Secretary, Ministry of Information & Broadcasting.

(ii) The maximum height of antenna permitted above the ground for the CRS shall not exceed 30 metres. However, minimum height of Antenna above ground should be at least 15 metres to prevent possibility of biological hazards of RF radiation.

(iii) Universities, Deemed Universities and other educational institutions shall be permitted to locate their transmitters and antennae only within their main campuses

(iv) For NGOs and others, the transmitter and antenna shall be located within the geographical area of the community they seek to serve. The geographical area (including the names of villages/institution etc) should be clearly spelt out along with the location of the transmitter and antenna in the application form.

8. *Funding & Sustenance*

(i) Applicants will be eligible to seek funding from multilateral aid agencies. Applicants seeking foreign funds for setting up the CRS will have to obtain FCRA clearance under Foreign Contribution Regulation Act, 1976.

(ii) Transmission of sponsored programmes shall not be permitted except programmes sponsored by Central & State Governments and other organisations to broadcast public interest information. In addition, limited advertising and announcements relating to local events, local businesses and services and employment opportunities shall be allowed. The maximum duration of such limited advertising will be restricted to 5 (Five) minutes per hour of broadcast.

(iii) Revenue generated from advertisement and announcements as per para 8(ii) shall be utilised only for the operational expenses and capital expenditure of the CRS. After meeting the full financial needs of the CRS, surplus may, with prior written permission of the Ministry of Information & Broadcasting, be ploughed into the primary activity of the organisation i.e. for education in case of educational institutions and for furthering the primary objectives for which the NGO concerned was established.

9. Other Terms & Conditions

(i) The basic objective of the Community Radio broadcasting would be to serve the cause of the community in the service area of the Permission Holder by involving members of the community in the broadcast of their programmes. For this purpose community shall mean people living in the zone of the coverage of the broadcasting service of the Permission Holder. Each applicant will have to specify the geographical community or the community of interest it wants to cover.

The Permission Holder shall provide the services of his CRS on free-to-air basis.

(ii) Though the Permission Holder will operate the service under these guidelines and as per the terms and conditions of the Grant of Permission Agreement signed, the permission shall be subject to the condition that as and when any regulatory authority to regulate and monitor the broadcast services in the country is constituted, the permission holder will adhere to the norms, rules and regulations prescribed by such authority from time to time.

(iii) The Permission Holder shall provide such information to the Government on such intervals, as may be required. In this connection, the Permission Holder is required to preserve recording of programmes broadcast during the previous three months failing which Permission Agreement is liable to be revoked.

(iv) The Government or its authorised representative shall have the right to inspect the broadcast facilities of the Permission Holder and collect such information as considered necessary in public and community interest.

(v) The Government reserves the right to take over the entire services and networks of the Permission Holder or revoke/terminate/suspend the Permission in the interest of national security or in the event of national emergency/war or low intensity conflict or under similar type of situations.

(vi) All foreign personnel likely to be deployed by way of appointment, contract, consultancy etc by the Permission Holder for installation, maintenance and operation of the Permission Holder's services shall be required to obtain prior security clearance from Government of India.

(vii) The Government reserves the right to modify, at any time, the terms and conditions if it is necessary to do so, in public interest or for the proper conduct of broadcasting or for security considerations.

(viii) Notwithstanding anything contained anywhere else in the Grant of Permission Agreement, the Government shall have the power to direct the permission holder to broadcast any special message as may be considered desirable to meet any contingency arising out of natural emergency, or public interest or natural disaster and the like, and the Permission holder shall be obliged to comply with such directions.

(ix) The permission holder shall be required to submit their audited annual accounts to the Government in respect of the organisation/division running the CRS. The accounts shall clearly show the income and expenditure incurred and the Assets and Liabilities in respect of the CRS.

(x) A Permission Agreement will be subject to such other conditions as may be determined by the Government.

(xi) The Government shall make special arrangements for monitoring and enforcement of the ceiling on advertisements, particularly in those areas where private FM radio stations have been granted licenses.

Source: http://mib.nic.in/CRS/CRBGUIDELINES041206.pdf, last assessed 23 August 2007.

REFERENCES

Abbot, Dina. 1997. 'Who Else Will Support Us? How Poor Women Organise the Unorganisable in India,' *Community Development Journal*, July, 32 (3).

Agarwal, Bina. 1997. 'Environmental Action, Gender Equity and Women's Participation,' *Development and Change*, January, 28(1): 1–44.

AID (Alternative for India Development) website: http://www.aidindia.net/aboutus.htm, last accessed 5 May 2007.

AMARC. 1994. *Community Radio Charter for Europe*. Ljubljana, Slovenia: First AMARC Pan- European Conference of Community Radio Broadcasters. URL: http://legislaciones.amarc.org/The_Community_Radio_Charter_for_Europe.doc, last accessed 5 May 2007.

———. 1995. *Waves for Freedom: Report on the Sixth World Conference of Community Radio Broadcasters*. Dakar, Senegal, 23–29 January.

———. 1998a. *The Milan Declaration on Communication and Human Rights*. URL: http://wiki.amarc.org/index2.php?topic=milan_declaration&lang=EN&style=amarc&site=amarc and http://freestone.com/kpfa/milandeclaration.html, last accessed 5 May 2007.

———. 1998b. *What is Community Radio?* URL: http://wiki.amarc.org/index2.php?topic=What_is_community_radio&lang=EN&style=amarc&site=amarc, last accessed 5 May 2007.

———. 2000. *Communications Infrastructure for Citizens' and Community Media–An AMARC-Europe Response to the 1999 Communications Review*. URL: http://europa.eu.int/ISPO/infosoc/telecompolicy/review99/comments/amarc28b.htm, last accessed 5 May 2007.

———. 2003. http://www.itu.int/dms_pub/itu-s/md/03/wsispc3/c/S03-WSISPC3-C-0107!!PDF-E.pdf, last accessed 5 May 2007.

Anderson, Benedict. 1992. *Imagined Communities*. London: Verso.

Appadurai, Arjun. 1997. *Modernity at Large: Cultural Dimensions of Globalisation*. Delhi: Oxford University Press.

Arnst, Randall. 1996. 'Participation Approaches to the Research Process,' in Jan Servaes, Thomas L. Jacobson and Shirley A. White (eds.), *Participatory Communication for Social Change*. pp. 109–126. New Delhi: Sage Publications.

Atton, Chris. 1999. 'A Re-assessment of the Alternative Press', *Media, Culture and Society*, 21(1): 51–76.

Atton, Chris. 2001a. 'The Mundane and its Reproduction in Alternative Media', *Journal of Mundane Behavior.* Special Issue: Media/Mundania. February. 2(1). URL: http://www.mundanebehavior.org/index.htm, last accessed on 5 May 2007.

———. 2001b. *Approaching Alternative Media: Theory and Methodology*. Scotland: Napier University. URL: http://www.ourmedianet.org/papers/om2001/Atton.om2001.pdf, last accessed on 5 May 2007.

———. 2002. *Alternative Media*. London: Sage Publications.

Australian Broadcasting Authority (ABA). 2002. *Community Broadcasting Codes of Practice*. Sydney: ABA.

Bagdikian, Ben H. 1992. *The Media Monopoly* (Fourth Edition). Boston: Beacon Press.

Bamberger, Michael. 1988. 'The Role of Community Participation in Development Planning and Project Management'. EDI Policy Seminar Report No.13. Washington D.C: The World Bank.

Baran, Paul A. 1957. *The Political Economy of Growth*. New York: Monthly Review Press.

Barnard, Stephen. 2000. *Studying Radio*. London: Arnold.

Baruah, U.L. 1983. *This is All India Radio*. New Delhi: Publications Division, MIB.

Bell, Daniel. 1974. *The Coming of Post Industrial Society: A Venture in Social Forecasting*. Harmondsworth: Penguin.

Benjamin, Walter. 1934/1982. 'The Author as Producer', edited translation in Francis Frascina and Charles Harrison (eds.), *Modern Art and Modernism: A Critical Anthology*, pp. 213–16. London: Paul Chapman, in association with the Open University.

Berrigan, Frances J. 1979/1981. *Community Communications: The Role of Community Media in Development*. Paris: UNESCO.

Béteille, Andre. 1996. 'Civil Society and Its Institutions', The First Fulbright Memorial Lecture, Calcutta: USEFI.

———. 1999. 'Citizenship, State & Civil society', *Economic and Political Weekly*, 4–10 September, 34(36): 2588–91.

Bhasin, Kamla. 2000. *Understanding Gender*. New Delhi: Kali for Women.

Blumberg, Rae Lesser. 1989. 'Toward a Feminist Theory of Development', in Ruth A. Wallace (ed.), *Feminism and Sociological Theory*. Newbury Park/London: Sage Publications.

Boserup, Ester. 1970. *Woman's Role in Economic Development*. New York, NY: St Martin's Press.

Broadcasting Commission of Ireland (BCI). 1997. *BCI Policy on Community Radio Broadcasting*. URL: http://www.bci.ie/documents/comm_radio_policy.pdf, page 2, last accessed on 5 May 2007.

Buckley, Steve. 2000. 'Radio's New Horizons: Democracy and Popular Communication in the Digital Age', *International Journal of Cultural Studies*, 3(2): 180–87.

Calhoun, Craig. 1994. *Social Theory and the Politics of Identity*. London: Basil Blackwell.

Calhoun, Craig (ed.). 1992. *Habermas and the Public Sphere*. Cambridge, MA: MIT Press.

Canadian Radio-Television and Telecommunications Commission (CRTC). 2000. *Community Radio Policy* in Public Notices CRTC 2000-13, dated 28 January, and CRTC 2000-13-1, dated 2 February. URL: http://www.crtc.gc.ca/archive/eng/Notices/2000/PB2000-13.htm and http://www.crtc.gc.ca/archive/eng/Notices/2000/PB2000-13-1.htm, last accessed on 7 May 2007.

Carpentier, N., R. Lie and Jan Servaes. 2002. 'Making Community Media Work', in Jan Servaes (ed.), *Approaches to Development Communication*. Paris: UNESCO.

Chafetz, Janet Saltzman. 1988. *Feminist Sociology: An Overview of Contemporary Theories*. Itasca, IL: F.E. Peacock.

Chambers, Robert. 1997. *Whose Reality Counts? Putting the First Last*. London: Commonwealth Secretariat.

Chandoke, Neera. 1998. 'The Assertion of Civil Society Against the State', in M. Mohanty, P.N. Mukherjee and O. Tornquist (eds.), *People's Rights: Social Movements and the State in the Third World*. New Delhi: Sage Publications.

Chatterjee, Partha. 1998. 'Community in the East', *Economic and Political Weekly*, 7 February, 33(6).

Chatterji, P.C. 1991. *Broadcasting in India*. New Delhi: Sage Publications.

Civil Society Declaration to the World Summit on the Information Society. 2003. *Shaping Information Societies for Human Needs*. Geneva: WSIS Civil Society Plenary.

Community Media Association (CMA). 2005. URL: http://www.commedia.org.uk/news-amp-press/news-items/18-more-stations-licensed/ dated 6 October 2005, last accessed on 2 May 2007.

Collins, R., N. Garham and G. Locksley. 1988. *The Economics of Television: UK Case*. London: Sage Publications.

Cornwall, Andrea. 2000. 'Making a Difference? Gender and Participatory Development', Discussion Paper 378. University of Sussex: Institute of Development Studies.

Dagron, Alfonso G. 2001. *Making Waves: Stories of Participatory Communication for Social Change*. New York: The Rockefeller Foundation.

Dahlgren, Peter. 1995. *Television and the Public Sphere: Citizenship, Democracy and the Media*. London: Sage Publications.

David, M.J.R. 1992. 'Mahaweli Community Radio', in Bruce Girard (ed.), *A Passion for Radio: Radio Waves and Community*. Canada: Black Rose Books.

Deccan Development Society (DDS). 2000. *The Pastapur Initiative on Community Radio Broadcasting* (Appendix III).

———. 2005. *Deccan Development Society ... a Profile*. Andhra Pradesh: DDS.

———. Website: http://www.ddsindia.com/www/default.asp, last accessed on 5 May 2007.

———. 'DDS and Community Radio: A Short Introduction', by P.V. Satheesh, Director, Deccan Development Society. URL: http://www.ddsindia.com/www/radiostn.htm, last accessed on 5 May 2007.

Deshler, D. and D. Sock. 1985. 'Community Development Participation: A Concept Review of International Literature'. Paper presented at the International League for Social Commitment in Adult Education. Sweden: Ljungskile.

De Tocqueville, Alexis. 1945. *Democracy in America–Vol II*. New York: Vintage Books.

Downey, John and Natalie Fenton. 2003. 'Publicity and the Public Sphere', in *New Media & Society*. London, Thousand Oaks, CA and New Delhi: Sage Publications.

Downing, John D.H. 2001, *Radical Media: Rebellious Communication and Social Movements*. Thousand Oaks, CA: Sage Publications.

Elson, Diane (ed.). 1991. *Male Bias in the Development Process*. Manchester: Manchester University Press.

Enzensberger, Hans Magnus. 1976. 'Constituents of a Theory of the Media', in *Raids and Reconstructions: Essays on Politics, Crime and Culture*, pp. 20–53. London: Pluto Press.

Escobar, Arturo. 1995. *Encountering Development: The Making and Unmaking of the Third World*. New Jersey: Princeton University Press.

Federal Communications Commission. 'Low Power FM Radio: An Applicant's Guide'. URL: www.fcc.gov/lpfm, last accessed 7 May 2007.

Fielden, Lionel. 1939. *Report on the Progress of Broadcasting in India*. Shimla: Government of India Press.

———. 1960. *The Natural Bent*. London: Andre Deutsch.

Forde, Susan, Michael Meadows and Kerrie Foxwell. 2003. 'Through the Lens of the Local: Public Arena Journalism in the Australian Community Broadcasting Sector', *Journalism*, 4(3): 314–35.

Foucault, Michel. 1980. *Power/Knowledge: Selected Interviews and Other Writings, 1972-1977* (edited by Colin Gordon). Brighton: Harvester Press.

Frankson, Joan Ross. 2000. *Gender Mainstreaming in Information and Communications: A Reference Manual for Governments and Other Stakeholders*. London: Commonwealth Secretariat.

Fraser, Colin and Sonia Restrepo-Estrada. 2001. *Community Radio Handbook*. Paris: UNESCO

———. 2002. 'Community Radio for Change and Development', *Development*, 45(4): 69–73.

Fraser, Nancy. 1992. 'Rethinking the Public Sphere: A Contributon to the Critique of Actually Existing Democracy', in Craig Calhoun (ed.), *Habermas and the Public Sphere*. Cambridge: MIT Press.

Freire, Paulo. 1970/1983. *Pedagogy of the Oppressed*. New York: Continuum.

———. 1985. *The politics of Education: Culture, Power and Liberation*. New York: Bergin and Garvey.

Gaonkar, Dilip Parameshwar. 2002. 'Towards New Imaginaries', *Public Culture*, 14(1): 1–19.

Gauntlett, David. 1996. *Video Critical: Children, the Environment and Media Power*. Luton: John Libbey Media.

Girard, Bruce (ed.). 1992. *A Passion for Radio: Radio Waves and Community*. Canada: Black Rose Books.

Government of Nepal. 1993. The National Broadcasting Act, 2049. URL: http://www.nepalpressfreedom.org/documents/national_broadcasting_act.pdf, last accessed on 5 May.

Government of South Africa. 1998. *White Paper on Broadcasting*. Department of Communications, 4 June. URL: http://www.safilm.org.za/reading/whitepa2.html, last accessed on 7 May 2007.

Gramsci, Antonio. 1975. *Selections from the Prison Notebooks*. New York: International Publishers.

Guijt, Irene and Meera Kaul Shah. 1998. 'Waking up to Power, Conflict and Process', in Irene Gujit and Meera Kaul Shah (eds.), *The Myth of Community: Gender Issues in Participatory Development*. London: Intermediate Technology Publications.

Habermas, Jürgen. 1962. *The Structural Transformation of the Public Sphere: An Inquiry into a Category of Bourgeois Society*. Cambridge: MIT Press.

Hall, John A. 1995. 'In Search of Civil Society', in John Hall (ed.), *Civil Society: Theory History Comparison*. Cambridge: Polity Press.

Hamilton, James. 2001. 'An Alternative Practice of Alternative Media', unpublished manuscript.

Hantrais, Linda. 1996. 'Comparative Research Methods', in *Social Research Update*. England: Department of Sociology, University of Surrey.

Held, David. 1987. *Models of Democracy*. Cambridge: Polity Press.

Herman, Edward S. and Noam Chomsky. 1988. *Manufacturing Consent*. New York: Pantheon Books.

Hochheimer, John L. 1993. 'Organizing Democratic Radio: Issues in Praxis', *Media, Culture & Society*, 15(3): 473–86.

———. 1999. 'Planning Community Radio as Participatory Development', in Shirley A. White (ed.), *The Art of Facilitating Participation*. New Delhi: Sage Publications.

hooks, bell. 1989. *Talking Back: Thinking Feminist, Thinking Black*. Boston, MA: South End Press.

Humble, Morag. 1998. 'Assessing PRA for Implementing Gender and Development', in Irene Guijt and Meera Kaul Shah (eds.), *The Myth of Community: Gender Issues in Participatory Development*. London: Intermediate Technology Publications.

Institute of Development Studies (IDS). 2002. 'Community Radio in South Asia—Exploring the Way Forward—Recommendations and Report', Sussex: IDS. URL: http://www.mediasouthasia.org/communityradioworkshopforwebsite010604.htm, ast accessed on 5 May 2007.

Jacobson, Thomas L. 1994. 'Modernization, Post-Modernization Approaches to Participatory Communication for Development', in Shirley A. White, K.Sadanandan Nair and Joseph Ascroft (eds.), *Participatory Communication: Working for Change and Development*. New Delhi: Sage Publications.

Jacobson, Thomas L. and Jan Servaes. 1999. 'Introduction', in Thomas L. Jacobson and Jan Servaes (eds.), *Theoretical Approaches to Participatory Communication*, pp. 1–13. Cresskill, NJ: Hampton Press.

Jodhka, Surinder S. 2001. *Community and Identities: Contemporary Discourses on Culture and Politics in India.* New Delhi: Sage Publications.

Joseph, Ammu. 2005. 'Media with a message', URL: http://www.indiatogether.org/2005/mar/ajo-barefoot.htm, last accessed on 5 May 2007.

Kabeer, Naila. 1994. *Reversed Realities: Gender Hierarchies in Development Thought.* London: Verso.

Kaviraj, Sudipta. 1992. 'The Imaginary Institution of India', in Partha Chatterjee and Gyan Pandey (eds.), *Subaltern Studies VII.* Delhi: Oxford University Press.

Kaviraj, Sudipta and Sunil Khilnani. 2001.*Civil Society: History and Possibilities.* Cambridge: Cambridge University Press.

Keane, John. 1988. *Democracy and Civil Society.* London: Verso.

Kidd, Dorothy. 1992. 'Alternate Media, Critical Consciousness and Action: The Beginnings of a Conversation about Women and Grassroots Media', unpublished manuscript. Burnaby, Canada: Simon Fraser University.

———. 1998. 'Talking the Walk: the Media Enclosures and the Communications Commons', Dissertation. Burnaby, Canada: Simon Fraser University.

Knobloch, Ulrike. 2002. 'The Contribution of Martha Nussbaum's Capabilities Approach to Feminist Economics: Questioning the Gender-Based Division of Labour', Conference paper 9-10, September, Cambridge: von Hugel Institute, St Edmund's College, University of Cambridge.

Koirala, Bharat Dutta. 2002. An Interview in 'Briefing Document: Community Radio in India, Proceedings of an Internet Conference on The Hoot.org', URL: http://www.nepaldemocracy.org/media/interview_bd_koirala.htm, last accessed on 5 May 2007.

Kothari, Rajni. 1984. 'Communications for Alternative Development: Towards a Paradigm', *Development Dialogue,* 1–2.

———. 1988. *State Against Democracy: In Search of Humane Governance.* Delhi: Ajanta.

Kumar, Keval J. 1994. 'Communication Approaches to Participation and Development: Challenging the Assumptions and Perspectives', in Shirley A. White, K. Sadanandan Nair and Joseph Ascroft (eds.), *Participatory Communication: Working for Change and Development.* New Delhi: Sage Publications.

Kumar, Kanchan. 2003a. 'Kutch Mahila Vikas Sangathan (KMVS) Community Radio Initiative: A Case Study—Some Preliminary Observations', paper presented at the UNDP Consultation on ICTs and Development, 11 March, Bangalore: Indian Institute of Management.

———. 2003b. 'Mixed Signals: Radio Broadcasting Policy in India', *Economic and Political Weekly*, 31 May.

———. 2004. 'Community Radio Waiting to Go on Air', *Grassroots,* February, 5(2): 15.

Kutch Mahila Vikas Sangathan (KMVS). 2003. 'Kutch Mahila Vikas Sangathan: Sharing Experiences', a power point presentation at the UNDP Consultation on ICTs and Development, 11 March. Bangalore: Indian Institute of Management.

Laclau, Ernesto and Chantal Mouffe. 1985. *Hegemony and Socialist Strategy: Towards a Radical Democratic Politics*. London: Verso.

Langdon, Jeff. 1995. 'The Social and Political forces that led to the Development of Public Radio in the 1960's', URL: http://www.acmi.net.au/AIC/PUB_RAD_OZ_LANGDON.html, last accessed on 7 May 2007.

Lelyveld, David. 1996. 'Upon the Subdominant: Administering Music on All India Radio', in Carol A. Breckenridge (ed.), *Consuming Modernity*. Delhi: Oxford University Press.

Lerner, Daniel. 1958. *The Passing of Traditional Society*. Glencoe, IL: Free Press.

Lewis, Peter. 1993. 'Alternative Media in a Contemporary Social and Theoretical Context,' in Peter Lewis (ed.), *Alternative Media: Linking Global and Local*. pp. 15–25. Paris: UNESCO.

Lewis, Roger. 1972. *Outlaws of America: The Underground Press and its Context*. Harmondsworth: Penguin.

Lipschutz, Ronnie D. 1992. 'Reconstructing World Politics: The Emergence of Global Civil Society', *Millennium: Journal of International Studies*, 21(3).

López , Vigil José Ignácio. 1997. *Manual Urgente para Radialistas Apasionados*. Quito: ciespal/AMARC.

Ludden, David. 1992. 'India's Development Regime', in Nicholas Dirks (ed.), *Colonialism and Culture*. Ann Arbor: University of Michigan Press.

Luthra, H.R. 1986. *Indian Broadcasting*. New Delhi: Publications Division, MIB.

Lyon, David. 1988. *The Information Society: Issues and Illusions*. Oxford: Polity Press.

MacBride, Seán (ed.). 1980. *Many Voices, One World: Communication and Society: Today and Tomorrow*. Paris: UNESCO.

Mahajan, Gurpreet. 1999. 'Civil Society and Its Avtars: What Happened to Freedom and Democracy?', *Economic and Political Weekly*, 15–21 May, 34(20): 1188–96.

Malik, Kanchan K. 2005. 'For a radio of their own', Online edition of *The Hindu*, 7 August, URL: http://www.hindu.com/op/2005/08/07/stories/2005080703111600.htm, last accessed on 7 May 2007.

Manipal Institute of Communication (MIC). 2004. *A New Culture of Broadcasting: Training Manual for Radio with Community Orientation*. Manipal, India: Manipal Institute of Communication and Ford Foundation.

Mathur, J.C. Paul Neurath. 1959. *An Indian Experiment in Farm Radio Forums*. Paris: UNESCO.

Mattelart, Armand. 1983. *Transnationals and the Third World: The Struggle for Culture*. Massachusetts: Bergin & Garvey Publishers.

McAnany, Emile G. 1983. 'From Modernization and Diffusion to Dependency and Beyond: Theory and Practice in Communication for Social Change in the 1980s', Proceedings of a Midwest Symposium Development Communications in the Third World, April. University of Illinois.

McGuigan, Jim. 1992. *Cultural Populism*. London: Routledge.

McLuhan, Herbert Marshall. 1964. *Understanding Media*. New York: Signet.

McQuail, Denis. 1983. *Mass Communication Theory: An Introduction*. London: Sage Publications.

———. 1994. *Mass Communication Theory: An Introduction* (Third Edition). London: Sage Publications.

Melkote, Srinivas R. 1991. *Communication for Development in the Third World: Theory and Practice*. New Delhi: Sage Publications.

Melkote, Srinivas R. and H. Leslie Steeves. 2001. *Communication for Development in the Third World: Theory and Practice for Empowerment*. New Delhi: Sage Publications.

Ministry of Information and Broadcasting (MIB). 1966. *Report of the Committee on Broadcasting and Information Media*. New Delhi: Government of India.

———. 1977. *White Paper on misuse of Mass Media during the Internal Emergency; August*. New Delhi.

———. 1978. *Akash Bharati: Report of the Working Group on Autonomy for Akashvani and Doordarshan*. New Delhi.

———. 1982. *News Policy for Broadcast Media: Guidelines prepared by Advisory Committee on Official Media*. New Delhi.

———. 1985. *An Indian Personality for Television: Report of the Working Group on Software for Doordarshan*. New Delhi.

———. 1995. *Cable Television Networks (Regulation) Act*. New Delhi.

———. 1996a. *Report on Prasar Bharati* (Nitish Sengupta Committee). New Delhi.

———. 1996b. *Report of the Expert Committee on the Marketing of Commercial Time of AIR and DD* (Siddhartha Sen Committee). New Delhi.

———. 1996c. *Prasar Bharati Act 1990*. New Delhi.

———. 1996d. *Broadcasting Bill: Issues & Perspectives*. New Delhi.

———. 1996e. *National Media Policy* (Working Paper Submitted by the Parliamentary Sub-committee). New Delhi.

———. 1997. *The Broadcasting Bill*. New Delhi.

———. 2000a. *Prasar Bharati Review Committee Report*. New Delhi: http://mib.nic.in/nicpart/pbcont.html

———. 2000b. *The Draft Communication Convergence Bill 2000*. www.mib.nic.in

———. 2002a. *Mass Media 2002*. New Delhi: Publications Division.

———. 2002b. D.O. No. 212/100/2000-B(D) dated 11.01.2002. New Delhi.

Moore, Sylvia. 1986. 'Participatory Communication in the Development Process', *The Third Channel*, 2(2): 4.

Morris, Angela and Graeme Morton. 1998. *Locality, Community and Nation*. London: Hodder & Stoughton.

Moser, Caroline. 1993. *Gender, Planning and Development: Theory, Practice and Training*. London: Routledge.

Mowlana, Hamid. 2001. 'Communication and Development: Theoretical and Methodological Problems and Prospects', in Srinivas R. Melkote. and Sandhya Rao (eds.), *Critical Issues in Communication: Looking Inwards for Answers*. New Delhi: Sage Publications.

Mowlana, Hamid and Laurie J. Wilson. 1988. *Communication Technology and Development*. Paris: UNESCO.

Mtimde, Lumko. 2000. 'Radio Broadcasting in South Africa: An Overview', *International Journal of Cultural Studies*, 3(2): 173–79.

Mukhopadhyay, Bandana. 2000. 'Why AIR has Completely Ignored Community Radio', *Humanscape,* June, 24–25.

Nair, K. Sadanandan and Shirley A. White. 1987. 'Participation is Key to Development Communication', *Media Development,* 34(3): 36–40.

———. (eds). 1993. *Perspectives of Development Communication*. New Delhi: Sage Publications.

———. 1994. 'Participatory Message Development: A Conceptual Framework', in Shirley A. White, K. Sadanandan Nair and Joseph Ascroft (eds.), *Participatory Communication Working for Change and Development.* New Delhi: Sage Publications.

National Foundation for India (NFI). 2001. *Process Document for Community Radio Initiative*. New Delhi.

Negt, Oskar and Alexander Kluge. 1972/1983. 'The Proletarian Public Sphere', translated from the German by Stuart Hood, in Armand Mattelart and Seth Siegelaub (eds.), *Communication and Class Struggle, Vol. 2: Liberation, Socialism*, pp. 92–94. New York: International General.

Nigg, H. and G. Wade. 1980 *Community Media: Community Communication in the UK, Video, Local TV, Film, and Photography*. Zurich: Regenbogen.

Ninan, Sevanti. 1998. 'History of Indian Broadcasting Reform', in Monroe E. Price and Stefaan G. Verhulst (eds.), *Broadcasting Reform in India*. Delhi: Oxford University Press.

Nisbet, Robert. 1967. *Sociological Traditions*. London: Heinemann.

Noronha, Frederick. 2000. 'Who's Afraid of Radio in India?', *Economic and Political Weekly*, September: 3385–87

———. 2003. 'Community Radio: Singing New Tunes in South Asia', *Economic and Political Weekly*, 31 May.

Nussbaum, Martha. C. 1992. 'Human Functioning and Social Justice: In Defense of Aristotleian Essentialism', *Political Theory*, 20(2): 202–46.

———. 2000. 'Women and Work—The Capabilities Approach', *Little Magazine*, Issue I, URL: http://www.littlemag.com/2000/martha2.htm, last accessed on 7 May 2007.

———. 2005. Date: 06/02/2005, URL: http://www.thehindu.com/thehindu/mag/2005/02/06/stories/2005020600490300.htm, last accessed on 7 May 2007.

Official website of All India Radio, India. URL: http://www.allindiaradio.org/index.html last accessed on 7 May 2007.

Official website of Broadcasting Commission of Ireland. URL: http://www.bci.ie/index.html last accessed on 7 May 2007.

Official website of Bush Radio. URL: http://www.bushradio.co.za/ last accessed on 7 May 2007.

Official website of Independent Communications Authority of South Africa (ICASA). URL: http://www.icasa.org.za/ last accessed on 7 May 2007.

Official website of Ministry of Information and Broadcasting, Government of India. URL: www.mib.nic.in last accessed on 7 May 2007.

Official website of the Australian Broadcasting Authority (ABA). URL: http://www.aba.gov.au/

Outcome Document. 2000. Adopted by the UN General Assembly Session on Gender Equality, Development and Peace for the 21st Century, 5–9 June. New York. URL: http://www.un.org/womenwatch/daw/followup/ress233e.pdf last accessed on 2 May 2007.

Page, David and William Crawley. 2001. *Satellites Over South Asia*. New Delhi: Sage Publications.

Parpart, Jane L., Patricia M. Connelly, Tania Murray Li and Martha MacDonald. 2000. 'Feminism and Development: Theoretical Perspectives',in Jane L. Parpart, Patricia M. Connelly and Eudine V. Barriteau (eds.), *Theoretical Perspectives on Gender and Development*. Ottawa, Canada: International Development Research Centre (IDRC).

Patton, Michael Quinn. 1990 *Qualitative Evaluation and Research Methods* (Second Edition). Newbury Park, CA: Sage Publications.

Pavarala, Vinod. 2003a. 'Breaking Free: Battle over the Airwaves', *Economic and Political Weekly*, 31 May.

———. 2003b. 'Building Solidarities: A Case of Community Radio in Jharkhand', *Economic and Political Weekly*, 31 May.

Pavarala, Vinod and Kanchan Kumar. 2001a. 'Legislating for Community Radio: Policy Framework from other Countries', *Voices for Change: A Journal on Communication for Development*, May, 5(1): 13–17.

———. 2001b. 'Broadcasting in India: New Roles and Regulations', *Vidura*, July–September, 3.

———. 2002. 'Civil Society Responses to Media Globalization: A Study of Community Radio Initiatives in India', *Social Action*, January–March, 52(1): 74–88.

———. 2004. 'Enabling Community Radio: Case Studies in National Broadcasting Policy', *MICA Review*, 1(3): 5–23.

Pieterse, J. Nederveen. 1994. 'Globalization as Hybridization', *International Sociology*, 9: 169–84.

Prakash, Amit. 2001. *Jharkhand: Politics of Development and Identity*. New Delhi: Orient Longman.

Prasar Bharati. 2002. *All India Radio 2002*. New Delhi: Prasar Bharati.

———. 2004. *All India Radio 2004*. New Delhi. Prasar Bharati

Price, Monroe E. and Stefaan G.Verhulst (eds.). 1998. *Broadcasting Reform in India*. Delhi: Oxford University Press.

Price-Davies, Eryl and Jo Tacchi. 2001. 'Community Radio in a Global Context: A Comparative Analysis', unpublished Report. London: Community Media Association.

Ramachandran, V. and A. Saihjee. 2000. 'Flying with the Crane: Recapturing KMVS's Ten-year Journey'. Bhuj: KMVS (unpublished—for internal circulation; copy with the authors).

Riaño, Pilar (ed.). 1994a. *Women in Grassroots Communication*. Thousand Oaks, CA: Sage Publications.

———. 1994b. 'Women's Participation in Communication: Elements of a Framework', in Pilar Riaño (ed.). *Women in Grassroots Communication*, pp. 3–29. Thousand Oaks, CA: Sage Publications.

———. 1994c. 'Gender in Communication: Women's Contributions', in Pilar Riaño (ed.), *Women in Grassroots Communication*. Thousand Oaks, CA: Sage Publications.

Robertson, Roland. 1992. *Globalization: Social Theory and Global Culture*. Newbury Park, CA: Sage Publications.

Rodriguez, Clemencia. 2001. *Fissures in the Mediascape: An International Study of Citizens' Media*. Cresskill: Hampton Press.

Rogers, Everett M. 1962. *Diffusion of Innovations*. New York: The Free Press.

———. 1976. 'Communication and Development: The Passing of the Dominant Paradigm', in Everett M. Rogers (ed.), *Communication and Development: Critical Perspectives*. Newbury Park, CA: Sage Publications.

Rogers, Everett M. and F.F. Shoemaker. 1971. *Communication of Innovations: A Cross Cultural Approach*. New York: The Free Press.

Sanjay, B.P. 1991. 'Broadcasting Policy in India: An Outsider's view', paper presented in the technical symposium-cum-exhibition by Broadcasting Engineering Society, 7–8 December, New Delhi.

Satheesh, P.V. 1999/2000. 'An Alternative to Literacy', *Forests, Trees and People*, Newsletter No. 40/41.

Schramm, Wilbur. 1964. *Mass Media and National Development: The Role of Information in the Developing Countries*. California: Stanford University Press.

Schumacher, Ernst Friedrich. 1973. *Small is Beautiful*. New York: Harper and Row.

Sen, Gargi. 2000. 'An Interview with Kiran Karnik', *Alternative Media Times*, 1(3).

Servaes, Jan. 1996. 'Linking Theoretical Perspectives to Policy', in Jan Servaes, Thomas L. Jacobson and Shirley A. White (eds.), *Participatory Communication for Social Change*, pp. 29–43. New Delhi: Sage Publications.

———. 1999. *Communication for Development: One World, Multiple Cultures*. Cresskill, New Jersey: Hampton Press.

———. (ed). 2002, *Approaches to Development Communication*. Paris: UNESCO

Servaes, Jan, Thomas L. Jacobson and Shirley A. White (eds.). 1996. *Participatory Communication for Social Change*. New Delhi: Sage Publications.

Sharma, Kumud. 2001 'Rethinking Social Development with Women: An Arduous Journey Ahead', in Debal K. SinghaRoy (ed.), *Social Development and the Empowerment of Marginalised Groups: Perspectives and Strategies*. New Delhi: Sage Publications.

Shiva, Vandana. 1988. *Staying Alive: Women, Ecology and Survival*. Delhi: Kali for Women.

Simon, Roger. 1982. *Gramsci's Political Thought*. London: Lawrence and Wishart.

Singhal, Arvind and Everett M. Rogers. 2001. *India's Communication Revolution*. New Delhi: Sage Publications.

Singha Roy, Debal K. (ed.). 2001. *Social Development and the Empowerment of Marginalised Groups: Perspectives and Strategies*. New Delhi: Sage Publications.

Siochrú, S.Ó. 2004. 'Social Consequences of the Globalization of the Media and Communication Sector: Some Strategic Considerations'. Working Paper No. 36. Geneva: World Commission on the Social Dimension of Globalization: International Labour Office.

Soni, Preeti. 2004. 'Community Radio-Kutch Mahila Vikas Sangathan (KMVS)', in *ICTs for Development—Case Studies from India*, an ICTD Project Compilation, pp. 89–91. Hyderabad: National Institute for Smart Government. URL: http://www.nisg.org/ictd_docs/ICT%20case%20studies.pdf last accessed on 7 May 2007.

Soni, Preeti and K. Stalin. 2004. 'Radio Ujjas: Greening the Ears for the Kutch People', i4d Monthly, August. URL: http://www.i4donline.net/aug04/greening.asp last accessed on 7 May 2007.

Spivak, Gayatri Chakravorty. 1988. 'Can the Subaltern Speak?', in Cary Nelson and Lawrence Grossberg (eds.), *Marxism and the Interpretation of Culture*. pp. 271–313. Urbana & Chicago: University of Illinois Press.

Strauss, Anselm L. 1987. *Qualitative Analysis for Social Scientists*. Cambridge: Cambridge University Press.

Streitmatter, Rodger. 2001. *Voices of Revolution: The Dissident Press in America*. New York: Columbia University Press.

Supreme Court Judgement. 1995. *Ministry of Information and Broadcasting v. Cricket Association of Bengal*. Official website of MIB, URL: http://www.mib.nic.in/informationb/POLICY/frames.htm last accessed on 7 May 2007.

Tabing, Louie. 2002. *How to Do Community Radio: A Primer for Community Radio Operators*. New Delhi: UNESCO.

Taglang, Kevin. 2000. 'Community & Broadcasting', *The Digital Beat*, February, 2(24): Benton Foundation. URL: http://www.benton.org/PUBLIBRARY/digitalbeat/db020300.html last accessed on 7 May 2007.

Taylor, Charles. 1995 'Invoking Civil Society', *Philosophical Arguments*, pp. 204–24. Cambridge MA: Harvard University Press.

The Bangkok Declaration. 1994. February.

The Beijing Declaration and the Platform for Action. 1995. United Nations Fourth World Conference on Women, Beijing, China. New York: United Nations. URL: http://www.un.org/womenwatch/daw/beijing/platform/declar.htm and http://www.un.org/womenwatch/daw/beijing/platform/plat1.htm last accessed on 2 May 2007.

The Rockefeller Foundation. 1999/2002. *Communication for Social Change: Working Paper Series*. New York: The Rockefeller Foundation

Thomas, Pradip. 1994. 'Participatory Message Development Communication: Philosophical Premises', in Shirley A. White, K.Sadanandan Nair and Joseph Ascroft (eds.), *Participatory Communication: Working for Change and Development*, pp. 49–59. New Delhi: Sage Publications.

Thomas, T.K. (ed.). 1990. *Autonomy for the Electronic Media: A National Debate on the Prasar Bharati Bill*. New Delhi: Konark Publishers.

Thompson, John B. 1995. *The Media and Modernity: A Social Theory of the Media*. Cambridge: Polity Press and Stanford: Stanford University Press.

Tomaselli, Keyan and Eric Louw. 1990. 'Alternative Media and Political Practice: the South African Struggle', in Marc Raboy and Peter Bruck (eds.), *Communication for and against Democracy*, pp. 203–20. Montreal: Black Rose Books.

Tönnies, Ferdinand. 1955. *Community and Association*. London: Routledge and Kegan Paul.

Toronto Platform For Action. 1995. 'International Symposium on Women and the Media: Access to Expression and Decision-Making', Final Declaration. UNESCO.

Traber, Michael. 1985. 'Alternative Journalism, Alternative Media', *Communication Resource*, 7 October. London: World Association for Christian Communication.

———. (ed.). 1986. *The Myth of Information Revolution*. New Delhi: Sage Publications.

United Nations Development Programme (UNDP). 2005.*Community Radio in India: Step by Step*. New Delhi: UNDP and VOICES.

Upadhya, Carol. 2001. 'The Concept of Community in Indian Social Sciences', in Surinder S. Jodhka (ed.), *Community and Identities: Contemporary Discourses on Culture and Politics in India*. New Delhi: Sage Publications.

Verma, Vidhu. 2004. 'Engendering Development—Limits of Feminist Theories and Justice', *Economic and Political Weekly*, 4 December.

Virmani, Shabnam. 2000. *Listen to the Sarus Crane*. URL: http://www.thehoot.org/story.asp?storyid=w2khootL1K06130212&pn=1 last accessed on 7 May 2007.

VOICES. 1996. 'Bangalore Declaration on Radio'. (See Appendix II)

———. 2002. 'Namma Dhwani Local ICT Network', Project Document for UNESCO Partnerships Project *Assessing Impact of ICTs for Poverty Reduction*. Bangalore.

Walker, Jesse. 1997. 'With Friends Like These: Why Community Radio Does Not Need the Corporation for Public Broadcasting', *Cato Policy Analysis*, 24 July, 277.

White, Robert. 1994. 'Participatory Development Communication as a Social-Cultural Process,' in Shirley A. White, K. Sadanandan Nair and Joseph Ascroft (eds.), *Participatory Communication: Working for Change and Development*, pp. 95–116. New Delhi: Sage Publications.

———. 1999. 'The Need for New Strategies of Research on the Democratization of Communication', in Thomas L. Jacobson and Jan Servaes (eds.), *Theoretical Approaches to Participatory Communication*, pp. 229–62. Cresskill, NJ: Hampton Press.

White, Shirley A. 1994. 'The Concept of Participation: Transforming Rhetoric to Reality', in Shirley A. White, K. Sadanandan Nair and Joseph Ascroft (eds.), *Participatory Communication: Working for Change and Development*. New Delhi: Sage Publications.

———. (ed.). 1999. *The Art of Facilitating Participation*. New Delhi: Sage Publications.

White, Shirley A. and Pradeep K. Patel. 1994. 'Participatory Message Making with Video; Revelations from Studies in India and the USA', in Shirley A. White, K. Sadanandan Nair and Joseph Ascroft (eds.), *Participatory Communication Working for Change and Development*. New Delhi: Sage Publications.

White, Shirley A., K. Sadanandan Nair and Joseph Ascroft (eds.). 1994. *Participatory Communication: Working for Change and Development*. New Delhi: Sage Publications.

Williams, Raymond. 1980. 'Means of Communication as Means of Production', in Raymond Williams (ed.), *Problems in Materialism and Culture: Selected Essays,* pp. 50–63. London: Verso.

———. 1983. *Towards 2000*. London: Chatto and Windus/Hogarth Press.

Wilson, Rob and Wimal Dissanayake. 1996. *Global/Local Cultural Production and the Transnational Imaginary*. Durham, NC: Duke University Press.

Wimmer, Roger D. and Joseph R. Dominick. 1987. *Mass Media Research: An Introduction* (Second Edition). California: Wadsworth.

World Association for Christian Communication (WACC). 2005. 'Women Empowering Communication and Bangkok10', *Media and Gender Monitor,* 15, URL: http://wacc.dev.visionwt.com/wacc/publications/media_and_gender_monitor/issue_15/forum_women_empowering_communication_and_bangkok_10 last accessed on 7 May 2007.

Wresch, William. 1996. *Disconnected: Haves and Have-nots in the Information Age*. New Jersey: Rutgers University Press.

Yashpal. 1983. 'Communication Technology for the people', *Communicator*, July–October, 18(3 & 4), New Delhi: IIMC.

Yin, Robert K. 1984. *Case Study Research: Design And Methods* (1st ed.). Beverly Hills, CA: Sage Publications.

———. 1993. *Applications of Case Study Research*. Newbury Park, CA: Sage Publishing.

———. 1994. *Case Study Research: Design and Methods* (Second Edition). Thousand Oaks, CA: Sage Publications.

Yoon, Chin Saik. 1996. 'Participatory Communication for Development', in G. Bessette and C.V. Rajasunderam (eds.), *Participatory Communication for Development: A West African Agenda*. Ottawa: IDRC and Penang: Southbound.

———. 2004. 'Participatory Communication for Development', Southbound, URL: http://www.southbound.com.my/communication/parcom.htm last accessed on 7 May 2007.

INDEX

ABOUT THE AUTHORS

Vinod Pavarala is Professor of Communication and Dean, Sarojini Naidu School of Communication, University of Hyderabad. After completing a dual Masters in Communication & Journalism and Sociology, he obtained his PhD from the University of Pittsburgh, USA. He has taught at the University of Pittsburgh, Virginia Tech (Blacksburg, USA), and the Indian Institute of Technology, Mumbai, and has been a Visiting Fellow at Princeton University. For over five years he has been one of the leading campaigners for a national policy on community radio and has played a significant role in the drafting of the policy approved by the Union Cabinet in late 2006, permitting community-based organizations to start their own radio stations. Pavarala is the author of *Interpreting Corruption* (Sage, 1996) which looks at the social construction of corruption in India.

Kanchan K. Malik is Lecturer, Sarojini Naidu School of Communication, University of Hyderabad. She has a dual Masters in Economics and Mass Communication from Panjab University, Chandigarh, and a PhD in Communication from the University of Hyderabad. She worked as a journalist with *The Economic Times* before taking up a career in academics. Through her empirical work in Jharkhand, Gujarat, Karnataka, Andhra Pradesh and New Delhi, Malik has systematically engaged with the processes of media interventions by NGOs for empowerment at the grassroots level. Her research interests include print journalism, communication and development, community media, communication research, and media, gender and social change.